MESSAGES FROM METATRON
A Course in Self-Transformation

By Devi Nina Bingham

Combined Volume

_____

Text

Workbook for Students

"And the angel that talked with me came again, and waked me,

as a man that is wakened out of his sleep."

-Zechariah 4:1

Dedication

It is with warm affection and utmost respect that I dedicate this book to Lord Archangel Metatron who taught me to be unafraid of channeling, and unapologetic about believing in things that cannot be seen. These lessons are dedicated to the Light Workers who will rescue Mother Earth and her children, for you are the light of the world.

Table of Contents

Forward from the Author 1

Message 1-Letter to the Miracle Workers............................16

Message 2-Father God 25

Message 3-Mother God 33

Message 4-Letter from Mother God 37

Message 5-Love & Forgiveness..40

Message 6-Christ & The Avatars 49

Message 7-Spirit Guides & Angels...55

Message 8-Hungry Ghosts 60

Message 9-Enlightenment & the Buddha 70

Message 10-The Human Experiment....................................75

Message 11-Soul Work 81

Message 12-Illness & Healing 93

Message 13-Happiness...98

Message 14: Original Souls 109

Message 15-Transgenderism..117

Message 16-Soulmates...123

Message 17-Nothing to Fear 129

Message 18-Your Life Plan & Karma 140

Message 19-Decisions, Decisions, Decisions 148

Message 20-Practical Spirituality 153

Message 21-Good, Evil & The Material Lie......................................164

Message 22-The Anarchists of Light 174

Message 23-Intuition & ESP...184

Message 24-Destiny, Intention & Thought Forms............................190

Message 25-The Multiverse, Parallel Universes & Holographic You
....195

Message 26-The Oversoul..204

Message 27-Aliens & A Cosmic Religion 209

Message 28-Meditation 213

Message 29-The Stuff That Dreams Are Made Of 226

Message 30: The Butterfly King & The Rainbow Mother 229

Epilogue from Archangel Metatron 235

Workbook: Messages From Metatron..239

   LESSON 1-Judge Not..239

   LESSON 2-Not My Will 243

   LESSON 3-You'll Always Have a Mother 248

   LESSON 4-A Mother's Love 252

LESSON 5-Using the Soul to Forgive...256

LESSON 6-Religion & Science..261

LESSON 7-Your Karmic Team...264

LESSON 8-Biases..267

LESSON 9-The Buddha in The Mirror 272

LESSON 10-Change Your Thinking..275

LESSON 11-Your Invincible Soul 278

LESSON 12-Good Medicine 282

LESSON 13-Letting Karma Settle The Score 285

LESSON 14-Your Life Mission 289

LESSON 15-The Body Is Not You 292

LESSON 16-Learning From Soulmates 295

LESSON 17-Defeating Fear 299

LESSON 18-The Best Laid Plans...303

LESSON 19-Making Good Decisions 306

LESSON 20-Religion vs. Spirituality...310

LESSON 21-Renunciation...314

LESSON 22-Your Rebel Soul 317

LESSON 23-The Gift of Intuition 320

LESSON 24-You Are What You Think 324

LESSON 25-The Multiverse, Parallel Universes & Holographic You...327

LESSON 26-The Oversoul 331

LESSON 27-Cosmic Concerns..334

LESSON 28-Why Meditation..337

LESSON 29-The Stuff That Dreams Are Made Of....................341

LESSON 30-The Akashic Record & The Future 344

Bibliography...349

Forward from the Author

A new chapter of my spiritual journey commenced on the second anniversary of my daughter's death. Moriyah was smart and gorgeous, but she struggled with family-inherited depression. When her father died suddenly of ALS, or Lou Gehrig's disease, she was age eleven, and it sent her into a downward spiral. At the age of fifteen, she secretly stopped taking her antidepressant which proved to be a fatal mistake when she took her own life. I wrote about my grief recovery and her after-death visitation in my autobiography, *"Once The Storm Is Over: From Grieving to Healing After the Suicide of My Daughter" (Big Table Publishing, 2015)*. Three days of unexplainable phenomenon had removed any doubt from my mind that she was still alive on the Other Side and could communicate with me. So, when a male's relaxed but authoritative voice first tapped across the stage of my mind in June 2015, I wasn't completely surprised. In addition to my daughter's after-death visitation, since the age of eleven I'd had psychic abilities. I'd never called myself a psychic because I didn't want to be labeled as weird, or worse, a heretic. I was raised in a conservative Christian household where anything "New Age" was considered evil, or at least highly suspect.

The first time Archangel Metatron made contact I was age 51. Walking for me had become a therapy, and as I walked in the cool glow of summer's dusk, I missed Moriyah. The dreaded second anniversary of her death was approaching, and I fought back tears as I pictured how she might look: I could imagine her celestial, glowing face when I distinctly heard her voice. It startled me so much that I came to a complete stop, because she hadn't made contact since the visitation. She was a quiet child, so true to form, she kept it brief: "Mama, listen for the voice." Did I hear right? Did Moriyah speak to me, or was it my imagination? As the moon lit the path ahead, I slowly walked on, puzzled over the mysterious message. I hadn't the slightest idea what voice she was talking about, but I promised her that I would be listening for it.

Several months later I received the first message from Metatron in the middle of the night. I researched angel visitations and found that the Hebrew word for angel translated to "messenger." Angelic encounters and visions of angels have been reported since before the time of Christ. Martin Luther the Reformer prayed that he would never meet an angel, because they can be quite frightening to humans. In fact, the first thing angels are recorded as saying is, "Be not afraid" (Luke 2:10). Real angels are far from the decorative, chubby cherubs depicted in art. I am very grateful I've never actually seen Metatron, because being his channel was enough of a challenge. On the day of his last message, he jokingly asked if I was ready to see him. I replied, "Absolutely not! I don't want a heart attack," causing him to chuckle. Metatron had a distinct personality just as humans do, which included a wry sense of humor. His manner of speech was formal, so he could sound matter of fact or robotic, but despite his high intellect, this erudite Archangel was sympathetic to the human condition. Mostly I experienced Metatron as a tender and infinitely wise grandfatherly presence.

In my mind's eye, I pictured him as wizardly Father Time, keeper of the Akashic Record.

According to the Jewish Kabbalah, Metatron is the "top" Archangel, the Archangel "boss" who was once a human, mentioned in the Old Testament as Enoch, so pure that he was taken to Heaven while still mortal. He is described as an authority in the spiritual realm, but Metatron was surprisingly understanding of my limitations as an inexperienced channeler. He seemed to know my capacities well; he was "tuned into" me. The messages would stop flowing when I became fatigued, when my hand cramped from furious scribbling, or when my schedule didn't afford the luxury of spending whole afternoons channeling.

Words and pictures came in a flurry, often too fast to write down; a hailstorm of esoteric concepts. He spoke at such a quick pace that for the first three months I taped the messages on a hand-held voice recorder as he used my voice to speak through me. I'm so glad I did, because when I played the recordings back, I was astonished by what I heard. First, it didn't sound like me. While it was my voice, a male personality was being expressed. In addition, he had a formal, old-world detachment that wasn't my style. I would take in deep breaths before I started channeling and let out long sighs after the message was finished, almost as if I were drawing him in and breathing him back out.

After channeling for sixty to ninety minutes, I couldn't recall most of what I'd said. Because I am a Hypnotherapist, I knew amnesia was real. I'd witnessed my client's amnesia after their sessions, but now it was happening to me. One of the most fascinating things about this process was that He would stop mid-sentence, only to pick up ten minutes later in the exact spot where he'd left off. I marveled at this, because at my age, it wasn't uncommon for me to go into the next room and forget what I'd gone in there for! I've concluded that these interruptions were due to the great distance these transmissions had to travel between His realm and mine. This was perhaps the most convincing evidence that I had nothing to do with these expositions. My memory isn't good enough for a trick like that.

The presence of Metatron was later confirmed by a well-respected and renowned psychic from the United Kingdom. I called her radio show because she was giving complimentary readings and I wanted to see if she could pick up on what was happening to me. The phone lines were jammed, and I figured I wouldn't get in, but when she agreed to take one last caller it happened to be me. I didn't want to give anything away, so all I said was: "What do you get about me?" Right away, the psychic said there was "an angel sending me messages." She had no prior knowledge whatsoever of my situation, so I giggled nervously, and the psychic said, "You are a psychic! Do you know that? You are...very psychic, though you've never called yourself one." I confirmed it was true, and I asked the name of the angel who had been sending me messages. She's never going to get this right, I thought. To my amazement, she replied: "It's an

Archangel!" She paused, then continued: "It's Archangel...Metatron." That is the point at which I was convinced what was happening to me was real. Until that moment I doubted myself and wondered if I had an overactive imagination. But how could this be a coincidence? She told me that I would write an important book that would be dictated by Metatron and asked if I was ready for big changes in my life.

Because I am a skeptic, but an open-minded one, I turned to quantum physics to see if Metatron's fantastic cosmology was backed by scientific fact. After his message about how we are holograms living in a holographic world, I stumbled upon a hypothesis that sounded a lot like what Metatron had described. In a research paper by Oxford University's Nick Bostrom entitled, "Are You Living in A Simulation?" (2003), Bostrom asserts that "members of an advanced "post-human" civilization with immense computing power are running simulations of their ancestors in the universe," and he believes we are that simulation, a 3D projection of our ancient ancestors. When I read this, I recalled what Metatron kept saying about our world: that what we call reality is nothing more than a simulation, and we are being projected here in holographic form. At that same time, a Facebook friend posted a video about Holographic Mass, a theory that mathematically points to a holographic world. I did more digging and found that a good number of physicists, including the late theoretical physicist Stephen Hawking believe in a multiverse and parallel universes. Without getting too technical, the multiverse theory states that our universe is not the only one, but many. Other universes cannot be seen by us only because they are beyond our field of vision. And a parallel universe is a hypothetical self-contained reality co-existing with ours, in which each of us exists in an infinite number of other dimensions. How can this be possible? The theory states we could be beamed or projected by a laser due to shadow photons. David Deutsch, a physicist at Oxford University authored the book, "The Fabric of Reality" describing the Double Slit Experiment. In this simple experiment, he uses only a red laser pointer to show that parallel universes could exist. Upon learning about these theories, I breathed a huge sigh of relief. The scientific world suspects what indigenous peoples and the Eastern religions have been saying for centuries: that we live in a world of Maya, of illusion; that there's more going on behind the scenes than we perceive.

The concepts so fascinated me that I moved into a 23-foot travel trailer, so I could afford to continue my channeling and research, as I wasn't receiving a regular paycheck while writing. I knew that if I toughed it out and minimized expenses, I could continue to write full time. Though I'm not one to complain, the winter was miserable! When it snowed, the water froze, and I went without water. It was the first time I had ever roughed it for longer than a weekend camping trip, but I was getting to do what I loved so I persisted. While channeling the second book, *Ten Archangels Teach You How To Live An Inspired Life,* I formally converted to Hinduism. I considered myself an unofficial renunciate, but instead of living in a Himalayan cave, I was living in a tiny travel trailer.

I've taken what I was told and have tried to stitch it together to present a unified explanation of how the universe is structured. More importantly, the book answers larger existential questions, including: who is God, and what is our purpose? The most creative and exciting time of my life happened when I was utterly isolated, living a minimalist life. I found scientific evidence of what I was channeling and was getting more and more information about the Other Side, and the invisible, quantum world. The pieces were coming together, and I was having moment after moment of illumination in rapid succession, awestruck to find that Metatron's messages were verified by physics. It took three years to get all thirty messages and the study guide into coherent book form because I struggled to understand the scientific concepts. But from the beginning of this exploration, I felt I was channeling something profound, so I stuck it out. *Messages From Metatron* confirms that our universe is holographic in nature and that our thoughts create reality.

Once the initial resistance to channeling wore off, I resonated with the idea of being connected to my daughter's world. The desire to communicate with otherworldly beings is timeless. Communicating with gods while in trance was a highly prized ability among the ancient Egyptian priests, and ancient Greece had their oracles. The early Chinese, Tibetans, Japanese, Indians, Babylonians, Assyrians, and Celts channeled discarnate spirits. Judaism, Christianity, Islam and other religions received divine guidance via channeling prophets. It wasn't until Jane Roberts published her Seth books in the late 1960s and early 1970s that channeling saw a resurgence in mainstream popularity, and the 1980s saw a slew of channeled material. Channeling can occur spontaneously or be induced, and while some channels have learned to control the process at will, mine is spontaneous; so spontaneous that a message can wake me from a deep sleep in the dead of night. Mental channeling, which is what I do, is done in a slightly dissociated state, meaning that I'm not completely aware of the world around me. My personality recedes, and Metatron uses my voice, like the direct-voice mediumship of Jane Roberts, or JZ Knight (Ramtha). My voice changes only slightly; it drops in pitch, the words are articulated differently, with a more dramatic flair. Psychic information also comes to me by impressions and feelings. However, I believe anyone can learn to be a channel by developing her or his intuition and through meditation. This ability is not exclusive to an anointed few; anyone can learn to hear the angels if they are willing to tune in.

While I used two methods to write this book (voice recording, and automatic writing), the messages had one theme in common-that of unity. They all seem to be saying: we are one. Another favorite theme of these messages is that of reality. I found myself asking: What is real? Our subjective perspective defines our reality. If we could see through our biases, perhaps we would see things as they really are. From an angel's perspective, reality is not only the world of matter but the world of thought and feeling-that is an angel's realm. The brain is a rational machine, denying other dimensions and entities so we can focus on today, on the present moment. Only psychedelic drugs and spiritual experiences can remove that barrier and liberate the confined mind, giving us a peek into unseen worlds.

Unlike Eastern cultures who esteem ancient spiritual wisdom, Western society has prized materialism and science to the exclusion of spiritual knowledge. The West continues to ignore the metaphysical, while energetic frequencies vibrate all around us. Quantum Physics tells us that we are a materialized frequency, and Metatron says that your vibration will change and be altered upward as you evolve. Your Soul's frequency cannot be destroyed because frequency is a form of energy, and energy cannot be destroyed, it only changes form, so you are an eternal being. Incarnating is an opportunity for your frequency to move upward into a purer, nobler form. Each time you learn a life lesson, your consciousness expands a little farther. While each Soul emits a frequency, it may be easier to think of yourself as a light that shines brighter with each lesson learned. As your light shines brighter, it expels the collective darkness. This is the

Soul's most important task: to raise the collective vibration of the whole so that eventually no one walks in darkness. Do you see how vitally important your contribution is? You are a piece of the universal tapestry which affects the entire fabric of the Cosmos. You are a vibrational reality interacting with countless other vibrations and without you, there would be a tear in the perfection of the universal fabric.

Prior to 2016, I was using a voice recorder, but then I began automatic writing. As the pencil spills out words on the page, up to 30 pages at a time, my mind is completely devoid of my own thoughts. It is as if I'm taking dictation; the pencil seems to move of its own accord. Historically, the act of automatic writing has produced astounding results that supersede the knowledge of the writer. Automatic writing has been a big help, because I don't have the laborious task of transcribing the messages from the tape recorder to the paper and from the paper to the computer. They flowed fluidly and were longer, but there was a hitch-many of them came in the middle of the night. Between 1 to 3 am, my eyes would pop open as if an invisible hand had awakened me. I'd make excuses to stay in my warm bed: "I can write it down in the morning." But I knew by the morning the message would be gone. I'd drag myself out of bed, grab my robe, and brew a wicked strong pot of coffee. After taking a few sips of the reassuring brew, I'd sink into the couch and tune in. While there have been cases of automatic writing happening involuntarily, I'm always aware that I'm writing, though I couldn't tell you what the next word will be. Sometimes my hand is writing so furiously that it cramps, and the script is more expansive than normal and difficult to read (as if my handwriting wasn't bad enough).

Truth be told, I still don't understand very much about the mystical, magical process of channeling. But as I promised my daughter, I will keep listening for the voice-even when it comes in the middle of the night.

Devi Nina Bingham, 2019

Message 1-Letter to the Miracle Workers

Greetings from Heaven! Dispensing with formalities, shall we get right to it, then? In addition to angels, other Heavenly beings are eager to address you, but our superiors have asked us not to spoil the fun, so I will stick mainly to information about angels and humanity in this book. What is the use of telling you everything about the Other Side before you get here? That's like reading the end of the story before you've finished the book.

When most people think about Heaven, what they are immediately concerned with is the possibility of a surprise ending. You don't want to be ambushed at the end of your life, and I don't blame you. You also don't like to think of your mistakes, errors, missteps, and especially calculated wrongdoing haunting you on the Other Side. So, let me reassure you: truly, it will not-it cannot. There is no retribution for your errors awaiting you in Heaven. There is no eternal damnation for any Soul. In fact, there is no punishment at all in Heaven. Now you may be wondering: where is the justice in a system like that. Why live life unselfishly if there are no consequences?

Souls that have thought only of themselves and who have hurt others purposely-the Souls you call "evil," will continue to reincarnate. Wrongdoing is visited upon you in successive lifetimes, not in Heaven-and this is known as karma. I wish to draw a distinction between wrongdoing that is intentional and mistakes that are unintentional, because humans are coded for error. You are a creature that learns by its mistakes. Because of this, in the afterlife, you will be given the opportunity to review every aspect of your life, every choice you made. Upon review, you'll see how some of the choices you thought were benevolent produced a poor outcome, and some choices you regarded as malevolent, even calculated malevolency, were used for the greater good. The concept of morality-of you being able to distinguish good from evil, is ludicrous. You cannot know the outcome; you cannot see the final impact an action will have. To see the outcome, you must observe it over centuries of time, filtering its way down through your lineage, through your posterity. Therefore, how can you judge history, even your own history, and say with impunity, I am vindicated, or, they have sinned? Perhaps the greatest error of the human mind is the rush to judgement.

In eternity, there is no sin or grievance that is worse than any other because all sins are equal in the world of karma. What I mean is, all Souls are equally in need of redemption. Before a Soul's perfecting, one sin is as egregious as any other. We see all entities as equal for all need the same grace. I hope you realize by this time that you are no worse and no better off than any other. There is equality in the eternal world that makes no sense to the human mind which weighs and measures. In the end, all Souls will justify themselves through the practice of good works and devotion, and all errors will eventually be redeemed by karma. Contrary to popular religious notion, nobody is going to save you; you will save yourself. How will you do this? All Souls will incarnate until their perfection is attained. When you look at yourself, see your brothers and sisters reflected in the mirror. And when you look at your brother or sister, see your own sins and weaknesses reflected in them, for there is a little of you in everyone.

I would like to distinguish how angelic beings are different from mortal Souls. First, angels aren't born, nor do they die. They don't have a beginning (a birthday) nor an ending (death) the way mortals do. And angels have the power of foresight; we can see your Soul developing over the course of a lifetime. Just as you watch flowers push their way through the soil as they warm in the spring, angels observe your Soul as it sheds its false beliefs and erroneous thinking and finally blooms. As the Soul ripens, angels know its trajectory, and they anticipate how glorious will be the day when it discovers itself to be everything it needed and wanted. This "growing into," this ripening of the Soul, we watch.

Angelic beings are divine authorities who assist, serve and govern, much the same as law enforcement adjudicates morality on earth. But we don't need to carry billy-clubs and guns that intimidate. We don't use force and threats of punishment; our purpose is to protect and serve in the truest sense. We also cannot inflict any harm on you. *Most importantly, we cannot change the outcome of your decisions.* In the realm of free will, angels are prevented from intervening. When you've chosen, once you've made a conscious decision to go right or to go left, the natural consequences of that decision must play themselves out. Angels cannot change the natural consequences of any choice. Still, we get countless requests to bend the outcome in your favor and to overt catastrophe before it strikes. This is the greatest lesson: that you are the creator of your world. Because of this, angels are prevented from interfering with consequences. You might wonder: What good is it to pray, to ask for help in times of trouble?

There are parameters of response we can maneuver in. Like law enforcement wherein officers aren't allowed to search your home without a court order, likewise, angelic beings cannot interfere with the natural progression of things. Angels have rules to obey, too. There are laws that govern every form of existence. So as not to abuse our power, we must obey the law that says: "That which you sow, you shall also reap." Though Christ cried out, "'Take this cup from me,'" even He was required to fulfill his sacred contract, however painful, however humiliating it was. He knew the law of karma; He helped to write it. Yet stuck in a weakened and fearing body, He trembled at what stood before Him and wished to be delivered from it. This shows that even Gods can be afraid.

Throughout time, angels have witnessed your trials and tribulations. We protect, guide, and comfort you as much as allowed. The agreements you made with Soulmates, the destiny you shook hands with and agreed to meet face to face, you most certainly won't avoid because you cannot escape fate. It's true that everything happens for a reason. You may have sensed synchronicity; feeling as if things were being arranged or rearranged ahead of you. While we can't interfere with the outcome of conscious choice, we can comfort and assist during "close-calls." Remember that time you got extra lucky, or the time you narrowly avoided disaster? It wasn't random chance falling in your favor. Those were moments when your Oversoul had agreed to our help long before you entered the situation. There is no "good luck" or "bad luck," there is only "dumb luck" (chuckles). See, even angels can joke.

While angels are important agents of mercy, we can't stop what is fated. Pray as you wish-ask for help, wisdom and strength. We will hear you and take your requests to the Counsel of True Judges. We will say, "This human didn't realize what they were doing when they agreed to this. May we intervene?" And the directors of your destiny will find in favor of you, re-arranging events so you may learn your lessons in the most expedient way. Only the Counsel can re-order your Life's Blueprint or Chart. Angels go and plead your case, and the Intergalactic Council hears it, for they are sympathetic to an angel's compassionate heart. The Counsel can make certain adjustments to accommodate you, but sometimes they aren't able to do as much as they would like, as there are many Souls in your Life Chart to be considered. This intergalactic system of justice that I describe is beyond your comprehension. Still, I will paint a crude picture of the afterlife, of what to expect, because I don't want you to be afraid of death. I don't want you to be afraid of living, either. And I don't want you to fear otherworldly beings like angels, spirit guides, and your ancestors who have, from the moment of your inception, been with you, silently guiding you. Your karmic team, those who are your spirit guides, guardian angels and ancestors, are witnesses who feel *with* you. Even at your worst, when you were terrified and suffering, in those anguished moments, they were feeling with you. They have sorrowed with you, rejoiced with you, and been in awe of you. In awe, because you agreed to take this epic journey, including every frustrating, miserable moment, as well as to every beautiful, awesome moment. These merciful guardians feel your every tear, your every smile. Very simply, they are deeply devoted to you and will never leave you.

You are not superior creatures because of the things you own, the way you look, your talents and abilities, or even your intellect. You are not great because of what you have created, though we've been quite impressed with what you've been able to pull off. What we admire most is your indomitable human spirit that never gives up, and never gives in to hopelessness-this is what makes you great in our eyes. Adaptable you-ingeniously making the best of a bad situation. Your willingness to endure this haphazard journey is priceless. Only mortals can overcome earthly evil, making something good out of something that was broken. This is your lasting beauty, to make a meal for so many out of so few loaves and fishes. To be broken, and then to stand in your brokenness and declare: 'I shall be unbroken.' This is what makes you special, admired by so many on the Other Side.

Those creatures who have never been human before, who do not endure heartbreak, loss and imperfection; those who have only known the perfection of the Other Side look at your struggle to become something greater and exclaim: "These are the miracle workers." It doesn't matter if you don't feel like a miracle worker. Feelings will fool you into believing you're nothing more than your feelings. The truth is: You are profoundly more interesting to us than you know, and you're not doing it alone-especially in your darkest hour. Your loved ones on the Other Side, perfect now in every way, can see where you're headed, how you're growing, and when you've gotten stuck. With all this attention, will you please try to remember that though you feel like you have failed, you cannot? Ultimately, you are destined to grow into the most perfect form of you that you can be. You cannot fail to perfect that which looks so imperfect to you now. Yet all the while, you will be in the experience of your imperfections, acutely.

You began your earthly journey as a helpless, dependent infant who was placed in the arms of terribly imperfect parents. These imperfect people agreed to bring you into the world, but when you arrived, perhaps they couldn't take care of you. Perhaps they failed to try-failing completely. But this has nothing to do with your worthiness, because earth is not your home, and they are not your real parents. They were playing a role in the drama you designed for your ultimate growth and development. You chose them, and they chose you before you stepped into this play called your life. You agreed to accept everything that has happened to you, so trust that a divine plan is unfolding. To trust that something good will come of it is the most eloquent execution of living that you can hope to achieve. Try to accept circumstances and people as they are. Trust that the Universe knows what it's doing, and that most of the time, you do not. Not because you're too simple, but because you are in human form, walking through Hell, and with all that smoke, it's difficult to see anything clearly.

I'd like to discuss tests and trails. Know that every one of you will be tested. You are tested to show what you have learned, and what you have yet to learn. Naturally, you will wish to turn away from these trials and tribulations. Nevertheless, trauma is allowed so you see what you are made of. Can you find gratitude for what you've been given, or do you despise your circumstances? If you walk towards the Light, you will be given the strength to prevail. Yet be certain of this: you cannot do it alone. Even Christ did not face his cross alone. He surrounded himself with loved ones and appealed to the Heavens for strength. Why would you think you must go it alone? You are never alone, not even in the loneliest of moments. Your Spirit Guides, Guardian Angels, even your Ancestors-a great 'cloud of witnesses' (Heb. 12:1) can see you, especially when you call. Just because you cannot see them does not invalidate their presence. In your tests, trials, tribulations and traumas, we are *for* you, meaning we are rooting for you. We believe you will do great things; that you will use each moment as if it were fleeting and precious, for truly, you are more than halfway to Heaven. Death itself is the final tribulation, the final letting go. As soon as you cross from death to life, you will be on this side of the looking glass, watching your children, partner and loved ones, with hopeful anticipation for what they will accomplish in your absence.

On the Other Side you'll be reunited with Souls now forgotten to you-Soulmates from other lives. It will all come rushing back; all the pieces of you that were scattered will magnetically be drawn together again. And what you learn from the game that you called your life will be examined by you and many others as well. All others you touched for good and for ill will witness the drama that unfolded in your life. Upon inspection, even the worst traumas will seem nearly inconsequential when you see how they were fashioned perfectly for your Soul's evolution. You won't be judged by anyone: each of you will judge your own deeds. Heaven's many dimensions, or what we call 'Kingdoms' are higher vibratory systems, and you will enter these systems through stargates, or wormholes. In these dimensions, absolute truth is known in an instant, in 'the twinkling of an eye' (1 Cor. 15:52). There will be no escaping the truth; there is no denial in Heaven. There is nothing but the whole truth and nothing but the truth (so help me, God). Of course, there are consequences for every action: "For every action, there is an equal and opposite reaction" (Newton's Third Law). This is also true in the Heavenly realms. Those who caused suffering will submit to the appropriate counsel, and those who prevented suffering will be rewarded. Thankfully, benevolent deeds are far weightier than errors; the scales of Heavenly justice are always tipped in your favor. This is called mercy; Heaven is big on mercy. Once a Soul submits to the consequences of its actions, we are quick to forgive, sending the angels to save, comfort and restore. Given enough time, all Souls will be regenerated; every darkness will be cleansed, and every injury healed. Our system of justice is impeccable-there is no shadow of turning in it.

Despite the reassuring news that your plight is seen and known, and though your pain is producing a Soul worthy of the glory of the Heavenly realms, you will lose this confidence when it grows dark and God seems to have fled. You will forget everything that's been said about the necessity of trials, and you will care not to learn from the present moment's pain. In fact, you may run in the opposite direction of the test sent your way, failing the test completely. A wonderful aspect of the Soul's growth is that as you evolve, you run less and less. As your Soul matures your progress becomes exponential. Isn't that a marvelous feature of the Soul-It "picks up speed" as it goes? This means you don't have to be stuck forever in an endless cycle of learning the same lesson. No, the Soul is smarter than that. My dear, your present life is but a school, and once you pass the test, you won't have to repeat the lesson. It follows that the students who are most eager to learn will graduate the fastest. When you're swamped by a trial, call for your Guides and Angels who are trained to respond with a shot of courage when you need it. When you want to abandon this life, call for your Guides, Angels, and Ancestors. As you do, shut your eyes and feel their reassuring presence, gentle hands resting upon your weary shoulders. They will stay beside you long after you have forgotten them, to infuse you with persistent determination, and to steady you. Ask that they flood you with peace. Even when it doesn't make sense to have peace, you can enjoy peace.

The next time you face a giant of a problem, remember: it is not the size of the warrior, but the size of the warrior's heart that matters. Giants are only lies that have been blown out of proportion. A single pinprick can deflate a giant; giants are easily taken down once you know what you're looking at. When you can't understand why you must suffer, on the Other Side you will see how every moment of your life was engineered for your Soul's perfecting. Then you will be grateful for the journey. It sounds impossible, to be grateful for the trials and to see it as a gift, because: "For now, you see through a glass darkly" (1 Cor. 13:12). Today all you see are the mistakes, while all we see is how hard you tried. I promise, you're doing better than you think. Therefore, smile a little. Laugh a little and love a little-because this journey will be over before you know it. It will end as it began in birth-when pain is transformed into new life. Your story has a happy ending-one you've written for yourself. After all, who knows you better than...you?

Lord Archangel Metatron

Message 2-Father God

That which you call God is nothing but a construct, a representation, a reflection of your own humanity. Your popular representation of God is a creation of fearful minds that demand answers and must fashion answers in their own image, but this is not God. God transcends any personality, God transcends any religious definition or description, and yet God relates to all aspects of His creation. It is difficult to grasp what God is, because God is an energy, and energy doesn't seem relatable. Spirit is pure energy-it is neither male nor female, for neither energy nor spirit has genitalia that defines it. But God has a personality and can be accurately described as: multidimensional, without borders or boundaries. Therefore, it is impossible, even ridiculous to claim you comprehend God, or even "have a relationship with Him." What you have is a relationship with your projection of God. Conceptions of God have been taught to you; men project human characteristics onto a transcendent being that eclipses human characteristics. Some say that God condones wrath or punishment but only because they condone it. Human characteristics are "part of" what God is, but by no means is God mortal. God is beyond human comprehension.

You also like to think that God is outside of yourself, controlling that which seems chaotic, for it is comforting to believe that something larger, something more advanced and intelligent, something more sympathetic than yourselves is in control. Yet the truth is a different story. Inside of each of you is this piece; a reflection of larger, more advanced life, and this is the Soul. As a part of the Creator, your Soul has been endowed with the ability to project your thoughts outward and to manifest physical form. This means you are as much "God" as God is. But you don't like to think of yourself in this auspicious role. You see yourself as human: fallible, erroneous, mistaken creatures at the mercy of an unknowable universe, yet you are an unthinkably superior creator. The sooner you see this the better, because accepting that you are a facet of God will allow you to make a smoother transition to the afterlife. Fortunately, your consciousness is always expanding, so if you cannot grasp this yet, you soon will.

Because you see yourself as limited, it is impossible for you to understand what kind of creature you really are, where you came from, and where you're going. It's easier not to see your potentialities, not to animate and bring to life this atomic-like power inside you. For then you would have to look to yourselves, to look within for answers rather than to the external world or to an externalized God. This concept, that God is within, is so foreign to your minds, yet is perfectly understandable to the Spirit that resides inside this entity called you. Because your doubting mind doesn't readily grasp this concept doesn't make it any less true. You once did not think it was possible to walk upright; your mind was not developed enough to comprehend standing on your own, a skill foreign to you as an infant. But someone was standing by, encouraging you to take the next step. Nature provided an elder who supervised you and kept you safe, teaching you what to eat, what to wear, and how to behave. Likewise, over the course of many incarnations you learn to stand on your own feet spiritually and morally.

You have come to rely on one another, especially members of your family. Those who took the role of your parents helped you to be nourished, to be safe, and to learn right from wrong-these are what your elders taught you. They showed you by modeling human behavior. But what they could not show you was how to embrace your divine inheritance. This is what I would like to offer; wisdom which is less human-based, and more spirit-led. I don't profess to have all knowledge necessary for the Soul's transmutation, for its ultimate development. While I have studied the Soul's evolution, my knowledge is limited; I am not as omniscient as God. Yet what I have, I freely give you.

There will come a point in your development when you realize you are a Spirit-based creature, bigger than what you perceive, more important than a body, greater than a single intellect. When you begin to feel your own divinity, you'll yearn for communion with The Other Side, because what the world offers won't be able to hold you captive any longer. You will come to the end of your understanding; to the end of your own answers and strivings, and you won't be satiated with simple entertainments any longer. When you come to this fork in the road, you must decide if you will do the will of your mind or the will of your Higher Self. This is a very good place to be.

Every human will be faced with a turning point in which their own solutions fail them, miserably and completely. While you'll feel frustrated and angry at your own impotence, and powerless to change the circumstances, these very tests forge you into something stronger. Christ spoke of a new life, and new life only comes once something has died, isn't this true? There is grief when a person or a dream has died; when you have lost a part of you that you thought you had to have. You will grieve this lost part and think you will never recover your happiness; that you will never be the same. Yet these sorts of tests are fore-fashioned to create a new birth, a new lens with which to see yourself and the world. These change-points, these trials, can be as painful as birthing a child and yet, necessary. If you're never under pressure, how will you change? If you never change, how will you grow? It is great pressure that creates a diamond, isn't it? A piece of coal is worth nothing; a diamond is only a piece of coal that has been placed under very great pressure. Trials come to reveal your true nature. There is an overcomer in you that wills itself to live despite great adversity. This is the eternal you, and no human can destroy it. No human effort can save you from the trials of life, either. Only you can transform your pain into strength. If you look back and see you were forged into something stronger, then you are seeing your divinity at work. You are made from the same indestructible, relentless Life Force energy that created the entire Cosmos. When you see strength born of pain, you sense you are a creature part human and part divine. This great partnership between your Soul and the Divine Source is tenacious and eternal. God is supplying you in every moment with nourishment, the will to live, and the strength to go on. There is a moment-by-moment communion with the Life Force that creates a constant interplay between this realm and that.

What has been called God is nothing more, I assure you, than your own Soul's light combined with billions and billions of other Soul lights. This makes a great light, and *this* is God. God is everywhere, because everywhere through time and space, there is life, and God is the source of all life. How can I describe the complexity of such a system, and yet, its profound unity? Words are insufficient. You must trust that inside of you is something bigger than your mind can comprehend, and it is connected evermore to the Other Side. This is the reason all humans crave the feeling of importance, that longing to feel special. Instinctively you sense that you are here for some higher reason than your own puny circumstances. You've felt since birth that you are marvelously important, yet fragile. God is also indestructible, yet fragile; fragile, because God depends on each of you.

How does God depend on you? You have a symbiotic relationship with God. God created Itself to be distributed in bits and pieces throughout the Cosmos, so It could be a part of everything. God is in everything; even in the molecules of the air you breathe. God is in each imperceptible bit of the invisible, subatomic world. When you return Home, you will see you are certainly a facet of God's intellect, part of God's all-knowing heart. Because you chose to come and experience life for God, you became God's beating heart to the world. This is how precious you are, an extension of the Great Light. Your existence is quite important, quite precious, and yet, tenuous. While you are on this epic journey, never forget who you are: a marvelous imprint of the Divine heart sent to this planet, at a specific time in history, to do something unique, and to leave something good behind.

Spiritual people among you understand that above all laws stands this truth: all are one. The Creator is one with you, and you are one with the Creator. None of you exists outside of the other; all of you need the light of the other which you yourselves cannot furnish. You depend upon one another for your very existence. The highest spiritual precept is that of oneness. If you would meditate upon the concept of oneness, you would see that all things are interconnected, and the truth of it would profoundly come to you. Your mind would be opened to see that you are not disconnected-you never were, you couldn't possibly be. You are distanced from your Source, and therefore you feel unplugged and disempowered, and at times, disillusioned-because you feel stranded, far from Home. Yet Home has not moved; it will be there when your assignment is finished.

When you review your life's work, I hope you can say: "I left something good behind, something to be proud of." Even if it seems insignificant now, things have a way of magnifying themselves in eternity. Therefore, try hard to see that God is not hiding somewhere outside of your consciousness. You belong to God, and God belongs to you; you belong to each other. Remind yourself that everyone is a part of God, and God needs all of you, a collaboration of Souls. Unless you see yourself as the all-powerful, loving, indestructible force that you are, you will be reduced to a fearing worm of a person who feels she can be stepped on and rubbed out at any moment. Fear will get the best of you, and you'll never know what good you could have done. This facet of God you've been entrusted with is the Soul, and it is magnificent beyond compare. Altogether, *you* are magnificent beyond compare.

At this point you may be thinking: If God cares so much about us, why does He not help the oppressed? Why do innocent children suffer? Why do the good perish while evil men prosper? How could a loving God sit by while we destroy each other? Where is the justice? Please hear this: On earth, there is no justice-there is only free will. It could be a different story, a veritable Heaven-on-earth if humanity would harness their potential for good, to build shelters instead of bombs, homes instead of prisons, and forge peace treaties instead of war. Can you imagine a lovely world wherein peacemakers were honored instead of ridiculed? Humans are as capable of tender acts as they are of monstrous acts. Having the ability to reason, to feel, and to create is an ominous responsibility. This is why you are sent into life: to exercise your powers as a creator, even if you've only assisted humanity an inch.

Before you incarnated, you decided what you wanted to contribute, but once you arrived, it became challenging to stick to the plan. Of course, you've forgotten all the promises you made to yourself and your Soulmates, those precious Souls who promised to see you through. You forget everything when you reincarnate. Jesus illustrated this in a parable: "It is easier for a camel to pass through the eye of a needle than for a rich man to enter the Kingdom of God" (Matthew 19:24). Why did He use such a strange analogy? He was illustrating the Soul's journey. Like a camel, the Soul is large. It is a beast of burden, for it carries with it past lives. It is laden with baggage (your many incarnations) and used for time travel. The Soul drops its memory of past lives when you take birth, storing its history and knowledge (its baggage) in your subconscious. It travels from the realm of Spirit and is squeezed into the space of a single cell at your conception, something like a camel passing through the eye of a needle! Christ was a master teacher who used allegories with hidden meanings. There was the obvious teaching, but He hid within them more complex ideas and concepts. Is it so hard to believe that Divinity could be profound when explaining life? Returning to Christ's statement that the rich will have a difficult time reaching enlightenment-is this true? A lot of good can be done for others with money, and philanthropists have done a lot of good with money. Christ was not calling money evil, He was simply observing that "power tends to corrupt, and absolute power corrupts absolutely" (1887, Dalberg-Acton). He was issuing a warning. He was saying: beware that wealth and power don't rob you of the real, immaterial treasures.

You will often wish God could take your pain away. But let's look for a moment at the purpose of pain. God isn't a sadist; He dislikes evil and injustice as much as you do. But the minute God steps in to rescue you, He has taken away part of the free will equation: the consequences. And while at times you'd like to be rescued, He cannot help because before you incarnated, you made an agreement. You promised to grow and to be brave, and God promised not to interfere so you could learn your lessons. The story of your life was written long before you arrived, and God vowed not to interfere. I know it is nearly impossible to believe that you would have approved your Life Plan, but your Higher Self, known as your Oversoul, has tremendous faith in you. Like a guardian, your Oversoul meticulously poured over your Life's Blueprint and submitted it for inspection to the Counsel of True Judges. These are the Cosmic Elders, or High Council Members, the Lords of the Cycles. Your Oversoul went back to the drawing board, over and again with each incarnation, and a plan was hammered out that would cause the most Soul growth in the least amount of time. Like planning a cross-country trip, you wrote in all the shortcuts you could. I know this isn't what you wanted to hear, that you yourself are responsible for the pain you've endured. But I am an angel, and you can always count on angels to tell the truth.

While humanity creates all kinds of unnecessary destruction and havoc, God's part in the great experiment is to love you, every one of you. Unconditional love is something you need, but not something you always get (or can give). You cannot watch injustice or cruelty without hating the perpetrator, especially when you are the innocent victim, but God can. After all, someone must love the unlovely or they would have no chance at redemption. Every Soul needs one necessary ingredient, and even the vilest among you craves it: unconditional love. Without God's unconditional love, humanity would fall into darkness. God has an abundance of the one ingredient that fosters growth. Because of this, every Soul has a chance at redemption. God goes on loving even when His children deny him or crucify him. Why? Because "They know not what they do" (Luke 23:34). It is ignorance of His love that keeps you separated from God and separated from one another. Lifetime after lifetime, God will keep loving you, for that is God's job. The idea of suffering is more palatable when you remember it isn't God who is to blame. There's a lesson hidden inside of every impossibly painful situation, and it's meant to generate Soul growth. Can you think of a better way to grow? After all, humanity can be very stubborn! So, there you have it, the purpose of pain. And the purpose of God? To love you-still.

Message 3-Mother God

Because Father God is beyond fathoming, The Immovable Absolute, Mother God is more readily accessible in Heaven. To use a cliché, it's as if Father is at work while Mother tends to the children. Father's work is holding together all created things, while Mother's work is teaching her Cosmic children to get along. Father God can be comprehended by humanity's simplistic understanding of a Creator, though God could assume any form and in truth, God is beyond form-an impartial creative force, completely without bias. God is pure intellect while Mother is pure heart. Many religions, including Hinduism and Buddhism, have recognized and venerated the Mother Goddess, for She is not some abstract figure of a well-intended but overactive imagination. Among enlightened avatars, having a vision of the Mother God is a sign of momentous favor. Only awakened Souls are given a vision of the ferocious Lover of All Worlds, the ever-embracing totality of God. She is the personification of life-giving earth, Mother Gaia, reflected in her life-sustaining properties. More than a nice idea of a nurturing maternal figure and benevolent cosmic power, Mother God is the very breath of life. She is the Sustainer and the Maintainer. Without Her constant guiding force there would be no life as you know it. This is how important She is, and why cultures encircling the globe including the indigenous people of the Americas, Egyptians, the Aztec, Sumerian and Mesopotamian, Greek, Roman, Celtic, Germanic, Slavic and Turk have venerated her. Why then do you still doubt Her reality?

There was an intentional wiping-away of Mother's memory by the Christian patriarchs. These warring men believed women to be inferior, so they eliminated Mother God's presence from the

Gnostic Scriptures. They wished to purge Her forever from the heart of humanity, but humankind could not forget Her, for Her knowledge is stored within the subconscious, ever-present. She has never withdrawn Her protective, sustaining love, even when those taking their breath by Her intended to end Her reign. But to enlightened beings, She is the resurrection of hope for a peaceful future. She has not died; She only sleeps. Her resurrection day is coming-the memory of Mother is returning to all Her precious beings. She has allowed Herself to be obscured and silenced for a time when She could have insisted that She be venerated. Instead, Mother withdrew her magic presence until such a time when females will be acknowledged as equals upon the earth, as they are in Heaven. When this occurs, Her memory and Her enduring qualities of respect, care and concern for all life will be restored to human consciousness. See what the patriarchal consciousness has come to: war and strife. Humanity is suffering for it is crying out for its Mother Divine.

How can you be sure that there is a Mother God? How can you know her favor and blessed peace? In meditation or in prayer, go to Her quietly and humbly and ask that Her reality be revealed to you. She will give you a sign; ask for a sign of Her presence. She is the flowering of all life, an ever-blossoming gift. Perhaps She will give you a flower to remind you that you are not without a true Mother. Ask Mother to bless you, Her child in need. Do not repress Her memory; say that you wish to remember and be taken into Her arms again. It is only fear of the unfamiliar that keeps you from knowing Her. In time, if you continue to have sincere longings for the Blessed Mother, She will leave you with Her jewels of grace and mercy; you will never feel unlovely in Her presence. When the Mother smiles upon you, you will see Her gem-like eyes glittering, filled with an ocean of compassion. Her arms will be outstretched, inviting an embrace, and your Soul will be filled until you are overcome with emotion. You will fall to your knees in gratitude when the Almighty One, She of All Worlds Known and Unknown, Mother of Universes and Worlds of All Time, embraces you. But for now, Divine Mother remains shrouded in obscurity. Yet each Soul's devotion can unlock the Mystery of the Mother. It is easy to miss Her, to rush past a treasure so quiet and unassuming. Although She has allowed Her name to be suppressed, do not underestimate Her feminine persistence and strength. She is the warrior-like Amazon, going before the righteous. When faced with a battle, when attacked or accused, She is your victory. Call down Her warrior Spirit, Her confidence and boldness to speak the truth. Let Her voice be yours. While She is the sacrificial lamb, She is also the fiercest opponent. Her eyes blaze with righteous indignation for the poor and oppressed. With a swift sword She cuts away ignorance and injustice and calls for the downtrodden to come to Her side. She wishes to feed them-She wishes to point to their wounds, and in so doing, for their wounds to heal. She is the incomparable Goddess of Compassion who offers a magic balm of healing. See Her always pouring forth sweet gifts to the peoples of the world. Those who oppose Her will be made to tremble. When Her sleep is over, She will be revealed, and those who denied Her will be ashamed; they will see their poverty. They will cast their pithy crowns at Her golden feet. Out of Her unlimited, pure heart, the Mother of Lights will call them back to Her forgiving embrace. She has mercy on the poor in Spirit, both now and forever. Pray this prayer, asking Mother to show you Her reality:

Prayer to the Blessed Mother Universal

Blessed be

the Mother who has always lived

always knowing my Soul.

Blessed be Her name

for eternity She remains

the Heaven's most precious and brightest star.

I bend my knee in reverence to Mother Divine

who loves me perfectly, and without flaw.

She is the glittering secret

the One who animates and liberates.

Her heart contains all the stars and worlds

and on her head is a crown of jewels.

All the people of the worlds, her children will glitter and glow everlasting

when Mother smiles upon them.

I receive your reality, Oh Mother of Lights

I receive your favor, Oh Living Song of the Heavens

I am the grateful recipient of thine beatific vision.

Oh, Thou Blameless and Holy

whose name is a wonder and a mystery

Magical Mother of Compassion call me to your side

never let me forget you

for You are the perfection of all peoples.

For all time and in all places

your name is remembered and venerated among the Seven Heavens.

Open the eyes of my heart, Mother Divine

and I shall see

reality.

Message 4-Letter from Mother God

(Archangel Metatron): I have been given special dispensation to deliver this message of undying love from the Divine Mother to her children of Earth:

My Dear Children,

If I am known by any name in Heaven, it is the Mother of Love, because I have a Mother's heart. I want to talk to you about opening your hearts to love.

It is easy to think that the only thing you've gotten by listening to your heart is heartbreak. But you must be aware by now that God and I are hopeless romantics; terribly sentimental! You can be sure of this, because at the center of each human heart is the yearning to be loved. Even the most black-hearted among you has tender feelings towards something if only toward a pet, their mother, or their children. Loving is never a mistake; it is what you were designed to do. It is why poets, artists, writers and musicians pay tribute to the age-old art of love. Falling in love is as close as you will ever get to Heaven on earth. If you've never allowed yourself to fall unreservedly, you should. An affair of the heart is the most exciting and thrilling of all human experiences, reserved for those who dare to love greatly.

If your heart has been designed to love as We love, which is unconditionally and without reserve, to resist doing so and to say about love that it is foolish, or worse, that it is a trap, is to say that the law of love, the highest of all universal laws, is flawed. Is it love that is flawed, or have you become so leery of love, so cynical that you have forgotten what you really desire? Is it love that has let you down or have you let yourself down by forsaking it? Perhaps you have steered clear of love, numbing yourself with activity. Perhaps you drown yourself in business, or addict yourself to some trifling pleasure so you don't have to risk giving your whole heart, so you don't have to open your heart's door wider and wider? I know this world is not an easy place in which to trust. But don't allow yesterday's heartbreak to keep you from imagining something better for yourself. Why let the possibility of love wither and die? Love is the only seed you have for happiness in this world! Deny this and you scatter your chances for happiness atop hard ground. Only soft soil can nurture a fledgling seed, and only a soft heart will nurture the fragile seed of love. To soften is to live soulfully; to proclaim aloud: I am bigger than fear!

Look back carefully on all the moments you dared greatly, whether they were for the cause of love or not, and you will be astounded by your little heart's bigness. Even if you failed, you tried; and in trying you were reminded that nothing could stop you, save one thing: forgetting your own greatness. Every time you have squelched your heart, the world got a little colder, a little smaller. Dreams are the embers of the Soul. Before they grow dark, push them around to see if you can find some sort of heart-glow. Be restless for what burns beneath. If someone rushed in and stomped out your flame of love, or if life, like a tidal wave, washed away your ability to hear the distant echoes of love, then lift your ashes to the wind. Stop this restlessness plaguing you. There is nothing you can't rise above if you have something passionate to say, and someone passionately to love. People have hurt you not because you weren't lovely enough, but because they were in pain-they were showing you their wounds. You had to walk away from the insult, of course you did, a Soul cannot thrive in poison. A Soul is made of the sun's rays and the petals of flowers, a mosaic so brilliantly lit from within that to bury it in another's ignorance would have been a sin. You are not anyone's savior; you are here to save yourself. By healing yourself, you give something profound to the world. In being tender to yourself, you resolve the wounds you carry. Perhaps it's time to live with a fiery passion again, even if it is messy and vulnerable, for there is more of you left to give. I say: Love first and ask questions later.

You resist the pain of loving, but isn't the pain of walking alone enough? You can trick the mind, but the heart is never fooled. It always steers you towards more authenticity, more connection, more passion. It keeps taking the reins right out of your fearing hands and urging: "Let's head straight for the abyss." And what is this abyss? It is the darkness in you-the hardness, the wild-eyed willfulness, and the cries for love you've smothered. Your heart always says: Go to love-go there now! Because the heart is not a brain it does not see the danger, it only hears the chains breaking. It does not know the word goodbye; it only knows the wondrous word hello. The mind wants to be assured while the heart yearns to feel alive. You don't have to be sure of love-the road will be built before you as you take the next step. The light will go on and you'll see how trustworthy your heart was. You will see that it was not as risky as you'd supposed. You will realize it was necessary to love, and how you never fooled anybody, because you needed love as much as anyone.

Then your heart will fill with laughter and song and begin to dance to music that only lovers can hear, and the wind will play the holes in your heart like a flute. It has been too long since you have forgotten yourself this way! Once the light floods in, you will see there was nothing in the darkness to fear. When you open the door to love, joy will rush in, and you'll be filled with a tender knowing without knowing how you know that it is right to love. You will mutter: "What was I waiting for?"

Only for yourself, dear, only for yourself.

Eternally,

The Mother Who Loves You

Message 5-Love & Forgiveness

You are here to accomplish one thing; you have incarnated for one central reason, yet this reason eludes you: as Mother has said, you are here to learn to love. But even using the word "learn" is misleading, for there is nothing to learn about love at all. You see, you are the embodiment of love. You were conceived in an act of love or at least an act of passion. The sperm that created you was a champion who out-swam all the others to find the ovum and join with it. If this isn't a passionate display of unity and a heroic undertaking, I don't know what is. Then you grew in the womb as cells divided and multiplied following your unique DNA. From your first breath, arms held you, welcoming you into the world. You do not need to learn what love is because love is you and envelopes you. You are swimming in a sea of love! Love is not elusive or hiding, you don't have to seek it. Love is not a thing you find; you can't hunt for love. Love is not a commodity you can store up like money or food, yet it is the most valuable asset you'll ever "have." You cannot have more love on some days and less on other days. Love is a state of mind; love is an attitude. Love is realized when you understand your identity. Though you say you are depressed or anxious, happy or sad, fulfilled or unfulfilled, these are merely passing emotions you mistake as yourself. Your authentic Self is all loving, all accepting, even all knowing. The genuine "you" is always in a state of relaxed sufficiency and abundance in all circumstances. You embody love; therefore, you need not go searching for it, for you are it!

If I say love cannot hurt you, you may object because you've been "hurt by love." But have you truly been hurt by it? Love is the gesture of sharing. Love extends outward-it gives something of itself; this is the nature of love. It is spontaneous and thinks of the other before itself. Love sets free, it is not possessive. Love is a benevolent act. Because love is unselfish and wishes to give, it cannot injure you. Love has never hurt you-only another person can do that. The act of loving is magnanimous; it only results in expansion of the Soul. It never takes anything away from you because love cannot be reduced like a pile of money; love only multiplies. The more you give of it, the more you have to give, for you have a divine capacity to love. Your origins are loving origins; you are here to love.

When your Soul returns to divine remembering, which is what Self-realization is, it automatically sets about the task of loving without any need to protect itself by building walls. Self-realization is not only the realization of truth but the realization of love. Your heart is not a fortress some poor unsuspecting suitor must conquer, proving love to you before you let down the castle drawbridge. Yet you think of love like it can be withheld or stolen, used or tarnished. When you remember what you came to remember, which is: that your very nature is loving, playful, and even affectionate, you'll begin to warm up. You must pass through a thawing process. I say process, because it's not a jolt when the lights of your Soul are switched on and you suddenly become loving. Rather, it is a gradual stripping away of the ego, a process that takes a multitude of incarnations. An enlargement of the heart chakra happens every time you love, so look for opportunities to continue loving. Remember: you are never depleted or hurt by love; this is a fallacy. If you have been hurt because someone didn't return your love, that someone was lacking in love. The only way love can hurt is when there is not enough of it. When a person lacks love, you blame them for hurting you, because they did not return love the way you wanted. What is mistaken for love is a measured sort of exchange: 'If you do this for me, I'll do that for you.' Only when there is a perceived shortage of love does it hurt. You've been disappointed because you expected love in return. You expected to receive in the same measure that you gave. But this is not love; this is the mind's way of protecting itself. Real love gives without counting the cost or measuring what it receives in return. This kind of love is pure-it is a spiritual love, and it is rare. Mortal love is conditional, and therefore not love at all. However, don't be discouraged and suppose that the love you've been practicing isn't "good enough." Any attempt you've made to love has been important progress, so keep practicing. So much of life is practicing until you get it right.

When you incarnated, your memory of pure, unconditional love was rinsed away, so now you struggle to "get out of the way" when you try to love someone, and this is normal. Everyone experiences jealousy and possessiveness in love because the mind favors holding on over letting go. Earthly love is riddled with these lower human emotions. The Buddha taught that attachment causes suffering, but he had to remember everything he'd forgotten before he could teach the doctrine of no jealousy, no comparison, no competing, and non-possessiveness. That is all enlightenment is, a remembering of what your Soul knows but your mind has forgotten.

At the heart of all suffering is the inability to let go. Think about the times you've really suffered in life, and you'll see they all share a common thread: the inability to set something free. When you can simultaneously love (give to) and release (detach), you are in a state of perfect love. "There is no fear in love, but perfect love casts out all fear" (John 4:18). When you love perfectly, fear is sent packing. When you set another free, you are liberated from the bonds of attachment for there is no more desire. Once you are desire-less, whatever the other person says or does cannot create fear in you, and this is a wonderful thing. It is a paradox, but when you set something free, you are set free. This is because setting free is the nature of love and will result in a more courageous state. But as I said, the Buddha didn't understand the nature of attachment until he had practiced letting go for a long while.

How does one love and yet hold on loosely? You must practice letting go of both things and people. When I say to let go, I am not advocating abandonment of responsibility. However, what you think of as your responsibility often isn't and was never yours to carry. A way to know if you are attached is to check your emotions. Are you jealous? Possessive? Competitive? Are you comparing yourself? Are you scheming or conniving to get the love you want? If you're working hard at earning someone's love or attention or working overtime to get more and more material things to impress, my advice is to cool it. Being too eager isn't attractive. Holding on loosely is an art; over many lifetimes you'll learn it. Setting free allows the Universe some room in which to work. The Universe needs elbow room, too. When you're always in control, you become inflexible and demand that life conform to your plan.

The first step towards achieving a greater state of play is to practice being more spontaneous and flexible. If you've engineered your whole life, it doesn't allow for the delightful twists and turns your life story could take. When everything must be your way, there's not a lot of room for surprises. Part of letting go is releasing the expectations you've laid on life. Just because you didn't see it coming doesn't necessarily mean it will turn out badly. The most unexpected turn of events can open doors you never imagined. I suggest you cultivate an attitude of openness, so you don't miss out on the unplanned fun. You've been taught to strive for security and safety and in doing so you have forgotten the wonder you feel when life unfolds without having to push it. Un-learning erroneous ideas like being in control is your life's work. It's a matter of remembering something your Soul already knows but has temporarily forgotten. As your Soul progresses, you will throw off layers and come to your right mind again. It is insanity to avoid love when love is the only sanity.

Christ admonished: "Love your neighbor as yourself" (Mark 12:31). This commandment has two factors: love your neighbor and love yourself. He understood that to love others you must first love yourself. But what does it mean to love yourself, to have a healthy self-esteem? Loving oneself primarily refers to full acceptance of oneself, all of yourself. For starters, be grateful for inhabiting a body. To inhabit a body, your Soul has taken extraordinary measures to arrange for the exact body you have, the family you were born into, the temperament you were born with, as well as your genetics. All these factors your brilliant Soul arranged for you. But you may look at your body and the family you were born into as imperfect, or worse, you may dislike what you were given. It is not easy to be grateful when you are born with a disability, have a serious health issue, or when your lot in life stunted your potential. It may be very tempting to think of your body as unattractive and reject it. You may envy those who are more attractive. It can be a difficult task to love yourself; a person who accepts all of themselves is very rare. You will be nearest to loving yourself in old age when your strength fails, and you're forced to accept your limitations. In the final stage of life, one takes an inventory. At the end, you may realize you've grown to appreciate yourself despite your shortcomings. It takes lifetimes to fully embrace yourself and to be grateful for the journey. Until you have learned to love yourself, you won't be able to love someone else the way they need to be loved.

Let me explain: When a person has low self-esteem, they suffer with feelings of inadequacy, feelings of not being good enough. If a person feels shame about even a part of who they are, they withhold themselves. They won't get close; they won't let themselves be fully known. This hiding goes on unconsciously; the person suffering with inferiority will not be able to see it but will cut himself or herself out of the equation. This withdrawal causes an inability to connect, which results in a lack of emotional intimacy. When the disconnected person is "out of reach," those trying to connect are left empty. When this happens, people tire of reaching and go somewhere else. It is incumbent upon you to learn to love yourself as you are, so you can have strong, vibrant relationships.

Another key to loving yourself is self-efficacy, or the power to act on your own behalf. The more you become your own advocate and reach for the goals you desire, the more empowered you will feel and the higher your self-esteem will rise. Self-esteem can only be increased one way: by repeatedly proving your integrity. What is integrity? Doing what you say you will do-it is as simple as that.

When you can be as good as your word, your self-esteem will skyrocket, because you stand confident in the knowledge that you can trust yourself, and other people can, too. Therefore, being a person of high integrity is important. If you can't trust yourself, you won't have a sturdy self-regard.

Next, I'd like to address the fear of failure, which is being afraid to try or not trying at all because it might lead to failure. You think of failure as a bad thing, so you avoid risky ventures and relationships because they might lead to another let down. But failure is a necessary and unavoidable element of every success. Let me explain: Every person who succeeded at anything saw many failures along the way. Failure happens to be how you learn anything-it's the steppingstone to success. In fact, failure is the only thing that produces lasting Soul growth. Think of a past situation wherein you failed. You'll see that right alongside the failure was a lesson to be learned. Pain is a master teacher; it always brings a lesson. While you consider pain and failure a negative to be avoided, your Soul understands the necessity of it. When you fail to try, you block your Soul's impending growth. Do you see this? Fully living requires a willingness to fail. When you try, even if you perceive the outcome to be a failure, you haven't failed-you have only tried. And while it may feel like your world caved in when last you failed, nobody else took much notice of it. Nobody has the time or interest to sit around contemplating how many times you tried and failed. Everyone is too preoccupied with their own perceived problems and failures to notice. Even if they noticed, you are the only one dwelling on it. In truth, failure is more valuable than success, because it tests the muscle of determination-whether you will do what you say you will do. From our vantage point, there's no better workout for the developing Soul than a stiff shot of failure! It will rouse you, showing how strong or weak your self-belief is. If you're in the habit of avoiding relationships because you might get hurt, or avoiding the possibility of criticism, you're avoiding the primary reason you incarnated: growth. The only mistake you cannot reverse is the failure to try; that is the true sin. To try and fail is so much better than not trying at all, because at least you've learned a little something along the way.

Now we will turn to the subject of forgiveness. On earth, forgiving someone is a difficult task, sometimes nearly impossible while trapped on such an unforgiving planet. But Heaven sees forgiveness differently than you do. The word "forgive" means to give something before it can be asked for (for-give). The Universe is forgiving, every single day, so you wake up with a clean slate. This is because the earth exists in a state of grace. What does it mean to live in a state of grace? It means you exist in an energetically benevolent state, a positive state. Each of you, no matter the number of wrongs you have done, is living in complete and total forgiveness. You may wonder: how is justice served if everyone is forgiven?

Christ came with a message. In essence, He said: 'When you come to earth, you forget everything. You forget about Heaven and its all-encompassing love and mercy. You forget who you are, which is a cosmonaut! You have traveled to many worlds and seen fantastic and wondrous things that have been wiped from your consciousness. You even forget why you incarnated, what your original plan was.' Christ shouted to the world one message that every Soul benefits from: "Father, forgive them, for they do not know what they are doing" (Luke 23:34). Christ was saying: 'I forgive you, for you are blinded by ignorance.' You are blinded by the lower vibratory construct of the earth. Because you live in a state of grace, you should try to extend grace to others.

I'm not going to attempt to explain the all-encompassing system of justice that rules supreme in the Cosmos. A simple book cannot explain it! Even though I am a General among the angels, one who has outlived a hundred thousand stars, I am not privy to all cosmic knowledge. If I could explain it, you would see that in the end each Soul will shine like the brightest star and be glorified; the glory of God will be manifest in it. And what is the purpose of life, all this suffering and redemption from suffering? What is it for and where is it all going? It is all for the glory of love, my dear and gentle Soul. None of the suffering you've endured will linger then. You'll be taken to places-castles and kingdoms so glorious and will dwell in complete oneness and unity; none of the dirt of earth will cling to you then. The Prince of Heaven has already declared your Soul clean, spotless, and part of the Everlasting Light, which is your heritage. When the evolution of your Soul is complete, you will stand so tall above the wrongdoing that your earthly life will seem like a speck of dust and you will simply blow it away. There will be no error in you-this is your ultimate destiny. This glory is every creature's destiny, for in time, every living thing will be redeemed and perfected. And the redemption process has already begun! The vilest among you will never be destroyed, for God always loves and never abandons a Soul.

Science will teach you in the future that you are a piece of the universal fabric and are all dependent upon one another for your very existence, as each atom is connected to all the others. Here is the key to love and forgiveness: remembering that you are all one. On a subatomic level, you are quite literally part of everyone else, and everyone is a part of you. The Christ Consciousness looks out to the world and says: "I can forgive you, because I am complete, totally without flaw, and unforgiveness is a flaw." Forgiveness is one of the laws of perfection; only the strong can forgive. In the Cosmos, your Oversoul exists in a state of blissful oneness, so you can hereby "act as if" you are the embodiment of your Oversoul. You embarked on one of the most difficult and trying of journeys, and you chose it because you wished to be an advanced Soul. You wished to learn to love yourself in this lowly state, and you wished to learn to love others despite their horrible imperfections. Every one of you has one thing in common (which of course you've forgotten), and that is: you took on the most difficult of assignments and vowed to hold one another up. Not just to survive planet earth, but to redeem it. You see, you are the new redeemers. This planet is yours to save, and it can only be saved if you forgive one another. Your Oversoul is so perfect, so "together," so full of acceptance and understanding because of the Christ Consciousness which is a component of your DNA.

You are not the wad of flesh that you see decaying in the mirror. That is a mirage-a ghost, a visage that will be gone in a few years. No, this is not you! When you look in the mirror, say to your reflection: "This is not me!" Then say: "I am the perfection of God, and I am wholly loved. I am an eternal being who has come to lend a helping hand, because I am a part of everyone, and everyone is a part of me. I am here to forgive those who have injured me, because we are interconnected. I am part of the Great Redemptive Plan. I am love and nothing but love: I am so much bigger than the hurt. I am nothing less than the light of the world, and this light fills me from the inside out. This light outshines every wrong word and deed. We don't have to walk in darkness, we can walk in each other's light. We are part of the same redeeming plan, and we are forgiven. All is forgiven."

Message 6-Christ & The Avatars

When you begin to discuss theology, God-ology, humans become very knowledgeable and opinionated about speaking for God. Scholars and clergy alike confess to know, without a shadow of a doubt, the origins of God, Jesus Christ and the angels. I do not mean to offend these well-meaning educated people, but even if you have dedicated your life to understanding divinity, to speak for God, you must be given direct, divine insight into the workings of the afterlife, reincarnation, and the Universal Plan. Many claim to know the truth but few have received it.

The human mind has but a few prime directives which are part of its operating system. One of these directives is to understand its origin. More than just wanting to know its earthly mother and father, humans are curious about how the Universe came to be and why. The first humans looked to one another for answers, and the patriarchs did their best to explain God and the afterlife in their egocentric way. Early civilizations, including the Egyptians, described a multitude of Gods and Goddesses who ruled the afterlife and the seasons. The Egyptians believed their pharaohs to be incarnations of these Gods. They left hieroglyphs of therianthropic beings that came from the sky, beings who described in detail how to prepare the Soul for its journey to the afterlife, as well as their belief in reincarnation.

This explanation of human origins should have been sufficient for successive generations, but with each society came an updated version of the old theology. The story of creation evolved to suit different ethnologies. Religions encircling the globe have changed their doctrines drastically over the centuries. The modern Catholic Church is not the same church of antiquity that denied the findings of science and burned at the stake those it considered to be heretical. The Church's own administration and policies have grown into kinder, gentler versions over the millennia. You see, the world's version of the story of creation has conformed to the needs of its peoples. Each culture has its distinct way of telling the creation story. Therefore, religions can be said to be ethnocentric, as they reflect the customs and ethical conduct of its own peoples.

It stands to reason that doctrines will change with the times. Buddhist practice and philosophy are different today than it was in Buddha's time. It reflects his teachings and philosophy, but an exact replica? Certainly not. The mistake of religion was to force the people it conquered to conversion. Forced conversion robbed people of their own traditions, customs and cosmology while allowing the conquerors to keep what they favored and throw the rest away. I am not saying that ancient bloodthirsty religious practice was right. On the contrary: murder doesn't please God, it will never satisfy God, and neither will money buy God's indulgences. God does not require blood or money! But to take away a foreign people's beliefs and practices because they don't conform to your own is misguided at best, and shameful at worst. Do not force your beliefs on anyone! The way you live your life should be testament enough. Conversion should not be coerced; true conversion is an individual matter of the heart. Talk about your beliefs and faith but be wary of "bringing" anyone to God. God doesn't need you to bring Him another Soul. It is God's job to redeem Souls, not yours.

As societies come and go, religions come and go. Your modern religions continue to change and evolve to match the needs of its peoples. Today's religions will seem antiquated and nearly comical to societies living thousands of years in the future. How can you claim to know the whole truth about God when your description of God is still in the process of revision? It is easy to think you have the truth, to put blinders on. You feel that what is accepted as the truth today will in fact always be the truth, and no one should question the authority of religion. It seems very real, very true, and very stable. Yet a study of history reveals how very changeable humanity's theology is. Cultures of yesterday honored different religions than are even known today, and so it will be in the future. The story of creation changes with scientific understanding. Once upon a time, the church taught that the world was flat, and they imprisoned any who said differently. As science proved the patriarchs wrong, they were forced to change their doctrine. What I am about to explain will challenge known "truth," so try and keep an open mind, as the full story of humanity is in the process of revision.

Of all religious figures central to the human drama stand these in particular: Christ, Buddha, and Mohammed, religion's trinity. From their teachings, three versions of humanity's story emerged, and more blossomed from these. Also did the Hindu Scriptures instruct about the Atman, or the Self, what I am calling the Soul. For simplicity's sake, I will focus on the religious figure most central to Western civilization: the personhood of Jesus Christ. Repeatedly Christ said: "I and my Father are one" (John 10:30). Why did Christ place such emphasis on this statement? Christ was saying: 'Pay close attention to this truth, it's important,' or He wouldn't have repeated it. In claiming He was one with the Father, what did He mean? Was Christ claiming to be God? Christ emphasized that He and God were one because He was a projection of the Father. I tell you the truth: Jesus Christ *was* God incarnate! Christ was God projected to this planet, just as your Oversoul has projected various representations of you throughout the galaxy. Father God projected His persona to earth in the form of a teacher. He reduced Himself to a single cell, which split into other cells, which grew into a baby. Jesus grew into adolescence with unparalleled knowledge of God that mystified and challenged the Jewish religious leaders.

There are many "lost years" unaccounted for in the story of Jesus, years that your version of the Bible does not give account for. These lost years will be revealed in the future. Until then, you know Christ as a man who started a movement that led to His demise. The Roman government and religious leaders despised Him for He inspired the people to hope, and because He was a relentless speaker of the truth. He introduced new thought; He taught something completely different: love, forgiveness, and eternal life. To the desperately oppressed people, Christ was their hope of liberation from the terribly oppressive Roman government. They wished to be saved from their government's cruelty, so when He said, "Leave all and follow me" (Luke 18:22), they did not understand this was a call to renunciation. Instead, they imagined He would lead them to overthrow the government. Christ taught: "Cure the sick ones in it, and go on telling them, 'the kingdom of God has come near to you'" (Luke 10:9). He was the Kingdom of God, incarnated-and the mysteries of the Universe were being offered through Him. He wanted the common people to know that God was available to them; that the spectacle of divinity was not far away, but within them. He was offering a completely new truth: You don't need an intermediary to go to God. You don't need anyone to tell you how to pray or to pray on your behalf. You don't even need a temple to worship in; you are the temple, and the way you live your life is your worshipful gift. He was shouting as loudly as He could: "The Father and I are ONE, we are all one!"

Christ was never a separate entity existing apart from God. God was in disguise when He came as a mortal, cloaking Himself in flesh to identify with His creation. The Father wanted to be born and to pass through the various stages of bodily development, and then to teach and heal. He came to earth because He lacked one thing, and that was the actual experience of living in human form. He assumed a clever disguise as a "Son" of God, projecting an image of Himself as a man to the world. He referred to Himself as a Son because had He announced Himself as God the Father, the greatest authority in Heaven and on Earth, He would have been branded a heretic. As it was, He was only given three years in which to open the minds of the simple people around Him. To their eyes, He was a man of flesh and bone. Had He declared: "I am God made flesh" He would have stood no chance whatsoever. Had He explained Himself as a projection, they would never have understood the complex concept. He knew He only had a short time to convey simple truths. Of course, He had foreknowledge of His crucifixion for God is omniscient.

What has been called "The Holy Spirit" are only the sons and daughters of God. Each Soul is this Holy Spirit. *You* are this Holy Spirit, for you are the Soul. After death, you may see the figure of Jesus Christ if this is your religious tradition, because the Christ projection is so virulent in the hearts and minds of Christians. Remember please that God can assume any form He likes-and He assumed a human form when He was projected to earth. In Heaven, God easily recreates the projection of Christ, so if you are a follower of Christ, you will likely see Him and dwell with Him in the Heavenly realms, just as the disciples dwelled with Christ on earth. *In the afterlife, God will appear and relate to you in a form most accessible to you.* Therefore, you can say with certainty that all religious paths lead to God, for God will take the visage of a divine being known and dear to you.

Your sciences have a limited understanding of how holograms work, so it is difficult to comprehend all this talk of projection. You have a measure of understanding of this technology because you've discovered lasers, and 3D projections. But you are yet to discover how to transport yourselves via thought. Someday this will be a reality if your sciences keep progressing. The biggest impediment to progress is the belief that what you see is all there is, or that you have seen all that is possible. There is far more that you don't know about the cosmos than you do know. What you can be certain of is this: God in His infinite wisdom allowed you to come to earth to take part in the Human Experiment. God cared enough to send part of Himself to experience the pain and joys of human existence. It is extraordinary when you stop to consider that the Maker of All sent a piece of Himself, so you could know that He is real, so He could assure you of a rich afterlife. To demonstrate His divinity, Christ "miraculously" healed via thought. Christ was demonstrating God's capabilities, His compassionate and friendly nature, and even His approachableness. Christ's message was: "Look and see-I am good, therefore, God is good. Think of yourself as one of my children. You are my disciples, we are family." He wanted humanity to believe in the afterlife, so He resurrected Himself. He didn't have to go through any of it, but He did, because you are that important to Him!

Next time you look up into the clear night sky, ask for a revelation of God's realness. No church can give this to you. God desires a spiritual relationship with you. Stay curious, willing to wait as long as it takes. Perhaps you'll have a mystical experience that is beyond explaining. The only way to know something completely is through direct contact, just as God demonstrated when He became human. It sounds fantastic and beyond belief, but it's true: Christ was a projection of God, so God could fully appreciate what humans go through. If anyone understands how hard this world is, He does.

Message 7-Spirit Guides & Angels

Angelic beings have not lived on earth in human form before. Only Spirit Guides may have lived earthly lives, and if they choose to, they may continue to incarnate. Angels are solely in Spirit form. This is mainly the difference between Spirit Guides and Angelic Beings. Also, Angelic Beings are privy to more advanced knowledge and information than most Spirit Guides are allowed. Spirit Guides work directly with human beings to influence, guide and teach them. They interact with you daily, though you never suspect that you're being influenced. So many things happen without you knowing; so many entities are around you. If you have developed clairvoyance, both the 2nd and 3rd chakras are open (the throat chakra being the psychic powerhouse of the body). These chakras function as antenna to receive downloads from higher dimensions. Both the 2nd and the 3rd chakra must be opened for you to receive what is known as clairvoyance, or clear seeing.

You may be asking yourself: how does one open their chakras? Many have fervently attempted to manipulate their "energy" or etheric body. While their desire to see into the spiritual realm is admirable, they have no power to affect a change in energy fields. You live in a dimension of matter, and the chakras exist in an etheric dimension. Consequently, the only ones capable of opening human psychic ability are that person's Spirit Guides and their Guardian Angels, and a benevolent act it is. While you have been told that it's possible to open these doors for yourselves, ask your Spirit Guides to open your third eye or throat chakra. These two chakras will be opened first when ascending from a lower dimension to higher dimensions. They must be opened before you can see and hear the spirit world. Even if an energy worker claims they can open your chakras directly, while their intentions may be honest, this is inaccurate. It is always through an intermediary of the Spirit realm that chakras are opened, adjusted, and cleansed. The worker of energy is not affecting the healing-they are being guided; they are a conduit. They are merely the bridge between two worlds. The Spirit Guide has the greatest responsibility. Your Spirit Guide is like the surgeon who takes the instruments, opens the skin, fixes the diseased organ, and closes so the healing can begin. They are something like an unofficial doctor, and the energy worker is the nurse. When a healing has occurred, it hasn't occurred by the power or magnanimous will of the human healer. No! Healing happens because the willing subjects have a Spirit Guide, even several Guides, and angels working alongside them. These beings are trained and able to affect the healing prescription. You owe your very life to these helpers. From your first breath to your last, they are working on your behalf.

    A Spirit Guide may be relieved of its duties if there is another Guide who, for whatever reason, is more appropriate for the assignment; the original Guide may be replaced. This happens on occasion. More likely, the Guide that was chosen for you at birth will be with you throughout your lifetime, enduring with you all you have endured-even seeing you to the door of death, and meeting you on the Other Side. When you see them again on the Other Side, you'll remember them. It will all come flooding back, how they stood by you, defended you, and patiently guided you. How they grieved with you, rejoiced with you and how greatly they loved you. And while they have cared about you since childhood, their love for you grows daily. It is something like parental love. The parent loves the infant and protects it, but as the child matures into a capable adult, the parent's love and respect matures. In the same way, your Spirit Guide is bonded to you. When you meet on the Other Side, you will remember having endured this life together, and they will assist in your Orientation Process. They will explain pivotal moments and decisions, and how they tried their best to reach and influence you.

While alive, most people will never know they have a Guide, or several Guides. The Guide will go unrecognized, and there will be no gratitude for this Soul's service until you reach the next dimension where you'll have full recollection of every moment that your Spirit Guide stood beside you, holding your hand and showing you the way. You'll see how angels protect you-how many times they stepped in to be a shield for you, how many times you were nearly injured or attacked, and how many times you were saved from despair or death because of their uplifting presence. Thousands of incidents you were spared thanks to their benevolent presence. When you see how regularly they interacted with you and how close they were-closer than a brother, and how willingly they submitted themselves in service to you, you will be astounded and feel tremendous gratitude. You might even say they are your best friends. Though you aren't aware of them, they are your constant traveling companions. They are eternal and true friends, and I wish that every one of you would sense their presence now and again. If you have clairaudience, you may hear them and sense them around you. If so, you are blessed indeed! If you can see, hear or feel them, then know you are quite an evolved being. Meaning, you have lived many hundreds or thousands of times, and you've known these entities on the Other Side, and they have known you. Be sure that if you have knowledge of them, you have known each other over a long span of time; you are entwined in a blessed union of Souls.

Because everyone has Spirit Guides, it only makes sense to talk to them. You may not know their names, but if you close your eyes and focus on them, you can feel their comforting presence, just as you don't have to see God to talk to God. I expect there have been many times in crisis when you called to God for help. In those crucial moments, it wasn't God who directly intervened; it was your

Spirit Guide intervening. In certain cases, Angels work with your Spirit Guide to affect a more positive outcome. God does not deal directly with you. That is akin to expecting the President to answer your phone call! The chain of command doesn't work that way. You wouldn't expect the President to stop his work for you. As it is below, so it is above. Representatives carry out God's work, and these are Angels and Spirit Guides. There are also totem or spirit animals that are attached to you, and you may have one, several, or a group of devoted animal helpmates. In fact, they are part of your karmic team. They even communicate with one another, yet each serves a different purpose. Nevertheless, your karmic team is working in perfect harmony for your evolution. Spirit animals serve mainly as protectors and to lend comfort. They can act as signals that attract certain positive energies, and they can repel dark energies. It may be that you are attracted to certain earthly animals, having an unexplainable affinity for them because they are your Spirit Animals. They serve you without thanks and without your conscious acknowledgement.

You don't stop evolving when you get to the Other Side. Oh no-it's only the beginning! Your evolution happens so gradual on earth-at a snail's pace compared to the speed at which you develop on the Other Side. On earth, everything is slowed by interference from dark forces, and because you exist in a Universe of matter. In Heaven, there are no interferences, for there is no evil or matter. You will evolve exponentially for there are no impediments. This is what is so relieving about Heaven. You can evolve as quickly as you choose, or you may take your time. No one tells you how fast you must go, or what choices you must make. Heaven is a very autonomous place. When Souls first arrive, they are surprised at how much time they spend alone. This is because you have reflecting to do, for you must plan your next steps. If someone else influenced these decisions it would mean that you could make mistakes. You must be the only one to determine which path to take.

This is the birthright of every Soul-to determine its own path. There is free will in Heaven, just as there is free will on earth. In Heaven, you're not influenced by others, and you're not concerned with what people think; you're free of those persuasions.

Remember this-when you feel lonely, you are never alone; it only feels that way. When you don't know which way to turn, ask your Spirit Guide. Get connected to your spiritual best friend through meditation, for this is the most important relationship you can develop. If you ask your Spirit Guide to reveal themselves to you, there's no doubt in my mind that you will find each other. Once the lines of communication are established, your inner ear will be tuned so you can more readily hear the voice of your Spirit Guide. The voice you hear in your head (the good one) is usually your Spirit Guide. In fact, your conscience is your Spirit Guide! And you may have more than one, you may have several; some people even have three or four Guides. Ask for their names, and if you hear more than one name it's because you may have more than one Spirit Guide. Don't be afraid of them, and don't be afraid if they talk to you. It's a natural relationship you've enjoyed since birth. Though they don't need your acknowledgement or gratitude, it's thrilling for them when they are acknowledged. Just as a parent doesn't need gratitude from the child, when the parent receives that child's appreciation, it means something. It's difficult to believe that a force that you cannot see, feel, hear nor touch is with you. But you can't see your breath, can you? And I daresay it is real! Neither can you see the microscopic world, but it influences your survival in every moment. So it is with your invisible advisors-they are influencing your survival on a continual basis. Become aware of their mitigating presence, and occasionally, show them a little appreciation.

Message 8-Hungry Ghosts

All earthly elements are a representation of Divine mind. Consider the element of water. You can learn a lot from water if you examine it. Water is one of the few essential components of life. Without it, there would be no life, there would only be thoughts and ideas. It is the birthplace of all life, as creatures give birth in water: sea creatures of all kinds, and freshwater animals use water as a birthing bed. Your own body is composed largely of water; what you perceive as solid flesh and bone is mostly water. At death when the blood stops pumping through your veins and the lubricating element of water stops flowing, your body will become rock-hard. This is because water allows all entities, even non-sentient matter to exist; it is an essential building block of life. To create anything, one must exploit a certain amount of water.

Next, consider for a moment the properties of water: it is pliable, translucent, permeable, and so flexible that it has no real shape. Water can be heated or cooled without destroying its molecular structure. It changes with its environment; it's highly adaptable. It can morph as quickly as the ocean tide. It's as flexible as the stream that rushes around a rock, but it can sit as still and placid as a solitary pond; it shows how peaceful life could be. It also has an innate sensitivity to its environment as water is profoundly affected by words and sound. Thoughts, attitudes, emotions, even the environment you're in have a scientifically verifiable effect on the water molecules within your body. The words you speak have a vibration, and even unspoken thoughts and emotions can influence water's molecular structure. Water has a memory, embedding the thoughts, attitudes, and feelings of the environment. Essentially, water is teaching you to be transparent, flexible, easily directed, and sensitive. It's also showing that your thoughts have a measurable impact on the environment around you, and even your own body. The vital element of water has many lessons to teach, but perhaps the most important lesson is that while it's good to be busy, it's just as important to be still. Water doesn't have to announce its importance to be important. It simply is, by its very nature, essential to the maintenance of life, and so are you.

The natural state of water is tranquil. Water is moved by the wind but without the wind, water is still. The interplay between the opposites of activity and stillness is known as balance. Spiritual master's practice to achieve balance. To practice only one half of the polarity is to be satisfied with only half of the answer. You may be very adept at being busy because you've been told that the more productive you are the more valuable you are. A mature person understands she is just as valuable in quietness, producing peaceful energy, as she is producing a result. Actions are important to satisfy the creative urge, but the advanced Soul practices the disciplines of silence, self-control and patience. These characteristics are more lacking in society and thus more valuable. Everyone is in a rush trying to produce a result and working under a deadline. Not everyone can say they are just as content in quiet contemplation. The person who appreciates solitude and silence is a rare gem. Enlightened beings strive to find contentment in every situation. Endeavor to develop a sense of well-being, whatever comes.

When you busy yourself, what exactly are you keeping busy? You are giving your mind a toy to play with. You are giving your curious consciousness something to do so it feels productive. When you feel productive, you feel worthwhile. Society says: The more productive you are, the greater your worth and the better you will feel. This kind of thinking makes sense to the mind because you have been genetically designed to be achievers and creators. This is why art and music are prized so highly; they are the highest representations of creative ability. You automatically create; you are always busy creating something. For some, the creative instinct has become more than a preoccupation-it has become a compulsion, an obsession in many societies. Modern civilization's idea of progress is full of noise, distraction, stress, and irritation. Most minds cannot keep still. Thoughts that are jumpy, anxious and restless are the accepted norm. With the development of the Industrial Age came dissatisfaction, and a longing for luxurious things. This yearning for more has caused a great amount of heartache, especially in Western civilization where affluence is measured strictly by material gain. Yet materialism hasn't added up to greater satisfaction. Instead, it is an empty promise. Material things can only give so much pleasure before you need more. The acquisition of things will never be satiated, because there is a feeling of momentary excitement or importance when you're the owner of something new, but shortly the feeling fades. You're fooled into believing that getting more is the way to gratify your hungry Soul, but your Soul goes on yearning. There will never be enough to fill the empty space inside the human heart. What will satiate this restlessness?

There are only two directions that human consciousness can turn: outward and inward. When you direct your consciousness outward, you're turning to your environment for happiness. When you find that nothing and no one can make you feel complete, you may despair. You may not realize that your Soul is tethered to the Other Side by the silver cord of life. This cord connects you to your real home and your eternal purpose. When you look within, you can trust that a great Providential wisdom is guiding you and there is no need to feel lonely. Aloneness is a false human concept. In meditation, you will discover that you are a dearly cherished child who has not been abandoned or rejected, and therefore, being alone becomes less objectionable. For many people, feeling alone is the greatest scourge, the worst possible circumstance, while admired spiritual masters have mastered the art of aloneness. They have learned the secret of perpetual delight: to be with themselves and to love their own company. This is what sets them apart. If you would spend time in reflective pondering, you wouldn't be as needy, and you'd see how whole and utterly perfect you are just the way you are. You'd give up the compulsion to prove yourself to critics. Instead of worrying or becoming depressed by your circumstances, you'd be confident in your capabilities and grateful for the opportunity to experience life in the material world. All joys and heartaches would be reframed.

Once you have established a regular spiritual practice, take care not to instruct anyone who has not asked for your wisdom. Withhold it until you have found a willing, eager ear. Otherwise, you may invite criticism and rebuke. There will be few students and even fewer true teachers. But there are many hungry Souls, so hungry that they cannot wait to be fed; they will go to the immediate source. And while it suffices for the moment, they aren't satisfied for long. The discontent returns, for the only teacher is within. No guru can give you anything; all insight is within…in-sight! A teacher only guides your Self-discovery. Some Souls wander like hungry ghosts searching for fulfillment for the whole of their lives.

If you are lost in the deceptive promise of the material lie, you will look for answers in sex, money and possessions. While it is good to enjoy all you've been given, do not be fooled into thinking these are the ultimate answer. If you're always wanting more of something: more sex, more food, more affection, more attention, more "things," then you are like a hungry ghost. Every Soul searches for the door to liberation. What will bring you to the door? What will draw you, I cannot say, nor do I know when you will find it. There's no sign above the door that says, "Enter Here." Your heart is the passageway to enlightenment, and you may have bypassed its wisdom many times. You may have even knocked upon the door but became impatient and went away. It is only opened when you stay long enough. You'll be starving by the time you stumble through the door. Then all other tasks will be a distraction from the real task of unraveling the mystery. You will be so enchanted that words will be a complete failure; you'll fall silent before the unspeakable. Reverence and devotion will settle in your heart like two love birds warming one another. Captivated, you'll be unapologetic about taking your leave. Hearts cannot belong to others completely when they are so taken. You will hold your breath all day until you're finally alone with the truth, and the reality you once squirmed from becomes the enchanting voice you long to hear.

You'll know you've found the door when you're not hungry for anyone or anything anymore. There's no more want there-no more heartache, no more loneliness, no more loss. There is only the sound of the wind whispering. While you're trying to sleep it will go on whispering to you. You'll long for the whispers of the wind. Because you are a child of the wind, it will caress and tickle you as it's instructing you. It will whip the leaves around you just for monkey business and you'll be its curious kite. The farther you sail, the farther you'll want to sail. How high will you go? Nobody knows…that is up to you, and that is the mystery.

While you have heard that happiness comes from 'within,' you are flesh-and-blood creatures with drives, desires and longings, so happiness seems to come by way of the five senses. While there is nothing wrong with the senses, do not believe that sense pleasures can fulfill you. If this were true, you'd always be satisfied, because you're ever enjoying the world through your senses, aren't you? You have seen that money cannot buy love, and love doesn't guarantee happiness (sometimes just the opposite!). Spiritual masters have found ecstasy through isolated meditation. They achieve bliss while sitting sensory deprived in a Himalayan cave, disconnected from the world. How is this possible? Monks and nuns have found this solace: the more they look inward, the less they need the world's delights or approval. This phenomenon-the ability to be content and joyful despite deprivation is achieved only one way: by spending time in reflection, plundering the depths of the Soul. Every spiritual master has taught this, yet still it eludes you. It is only the mind and its insistence on being entertained that keeps you from discovering it. The mind is bored by the thought of sitting in quiet repose; the very suggestion repels the monkey-mind which demands stimulation and craves pleasure. It argues: 'If everyone sat around meditating all day, nothing would get done! After all, aren't we put on earth to accomplish something?' Spiritual practice offers lasting contentment and satisfaction, yet the result-driven mind refuses to listen. Defy your mind! It is YOUR mind, is it not? YOU are the master of this house! Perhaps it is time to tell the monkey to sit down and stop tearing up your peace!

Ask yourself: What am I here to accomplish. Is it merely to survive, or is there something beyond survival? Philosophers have been debating existential questions like these for eons, but in easy-to-understand terms, let me remind you of the reason you are alive: to discover your divinity, and to learn to love. If during your short stay on this spinning blue ball you leave something good behind and become a spiritually attuned person, you've done an outstanding job! If you're working on discovering your spiritual self, happiness will be magnetized to you. You don't have to chase enlightenment; enlightenment is chasing you. And when I say leave something good behind, I don't mean you should ignore your needs and be the sacrificial lamb. God isn't impressed with self-sacrifice or "good deeds." Religions who claim that spreading their doctrine will get you into Heaven, or that good works elevate your position in the afterlife, are sadly mistaken. God loves you unconditionally-you don't earn your ticket to Heaven; it is a gift. God doesn't need to win converts, for over the march of many lifetimes a Soul evolves; converting to a religion cannot hasten that process. You are "saved" by making choices that are sober and that benefit all involved. When you're faced with a difficult decision, consider the impact your actions will have on everybody. In some incarnations, you'll make more bad choices than good, but do not despair-you have an unlimited cache of incarnations with which to work. Eventually, you'll get it right; take hope in that.

Please don't make the mistake of thinking that because you go to church that you are in right relationship with your maker. There's a saying I like very much: "Just because you go to church doesn't make you a Christian. I can go sit in the garage and it doesn't make me a car" (Joyce Meyer). Religion is not synonymous with authentic God-consciousness. Many people who have never been to church live a devoted life, for they honor the law of love. Their lives are filled with good deeds that nobody sees (except for God). This is what Christ meant when He said, "So the last shall be first, and the first last" (Matthew 20:16). Those who have suffered oppression and were told to sit at the back of the bus will be the honored citizens of Heaven. Things up here are reverse of what you might expect. The most common response of a returning Soul is awed surprise followed by a profound humility when they see how things *really* are. If you're certain about who is getting into Heaven and who isn't, you'll think again when you arrive, for: "The last shall be first."

Having a genuine relationship with God (or your Higher Self, if you relate to that terminology) hasn't anything to do with your devotion to a religion or your attendance at church. Hitler was an extremely religious person and look what his religious fervor produced. Don't depend upon church leaders to tell you what to believe or you may be led down the wrong rosy path. Just pray: "God, reveal Yourself to me." You don't need a degree in theology to discover God's magnanimous love. The best part of being devoted to anything is your loving connection to it. Open yourself to experiencing unconditional, transcendent love without having to understand it. Simply climb into Mother's lap and tell her everything. You'll see her jeweled eyes glittering, and her rapturous smile will wrap you in an embrace so tender and exquisite that you'll be left speechless…which is how you're most beautiful; when you have humbly accepted your place as one of Her dear children. If you come to Her with a head full of knowledge, she'll turn her face away; She's heard it all before. The Universal Mother wants your pilgrim heart. Only in the lap of the Divine will you find your way home.

Most people cannot see past the material world. It is not because they do not possess the ability to see into the spiritual realm but because they are not prepared to see it. You will only see what your mind is open to seeing. To grasp the spiritual realm, you must increase in self-awareness. You must become introspective. Most people are only aware of what's outside of themselves: the weather, their finances, their partners, their children, their coworkers, what food they're eating, what car they're driving, and how good they look that day. Most people relate solely to the stimuli around them. This is unfortunate, for it means that something environmental will determine your happiness. If the weather is miserable, a grey cloud follows them. If they're fighting with their mate, they feel frustrated and irritated. If they're having a bad hair day, they feel self-conscious and unattractive. When the outer dictates the inner, you are at the mercy of every unfortunate circumstance of which there are many. The only remedy is to be your own thermostat instead of being a thermometer. A thermometer takes the temperature of its environment and matches it, while a thermostat sets the temperature and maintains it. A pilgrim Soul sets its own agenda, it listens to the beat of its own drum. To see beyond the material world, you must be alone in order that you should hear. Hear what, you ask?

There are two voices vying for your attention: the voice of the Higher Self and the voice of the ego. The Higher Self has been called many things. In Psychology it is called the Super Ego. In Christianity it is called The Holy Spirit. Secularism refers to it as the conscience. Whatever you call it, its mitigating presence regulates moral decisions. But for our purposes, we will use the term Higher Self, also known in Psychology as the Wise Mind. The ego has been represented by religion as the devil, the evil that tempts you to do wrong. Let me clarify what the devil is: it is malevolent energy, the same low-frequency energy that is found in demons, poltergeist, and ghosts. These entities remain trapped in the lower realms of the underworld and are not permitted into Heavenly realms. To an angel, these realms are not unseen, and therefore are more "real" than your material world. In Heaven, your world is both the dream and the nightmare. Here, *you* are the ghosts trapped in a world of maya. Listening to your ego is just as unhelpful as listening to the devil. Being ego-driven will slow your progress, so practice defying the ego, which is not easily accomplished. You might say that the brain has a voice, and that voice is the ego. It insists on being heard and getting its way. If the ego isn't quelled and is allowed to dictate without discretion it becomes ruthless and tyrannical and will believe its own lies. Eventually it will not be able to distinguish right from wrong; it will live in a world of delusion, a fortress built of lies. The tyrannical ego would overtake common decency. The ego has one set of objectives while the Higher Self has another, and their agendas are seldom sympathetic.

Most people have no tolerance for the timelessness of the Higher Self that would have you stay in meditation with little regard for schedules and responsibilities. You see, the Spirit world has no such artificial constraints as time or deadlines. When you have the whole of eternity at your disposal, what's the hurry? Therefore, the yogis meditate with little regard for what they wear, how clean they are, or whether their body has eaten. It matters not to a Soul who spends more time in the spiritual world what the body or outside world is up to. These spiritual masters have crossed the invisible divide from the material world into dimensions unconcerned with the ego's shallow agenda. The Soul pays no attention to the gripes of the flesh; it ignores them. The Soul is only concerned with the impartation of knowledge and truth; the Soul is obsessed with truth. The Soul hungers for more cosmic knowledge; that is, insight which transforms thinking from carnal into spiritual.

Think for a moment about the composition of a spirit: it is a light wave and a vibration. There is nothing immovable in it, for vibration is continually shifting and fluxing in intensity. Because spirit is made of light, it dwells in the realm of light where truth is always shining. You may not want to hear the truth, but your Higher Self will always tell the truth. This is the secret to realization of the Self: to hear the truth, and to accept the truth. Sounds simple, doesn't it? Self-realized people do not play games, because for them, the truth is everything. If you come to a Self-realized individual hiding behind facades, putting on an "act," an authentic guru will, before any lesson begins, require you to take off the mask.

This shedding of the false self is the first lesson. She will require that you speak truthfully and will not spare you the truth. Because she communes with the pure laws of the Universe, she will be uncompromising in her standards. While it sounds simple, it is in fact impossible for those without a regular routine of meditation and introspection to deny the ego, for it can be quite virulent.

Message 9-Enlightenment & the Buddha

Seekers want to say they are an "old Soul," spiritually progressed or enlightened. But the enlightened are an exclusive club, and as with any club, to be a member, you must be willing to make sacrifices. What sacrifices? Let's examine the life of one enlightened avatar. But first, why should you strive to achieve this mysterious spiritual badge called enlightenment? Because you don't want to keep reincarnating, of course! Simply stated, life is hard; Heaven is not. The Buddha understood this, and subsequently, He set himself on a crash-course with enlightenment, becoming one of the brightest stars in the spiritual sky. Buddhists all over the globe have found an assurance of peace and wisdom in His teachings, and even if they failed to achieve enlightenment, they became a better person-and isn't that what spirituality is all about?

It's crucial to understand the process of Self-realization if you're going to achieve it. Enlightenment, the kind that Lord Buddha had, is an intentional slaying of the mind. It is the willingness to be proven wrong. It is the suppression of the ego-self; and once tamed, it is the final execution of that terrible tiger that roars, "I know." But how does one slay the ego? And why have an ego if you must smother it over the course of many lifetimes? An ego is an inflated sense of one's own importance. People with inflated egos are quite impressed with themselves, and can be self-centered, self-serving, and self-aggrandizing; in short, it's all about themselves. To a certain degree, loving oneself is healthy. But while egotistical people have a high self-regard, they also have a marked lack of one quality: compassion. If a person lacks compassion for her fellows, then she has yet to understand what she's doing in a reincarnated body. When you are aware of your own divinity, you begin to turn a compassionate gaze on everything, for you'll recognize the spark of God in all of creation. People and animals will become sacred to you, so you'll do your best to avoid harming them. This is why Eastern religions don't kill anything that doesn't need to be killed. They have trained themselves to see the preciousness of all life. Now that a fundamental understanding of enlightenment has been reached, we can proceed to the all-knowing man himself, The Buddha.

He wasn't always called the Buddha or Shakyamuni, which means: The Awakened One. He was born Siddhartha Gautama, the son of a governor in India. Siddhartha was born to a rich and powerful family who pampered Him to the extent that He wasn't allowed to go outside of the family's palace grounds. He had everything a young man could desire: the best teachers, loving parents, the most comfortable accommodations, fine clothes, and the best food. He even married and bore a son. The only thing denied him was his actual freedom, because outside of the palace walls, his father knew he would find suffering in the world, and his father would have liked to spare his precious son from that. The first lesson to be learned about enlightenment was learned before Siddhartha ever set foot in the real world: that the Soul wishes to be free. Because of his yearning to experience the world directly, Siddhartha left his wife and infant son in the care of his family and set off to see what he could see, which is the second lesson: you may have to leave things and people behind to go where the Soul is leading you. When Christ was asked what the disciples should do to find the Kingdom of Heaven, He responded: "Leave all and follow me" (Matthew 8:22). You may be thinking: "Perhaps this idealistic notion of enlightenment isn't for me." Perhaps you don't fancy having to say goodbye to the people or things you love. Then never mind-go back to your life and don't trouble yourself, because the way of the awakened is not an easy road; it is uphill. The easy road always leads downward. But if you're not keen on decline, then, continue reading.

Siddhartha wandered India, meeting other aesthetics who were searching for enlightenment. In a country steeped in the spiritual traditions of renunciation, Siddhartha was encouraged to deprive himself of the sense pleasures, even the basic human pleasures such as eating and sleeping, and certainly, sexual pleasure. He listened to his teachers' advice, depriving himself of anything that would divert his attention from the austere life of an ascetic. What he found were four noble truths in the world: death, sickness, old age, and suffering. The prince quickly realized that the world had promised pleasure but all it could deliver was pain. His father had been correct after all, but Siddhartha needed to experience the carnal world for himself. Christ described a similar scenario of a son who sets out on a search for meaning, known as The Parable of the Prodigal Son (Luke 15:11-32). Like Buddha and the prodigal son, you desire to be free from the tyranny of the mind and the only place to find this peace is in the presence of your Heavenly Father. But the world is so alluring, so convincing, that you have done exactly what these seekers did: you have sought it in the outer world, and for many lifetimes. Perhaps you are still caught in the clutches of maya: the delusion, the dream of finding your fulfillment in a bankrupted society, or in the arms of another. But let's press on, for you must learn of the Buddha's triumphant ending.

Siddhartha, worn and starving, had not apprehended God despite renouncing wealth, the world, and all sense pleasures. To his dismay, striving had earned him only the knowledge of a strange world and the stranger people in it. What does a pure-hearted and devout Soul have to do to become enlightened that Siddhartha had not done? He had prayed and meditated 24-7. He had fasted and deprived himself in hopes of a revelation of God. He'd kept company with spiritual masters who had shown him God-like abilities that defied the laws of the physical world, and he'd done everything his teachers instructed Him to do. Having sought everywhere and with everyone for the key to unlocking his mind from the dream of physical life, Siddhartha sat beneath a Bodhi tree and declared: 'I will stop chasing enlightenment. I will simply wait on God.' He stopped trying to earn God's favor. He stopped questioning and talking. He suspended the mind's plans and questions and humbled himself. Suddenly the earth began to shake, and reality gave way, crumbling before his eyes. Evil spirits attempted to frighten him from his place of surrender. Siddhartha only had to breath out, and his breath became a strong wind which swept the evil away. By humbling Himself, by "being" instead of "doing," the door to enlightenment was opened to him. Siddhartha took a new name: The Buddha, which means, "The Awakened One."

But what did the Buddha awaken to? The truth, of course! He realized what every person must realize: that physical life is just a crucible to destroy the false self, which is the ego, and that the world offers nothing more. He saw that the purpose of life isn't pleasure, but it isn't pain, either. The Buddha's life is an allegory; it shows where the seeker must look. Enlightenment isn't found in a religion, a church, synagogue or mosque; these are only buildings. It isn't even found in the company of spiritual teachers. Ultimately, spirituality is an individual process that happens within. Siddhartha was being made into the Buddha day-by-day, step-by-step. The suffering he endured was forging in him a surrender that was key to his unlocking. By looking within and not to the world, He found peace, comfort, and direction. And while we are examining the Buddha's life, an important distinction should be drawn between prayer and meditation. Prayer is asking, a time to make your requests known, while mediation is surrendered listening. It's important to ask, but it's also important to listen.

To hasten your evolution, do what the Buddha did: listen more than you speak. It's the still, small voice that will tell you the truth. If it's not telling you things that are hard to hear from time to time, it's not the right voice. Your internal guru will consistently require you to help others, to give, to be kind, and to become a more truthful person. Mostly it will require you to love selflessly and to forgive. Not with a codependent kind of love that sacrifices its own development for another; that is not love at all. The kind of love you must learn is considerate of others without denying itself. God asks that you grow and develop so you can be a model for others. Humans learn by observing; your parents modeled behaviors-some good, some bad that you observed and then repeated. You must inspire others by setting a good example. The highest compliment is for others to be so inspired by you that they want to emulate you. How long will it take you to become enlightened? Most Souls won't realize their full potential even after many lifetimes. But this Cosmic vehicle of the Soul is encoded with a prime directive: to see reality. Like the Buddha, you'll meet strange Souls in strange lands, because you're a stranger here. You're on loan to the world for a little while but eventually, you'll awaken from the dream of maya. You cannot fail to become one more All-Knowing, Awakened One.

Message 10-The Human Experiment

Christ came as a unifier; His purpose was to unify humankind. His mission was never to divide humanity. Any division is a trap of the mind. It is not a spiritual thing to divide people; that is decidedly un-Christ-like. Just as each Oversoul incarnates knowing what's ahead, so Christ came with foreknowledge about the persecution He would endure. He knew He would not be listened to by the masses, and few would understand the real meaning of His words. This is what He meant when he said, "Many are called, but few are chosen" (Matthew 22:14). He knew what would come of the message He offered; the hope for another life, and the forgiveness He taught-but He taught it anyway. He chose to sacrifice His life so there would be some light when there were very few lights at that time in history. As with Christ, the importance of your life won't be seen during your own lifetime. You cannot know the impact your life will have until many centuries have passed. Don't judge your efficacy yet, because you're not able to see the full effect your life has had until you've reached the Other Side. Simply do what you can now to bring more light into the world and try to remember the ripple effect; how even the smallest good you do will be amplified in eternity.

Every Soul is surprised in the Afterlife Review when they see the immense network of Souls their existence touched. You simply cannot know your worth here in the present, so don't be afraid to have an effect. Don't be afraid to bring healing; don't even be afraid to speak out against injustice, as much as you understand it. What each person gives is proprietress, and essential for the perfecting of unity. Fear is the only true enemy-your greatest opponent. In truth, the only opponent is debilitating fear. With the knowledge that you'll go on until your Soul has attained perfection, what is there to be afraid of? Don't be afraid to stand alone, or to take the path less traveled, and don't be afraid to be something that nobody's ever seen before. Don't be afraid to be different! Don't be afraid of yourself, whoever that is. You came here for a reason-so why downplay your importance? It's just disbelief of the mind again; of course, you can make a difference! It's easy to look around and think, "If I weren't here, nobody would notice." But the ripple effect makes this false. Even the smallest pebble tossed into the water makes a ripple. The tiniest act of kindness has a profound effect, too enormous to fathom. It would be wise to remember that most everything is beyond your comprehension, and if everything is unreal and beyond your comprehending, then it's best to remain humble. Watch out for those who say they have all the answers-very few know the answers. You may have one part of the answer, and someone else has the other. Don't be so quick to think you know anything. Instead, be quick to remember you are but one thread among billions and billions of threads. Stay away from judging. Just be a child; that's all your spirit is.

When you look at the violence and chaos of the world, you might think that the Human Experiment has failed. An eon of disregard for the rights of others doesn't seem like a success, and saviors sent to this world are persecuted. But the Human Experiment began with great hope for a successful outcome, as all experiments do. The Creator wished to share the power, not to hoard it; God wished to walk with humanity the way it is said in Genesis that He walked with the first humans who served as companions to Him. God couldn't commune with Homosapians until they could understand Him as their teacher and friend. When the Bible describes the first man and the first woman, it is describing the first *intelligent* humans, capable of language and symbolism. Once humans were able to intelligently relate, God was eager to share His knowledge. The life you are living is part of the greatest unfolding drama called the Human Experiment, and it will reach a conclusion, as all experiments do. An experiment must have a result, which either proves or disproves a central hypothesis. The Human Hypothesis states that as free-will beings, the whole of humanity will evolve towards Self-realization. If the hypothesis is proven wrong, humanity will reject spiritual development and pursue the insatiable hunger of the ego. As a self-governing species influenced by both genetics and environment, it is probable that humanity will evolve away from that which harms it, that which threatens it to extinction. After all, the survival instinct is the strongest of all human drives. Most of you would go to great lengths to preserve your existence, and some of you value life so highly that you would protect and defend the lives of others. Because of this, odds are in your favor that humanity will yet come to its senses.

In the future, the Human Experiment will reach a conclusion; I am talking about the end of the world. This is a sore subject. One that, like death, is sure to happen, but nobody cares to talk about. If you were to say to a friend, "Shall we discuss the end of the world?" I daresay most people would be repelled by the thought. Or they will tell you what religious folklore has prophesied. Curiously, it is common among societies to have a belief about the end of the world and God's return. Ancient indigenous civilizations like the Mayans and the Aztecs envisioned God returning from the sky and so has Christianity. This theme of God returning has existed throughout humanity's history. It stands to reason that a belief common to societies has validity and is worthy of consideration.

As stated, the Human Experiment is ongoing and will be in effect until technology destroys all life (Atom Bomb or Biological Warfare), or until you create a successful conclusion by building a utopia. It's impossible to say how it will end. Why am I discussing such dismal subjects? Not to scare you, because you don't need to be scared! If the world should end today-if a massive asteroid were to hit the earth and every heart stopped beating, you'd only be returning Home, and Heaven is a much easier assignment than an earthly existence, I assure you. I am reminding you of your mortality because it is both real and impending, and the earth's inevitable demise is real. However, the world may keep spinning for billions of years. Why worry now about how it will end? The point is: you don't need to worry, but you should do your part to make it a better world and begin the healing of your planet.

All kinds of people act as if there are no consequences for their actions. Even religious leaders act dishonestly, while preaching the opposite. This is because the mind feels it will never get caught. It feels there is always more time and it need not be overly concerned with its actions. Those who believe there is no life after death feel they have every right to get what they want without regard for the interest of others. Understandably, most people feel powerless to change the future and say: if their number's up, it's up. If an asteroid should hit the earth or a mad country finally drop the A-bomb, there's nothing to be done about it. What can the average person do to prevent disaster from striking? Quite a lot, as it turns out. The Human Experiment has a protocol of operation, as every scientific experiment has. This protocol is constructed as an algorithm. Computer scientists are familiar with the term, but you may not be. Simply put, an algorithm is a systematic set of operations with an intended outcome. Algorithms exist for the entire cosmos, including planet earth. Algorithms are an effective way to manage and order space and time as a way of containing the infinite, if you will. Beginning with no data or an empty state, instructions prescribe a computation that, when executed, produce an intended outcome.

There are two types of algorithms: deterministic, and random. A deterministic type has a foreknown conclusion, and a random algorithm allows for variations. Earth's algorithm is random. Its running time is changeable, as is the result. This means that God Himself does not know how the human story will play out because He built into it the element of surprise! He is playful, this Mastermind. God used computational complexity based upon the principles of something called random number generation when He designed the Human Experiment. According to random number generation, collective consciousness creates order in the world (See: The Global Consciousness Project). When large numbers of people think in unison, random outcomes are persuaded according to collective thought. Collective thought will decide the fate of humankind-not God. God does not hold the whole world in His hands-y*ou do!* Therefore, you are co-creating the outcome of the Human Experiment by the thoughts you think. As it was said: If you think you can or you think you can't, either way, you're proven correct (Henry Ford). Said another way: "For as he thinketh in his heart, so is he" (Proverbs 23:7). If the outcome of planet earth is your responsibility, then your thoughts matter. The fate of planet earth and the human species rests upon your collective ability to think positively. But how do you get everyone thinking in a positive direction?

The answer is: you don't. You cannot control anyone but yourself, and you shouldn't try to. All the world's ills have been the result of separatist thinking that states: the other fellow must change as my way is the best way, my way is the only way-and you must do as I say. You must live as I live, you must think as I think, you must look as I look. If your collective thinking perpetuates these ideals, your history will be grimly written, ending in disaster. Stop trying to control others and work on yourself. Every time you have the impulse to tell someone how to live, how to think, or what to believe, STOP! Mind your own business. Make it your business to become a positive force in the world. If everyone adopted a policy of personal positivity, if each of you concentrated and focused all your energy and attention on being more loving, more accepting and more sympathetic, the collective tide would turn. You are a powerful influencer, even if you don't want to be. Or, you are denying your responsibility as God's co-pilot. Wake up and help God to pilot the plane of your existence. Change the world by changing yourself.

Message 11-Soul Work

Every living thing serves a purpose. If it is sentient, if it is a sensing creature, it can be said to have a Soul. A Soul is nothing more than the essence of a personality. It is a construct that is completely energetic. Souls cannot be seen or touched, but they can be felt and sensed. You can sense the presence of those who have passed, even those long departed. A Soul can communicate, even after death, from one dimension to another. A Soul is an electromagnetic energy field that perceives itself as having an identity. When your Soul leaves the body at death, it is once again gifted with the ability to do what it can only do now in the dream state: it can fly, move through solid objects, and travel in the blink of an eye. Humans coexist with Spirits but don't perceive them, and you appear as a ghost to beings in other dimensions. Temperature variations and telepathic messages are often dismissed, yet they may be your loved ones from the Other Side visiting you. The Soul is always accepting, even when it must experience consequences for its actions, and there are certainly karmic consequences for all actions. Still, the Soul does not know fear; only the mind fears. The Soul is the bravest part of you, that which is unafraid to try. The Soul knows who you are and what you're capable of, and always tries to reason with your unreasonable mind. It knows your very essence; it knows your complete story. It is encoded with the Blueprint for your life and the unique lesson you agreed to, what is known as your Life Mission. Before you took a body, your Soul was already wise beyond any known human intelligence.

All animals have a Soul of sorts. Not as complex as a human Soul, but a Soul just the same. If a sentient creature has self-awareness, it has a Soul: a consciousness that you exist, and desires and preferences of your own. Even if a Soul conforms to its instincts, if it is aware of itself it can be said to have a Soul. Every Soul is eternal, even animal Souls. There is no such thing as a damned Soul or a "lost" Soul. How can a Soul be lost when it is part of the omnipresent Creator? How can it be lost when it is part of Eternal Oneness, ever existing and abiding within the Source of all life? A Soul cannot be lost or destroyed, nor is it unrepairable or unredeemable as you may have been told. A Soul is a light which is never in darkness for long. This is the purpose of reincarnation, it is a redemptive tool. A Soul reincarnates so it may shed its false self and its misunderstandings. Believe me when I say you cannot be "lost." Your Soul will always find its way back to the Light; being lost is an impossibility. If you believe this, it is a completely erroneous understanding.

Physics knows that energy cannot be destroyed, and the Soul is completely composed of energy. Therefore, it stands to reason that the Soul cannot be destroyed. The Soul only transmutes in death, it adopts another form. All Souls are bound to a passport that allows them to span one dimension to the next. When you move from the earthly realm to the Spirit realm, it is only like putting on a new set of clothes. Don't fear if anyone threatens you with Soul damnation; they have no power over your destiny and are speaking foolishness. Your destiny is totally authored by you to bring about ultimate growth in the personality and compassionate leanings. Your very essence is composed of light particles, of unseen energy; it is not solid and fixed, but ever changing and mutating. Even in one lifetime you are evolving closer to perfection. Those on the Other Side, your loved ones, are now so different that when you arrive, you wouldn't know them! They will come to you and introduce themselves and you will both laugh, because they've been transformed. They will appear to you in a form that you understand, otherwise you would not recognize them.

Humans fear what they cannot see. For instance, they fear darkness because they can't see what is there. But the Soul has unerring vision, it can see into the heart of another and read what's there, to say what is helpful, what needs to be said. If you learn to listen to your intuition, you'll have insight into hidden matters and many revelations. These revelations are the mystical and mysterious knowledge that people are hungry for. A Soul yearns to understand its own composition and to see good developing within them; to know they will keep progressing. Even if a person says they don't believe in a Soul, they have one-and won't they be surprised! The moment they leave the body, they'll be instant believers. It's possible to comprehend the unseen realm, even things the mind once feared, but it takes is a willingness to learn. It's not hard to understand your Soul, it is the very core of you. Your body is like ornamentation. At times, you can feel your Soul as it speaks and animates the body. You are essentially a Soul with a shell that moves and breathes and is a sensing organ that sends information back to the Other Side during sleep. While sleeping, you transfer information to the Other Side. There are multitudes of entities spread across the multiverse that are similarly experiencing and sending information back so that Cosmic Consciousness can continue to grow and expand, which is essential for the good of all.

In truth, there is no human "you." There is only a body and a brain that you discard at death. Then you will get your complete, integrated Soul back. A Soul is far superior to a brain because it doesn't need to be acknowledged, confirmed or praised. This truth is quite startling: that the "you" you can see really isn't *you*. While you'll always have an eternal Soul, it doesn't have a form per se, nor will it assign itself labels such as: names, titles, nor even the distinction of male or female. In the afterlife, you won't be known as anyone's partner, spouse, son, daughter or parent, nor will you have distinguishing physical features, unless you create a form to present yourself in, and this is only temporary. You won't look different than any other Soul. You will be an essence, and that's all you will be. An essence is a slight representation of something larger, a reflection. If this sounds rather generic to your ears, it's because you're familiar with form and boundaries that the body offers. To exist in a formless, boundaryless state may seem frightfully dull or too nebulous for you. But I assure you, on the Other Side bodies only serve to divide and separate. You cannot be a part of Heaven while insisting on your "personal style" in dimensions where unity and oneness are fundamental, absolute laws.

If you desire aloneness and separateness, you certainly can have it; many Souls separate themselves and operate alone or within their own parameters of relations, but they are not part of the inclusive world you call Heaven. Heaven is fundamentally a place of warm connection and vibrant exchange. It is a community bustling with purpose and what you would call "goals." Souls who are not prepared for such a place are not required to participate in a unified field of consciousness, which is certainly a relief to that Soul and those around it. Why put someone where they don't fit and would be ill-at-ease? All Souls go where they belong. If a Soul hasn't learned to bear with others, if it hasn't yet developed patience, then it can be alone until it wishes of its own accord to grow out of the old patterns and into a higher way of relating. Souls develop in their own time and on their own terms, just as they do on earth. It's not as if you die and all become equal. While you are loved and cherished equally, each Soul develops at its own pace and in its own way. The process of Soul evolution continues seamlessly on the Other Side. There are many different universes, to accommodate so many different types of Souls, each at a different stage.

Did you think you were going to Heaven to retire on a cloud? There is a joke in Heaven about this, because there's no such thing as retirement nor does the Soul enter its "rest." It's laughed about frequently, because you will learn so much and be so busy that at times you will call for a rest period because you cannot absorb another concept! Even learning has its limits. There is plenty of work, and plenty of recreation for the Soul-all work and no play make Jack a dull boy, as they say. It will be shocking how many, many choices you will have, both simple and complex. When you first arrive, you'll determine where you will reside, what work you will do, what you will learn, who you will meet, who will be your teachers...the choices are endless! You'll have more options and choices on the Other Side than you ever had on earth. Heaven demands development-a brand new version of you.

Those who enter death with a fixed idea of Heaven or Hell will create for themselves these landscapes, and many will stay in these self-induced environments until such a time as they are freed from self-imposed limitations or false belief systems. It cannot be stressed enough that all of creation operates within a free-will system. You'll be liberated to fly through the lessons of each Universe (and the worlds therein) as quickly as you determine to. Your own resistance is the only thing that can keep you from progressing. Nobody will judge you; nobody will stand in your way, nobody will tell you what you can or can't do. The Other Side operates on 100% free-will and 100% responsibility. You'll be responsible to grow or not to grow. Nobody's going to argue with you if you don't want to be part of something grander. If you wish to stay "stuck" then you are free to stay stuck for as long as it takes you to figure out. But it's like being invited to a great party-you won't want to be left out. Eventually you'll tire of whatever's been holding you back and gladly and willingly "move up."

The system of Soul evolution is quite complex and fascinating, and for those who enjoy human sciences, you can become a student of Soul Sciences, including: philosophy, psychology, theology, sociology and other "ologies" as well. For those of you inclined to less emotional and more logical subjects, you may find yourself pursuing medicine, mechanical or mathematical endeavors, architecture, aviation, or animal husbandry…the subjects are unlimited. Just the field of physics alone would keep you challenged for an eternity. You see, you most certainly are not coming here to rest as you've been told!

The scary thing about death is the unknown. There are so many ideas circulating about what happens when you die that it's hard to know what to believe. The surest thing is to read near-death accounts to see what they have to say. It's like interviewing someone who has already visited another country: while they had their own unique experience, they can give you a general lay of the land. While most near-death experiences are positive, some are less than positive; you might classify them as frightening. There are even people who relate stories of seeing Hell, or of being in an "in-between" place (described as Purgatory). Or they report a grey and depressing place, devoid of hope, happiness or light. Do you remember I said that every Soul will be placed where they fit? During near-death experiences some see evil, darkness or suffering, for their Soul must see what it had been creating in life. The Hell discussed in religion is nothing more than that Soul's own darkness; it sees its own misunderstandings. If it finds itself in the lower realms of consciousness-or worse, with evil, it can stay there to be sure, or it can change its ways and turn towards the Light that will surely be visited upon it. Less than positive near-death experiences aren't punishment for sins; this is a common misunderstanding. These realms are a natural consequence of actions and choices; that's an important distinction to draw. *God does not send anyone to a hellish afterlife. One's own choices do; its deeds do. You mustn't blame God for one's own free-will choices!* It is not God who punishes. God is all loving, all merciful, and all-forgiving. God doesn't have a mean bone in His body. Those negative experiences are the consequence of evil that the Soul has perpetuated or torment it has caused. It is the result of its own karma and these Souls will learn from such visions and then reincarnate.

You do not need to fear the afterlife if you are trying to do well. You don't have to be perfect or a saint to get into Heaven (nobody would if that were the case). You only need to be teachable. If you are trying to be more loving, kinder, and more helpful, then you have nothing whatsoever to fear! You will be welcomed, even celebrated-and you'll be surprised that it doesn't matter whether you were a "believer." Many so-called atheists will be in Heaven with surprised looks on their faces and many so-called "religious people" will have to work their way up the ladder, because they only pretended to be good. The system of justice is impeccable here. You cannot hide anything, even your thoughts; it's like being naked all the time. While on earth you can hide behind a façade of words or money, after death, everyone will see everything, and I mean everything. In Heaven you look at a Soul and see what it's made of. It's a wonderful equalizer, because there are no more divisions of educated or uneducated, male or female, rich or poor. There is only the bare Soul to be seen.

The best way to prepare for this starkly different environment is to begin living a moral life now. Learning is also helpful-the more education you have, the more your awareness grows. A Soul needs spiritual nourishment, though you must have realized by now that religion and genuine spirituality are not the same. You can be religious and be a horrible person. Some of the worst violence and injustice has been perpetrated under the guise of "God said." Being a spiritual person has nothing to do with where you worship or even if you worship! There are good Souls doing good works that have never heard the name of Jesus Christ, and they will be welcomed into Heaven. Should they be "damned" because they were born where Christianity was not taught? Why would a loving God condone such a thing? This does not make any sense! *Spirituality is not who you worship but the way in which you live your life.* A spiritual life is not a religious life (although a devout person may be genuinely good). A spiritual person follows her conscience, not a church doctrine. You must understand this concept: "You" are the sum of your choices; that is who you are. Concentrate on making better choices. Believe you can do good in the world and set your mind to do it. Don't worry as to whether you're pleasing God. If you're growing into a better person, God is pleased. Concentrate on living your life so people will say after you're gone: she was a good Soul; she was honest, she was caring. Your Soul will thank you for it later.

Life is a dramatic experience; painful at times, and there will be agonizing circumstances beyond your control but also ecstatic moments beyond your control. All such profound moments are engineered by the Soul; foreknown to it-the Soul is not surprised. Yet your mind has no memory of all this Soul work. You must see the mind for what it is-your nemesis; and yet, a great instrument for acquiring knowledge and for sensing and feeling. If you know there is both a Soul and a mind, you won't be caught up thinking that your thoughts are "you." The mind is not you-the Soul is who you really are; they are two different instruments. If you believe that what you see is reality, then you've been duped. This is a movie you're making, and at the end the curtain will fall, and you'll step away from the stage and see that you were playing the part you wrote. You authored this play to learn and experience something new, whether it was pleasant or painful. This experience is valuable-all of it, because it has allowed you to grow in understanding of yourself, and of divine mind.

After you've figured out what you came here to learn, you can finally turn your attention to the important work of showing others the difference between reality and unreality. Once you've realized the unreality of the world, you're ready to become a teacher. But there's a stiff prerequisite for teachers. True teachers must first have been the obedient student. If your Soul has chosen to speed your growth, your lessons may be painful, long, and grueling. In other lives, the lessons may be lighter and more enjoyable. But whether you are experiencing positive or negative life circumstances, every lesson is valuable. Your Life's Blueprint is neither all good nor all bad. It is an amalgam-some painful lessons, others pleasurable, but the exact mix you need before you report to the Other Side. This is why during this journey you have felt lost, alone and sad. The Soul in you remembers what you have given up coming here and yearns to return. As a result, you'll feel separated, abandoned, and not nearly good enough. But unlike the mind, the Soul knows it is loved; only the mind feels insecure. When you are at peace, wanting nothing from the world, you are living from the Soul. When you are at home within yourself, detached as the observer, you are living from the Soul.

I've said that everything happens to serve a purpose. There's a higher plan for each entity, so be curious about why you are here, about why things have happened the way they have. Keep asking yourself, "What am I supposed to be learning?" Keep inquiring of your Higher Self until you see for yourself your *Self*. It's tempting to think that what your eyes see is the only reality. And please try not to take your errors so seriously! In the end, all the parts of you that were scattered in this lifetime-the parts of you that were missing or got broken, and parts that were disowned will come back together and make you whole again. All the projections of you, spread across time and space, will be re-integrated. The Soul is programmed with a natural homeostasis; it regulates itself, pulling each creature back to wholeness, equilibrium, and purity. It is as the Dalai Lama has said: "The purpose of life is happiness." If you are frequently unhappy, you haven't arrived. Not to say that you won't go through periods of deep discontent or grief, because the valleys are to be expected. But after the storm is over, if you're wings still aren't working, be sure there is more for you. The story isn't over-perhaps it hasn't even begun. Be patient, because obviously, you're doing the best you can. Try to remember this about others, too; they're doing the best they can with what they know. They may be going about it the wrong way, but they are trying. Being human on an insane planet is cause enough to run and hide, and some people do. For those willing to show up, give them a little credit and hope they give you some, too.

If you've managed to find peace and it has nothing to do with your circumstances, it's coming from within. When it comes from within, no one can touch it; you are impenetrable. One way to increase your everyday portion of happiness is to be in a state of wonderment about ordinary things, then the world will appear extraordinary. When you're connected to your heart, the entire world is a mystery. Though the world has not changed, your attitude about it has-and its secrets will open to you. To those awake, the entire world is a delightful puzzle! It may take an entire lifetime not only to see the colors, but to appreciate them all. And while you are as complex as many different shades, people may only see one. It doesn't mean you're not colorful enough-it means they are colorblind. It is not your duty to heal someone's blindness. When they've been in the dark long enough, they will open their eyes and realize they had sight along. It may take a lifetime to see with your internal eyes, or you may have been born with extraordinary vision. Either way, life must be seen to be lived. Why not see all of what is there? Your Soul is on a never-ending hunt. It's looking for something that is missing. There's always a longing. It's on a hunt for answers to questions you haven't even asked yet. Until one day you will surrender all your longings, and on that day, you shall have the answers.

Your character is not the result of good or bad breeding, it's not the result of education nor of ignorance. Character is not even the result of genetics, and it isn't formed because of your circumstances. What then informs a person's character? Character is what you do when nobody's looking. What you do in secret will always determine your character. Small decisions add up over a lifetime to form either a selfish character or a selfless character. Character is formed whenever you refuse to surrender your values in exchange for popularity. Each selfish choice contributes to a weak character, weak in the sense of inability to love others more than self. An egomaniac, the Narcissist, is "His Majesty the Baby" (Freud, 1914), expecting to be served and insisting his way be the only way. Such bravado appears powerful and, masterful-but this kind of person is a weak link and can bring a whole house down. When I say weak, I mean insensitive. The ability to sense other's feelings and to read others is the sign of a diplomat. A strong leader takes into consideration the welfare of others. There are leaders who are truly great because they influence others to let go of the shore of certainty and reach for something higher. They inspire goodness by being good to others and encourage a courageous spirit because they themselves are willing to show courage. Weak leaders will threaten and intimidate to get their way. True leaders motivate instead of intimidate; they employ reason instead of force. They don't subjugate; they elevate. By lifting others up, they rise in the eyes of their followers. A truly great character is formed by a combination of empathy for others and clear vision. A true leader must never apologize if she is demanding greater equality and justice. She must not forsake her ideals to gain popularity, and she must strive to keep her word while forgiving herself for human mistakes. A Mahatma, a Great Soul, can redeem even the gravest mistake. I am bringing to your attention the qualities required in a good leader in order that you should become someone who can withstand criticism and the adversity that will certainly come with the mantle of leadership.

    Your Soul is encoded with a mission and so unerring is this mission that even if you wanted to, you could not escape it. If you can't accomplish your Mission in a single lifetime, there will be opportunities to complete it in subsequent lifetimes. You yourself have devised your Soul Mission, though you've forgotten it consciously. It was implanted within your subconscious, and if you were to dive deep beneath the layers of the subconscious you would discover its directions there. These silent but powerful protocols guide and inform your decisions throughout life. You don't need to be aware of what your Soul Mission is-your Soul was programmed with it. If your mind got wind of it, it would only get in the way and make it harder for you to accomplish it. The mind always complicates things. If your mind got wind of your Mission, it would "reason" you right out of it. Or the mind might focus on promoting and elevating you as an important figure. Or it might do the opposite: denigrate you, eroding your self-confidence. The mind always tries to steal the show or hijack your Soul's success. It will attempt to rewrite your Mission, so it is a Mind Mission. It is crucial to scrutinize the overactive mind, otherwise it can dismantle all the good work your Soul is trying to do. Don't worry about what your Soul Mission is-you are on autopilot. When you reach the Other Side, you'll be amazed and awed at how close you came to completing your Mission. Your Life Plan is as unyielding as the strongest titanium, leading and informing you in every minute. See what an invincible character you are? Off to conquer the world now, aren't you?

Message 12-Illness & Healing

Everything in the body responds to a command of the brain, and each system of the body functions in perfect accordance with the will. The brain receives your will's messages, encoded as electrical impulses, and these impulses activate the neurons controlling the bodily functions. Your brain responds to your conscious will, but it is also activated by your higher will, and what is this higher will except your eternal Soul? Think of your Soul as a transmitter that sent out an electrical signal the day you were born. This signal switched your brain on and gave your heart its first jumpstart. Nobody, not even the greatest scientific minds of your time, can replicate cell differentiation-how cells know to form specific body parts. It is still a very great mystery how cells can be so intelligent. This mystery is what natural sciences, mechanical sciences, and elemental sciences are striving to understand. But the catastrophes that would occur if they could create and animate life would be enormous, because most humans can't even control their own wills; how would they steward the entire planet? Your current science is quite fundamental, as the earth is in a dark cycle known as Kali Yuga, translated from Sanskrit Scriptures: the age of the demon Kali, or the age of vice. The "Kali" of Kali Yuga means "strife", "discord", "quarrel" or "contention". At present, earth is a dark planet existing in the moral dark ages, like the ages before the Renaissance when reason took hold and exploration began.

Mind-body medicine is not a new discovery, the Egyptians practiced it, but humanity has yet to rediscover the utmost importance of it. Mind-body medicine sounds "New Age" to you, but it's quite old-age, even stone-age. It's a good thing for your doctors and scientists, counselors and nurses, teachers and healers to keep in mind that humans are a gestalt; a whole. The body does not function separate from the brain; therefore, holistic medicine should be the medical focus of the future.

Speaking of the future, there will be universities where people will become educated in the science and practice of mind-body medicine. It will be the medical "wave of the future." As neurology continues to decode the brain's mysteries, the new frontier is not space, but the brain. The estimates that claim only a small percentage of your brain is utilized are true. Since prehistoric times, medicine has been evolving, and over the march of time you've come to discover technology. In less than a decade you've witnessed the birth of the technological age, but there is a second birth! This second renaissance is of mind and energy, utilizing energy for healing and even for construction. Your civilization is in its infancy. The elementary medical knowledge and systems now in use have been so institutionalized that very little attention is paid to integrated medicine. The medical community has profited from specialization, which is the separation of one branch of medicine from another and it has produced medical elitists. But it has not been entirely beneficial as your physicians are taught to treat the body and not the mind. Your counselors are taught to treat the mind and not the body, and so it goes, each specialist has knowledge in her respective field and no more. The sharing of knowledge and newer technological breakthroughs are not occurring worldwide as they should be. Mainly this is due to governmental regulation and interference for profit. Left to its own devices, the medical and scientific communities would foster a natural cooperation, and this would benefit the world tremendously.

The Egyptians understood the mind-body connection. They understood how to work with energy to heal, but they left little behind to show those coming after them their methods. You know from studying Egyptian archeology that what looks impossible for that time period was done, and that supernatural, energetic principles had to have been harnessed. However, certain Egyptian Kings and Priests used their knowledge to elevate themselves, and to suppress the masses, which is why they were not allowed to pass on their knowledge. It was taken back just as easily as it was given. Each civilization is only allowed as much knowledge as they can be responsible for. Otherwise it's a temptation to use supernatural, energetic technologies to the detriment and exploitation of others. There have been avatars who demonstrated that thought can heal, yet Western medicine rejects the proposition. This rejection of the most fundamental, elemental understanding of physics is a hoax. Every scientist knows that solid things are composed of energy, and you are discovering that quantum particles can be manipulated by thought. These principles are accepted facts of Quantum Physics, even in the West.

Why does the medical community deny what it knows to be true? Simply because they profit when they can prescribe a pill for the body's ills. The pharmaceutical company profits, the physician profits, the insurance profits. The only one who doesn't profit is the patient, because his body is host to many ill side-effects. If research were used to develop mind-body technologies, there wouldn't be the need for hospitals and pharmaceutical companies that have profited and proliferated. This is a travesty! The ones who are blocking this knowledge are the physicians themselves. Ironic, isn't it? The same ones who have taken the Hippocratic Oath to do no harm. At present, although the knowledge of mind-body science could be forthcoming, the very "healers" who say they are so eager help have blockaded it.

Now the Universal Community is simply waiting to see what happens, much as the eager partner waits expectantly in the delivery room for the long-anticipated newborn. What will your academics birth next? We don't know if they will continue to rebuff metaphysical knowledge or if they will deliver an ethical way of healing. Your energy healers have been given very few tools with which to work. Jesus prophesied that healers would come after Him with even greater miracles than He performed. We know metaphysical healing has happened and will happen again-Jesus said it would. But for now, your healers are working in the dark with crude tools. This news could be discouraging to those among you who are eager to treat illness by natural means. When I say "natural," I mean metaphysical. We on the Other Side are hoping that younger minds, hungry for knowledge and solutions will turn away from lobbyists, governmental control, and materialism. When this happens, solutions will come to this planet.

As you age, treasure in your heart the knowledge that those coming after you have the potential to unlock secrets for the good of humanity. The Universal Community is very concerned that humans be healthy and happy-as happy as they can be in their short and difficult assignments on earth. We want you to be as comfortable as you can possibly be, because earth is a dangerous Soul mission. We care very deeply about your welfare and don't take your suffering lightly. It is not a lack of concern on the part of your Creators but a societal blindness. A greedy, materialistic commerce is robbing you of the health and happiness you deserve. I wish I could give you better news. Right now, big business and the government controls and regulates its citizens health. These big businesses are as the pharaohs. They crush the workers to build their temples higher and higher. Your pharaohs are greedy corporations who have no genuine concern for the health and well-being of their people. Just as the Egyptians, humanity is faced with a choice. The pharaohs must surrender their maniacal ways, their worship of wealth and material things, and submit to a higher knowledge which is socialist and democratic in nature; concerned with the welfare of all-not just a wealthy few.

We are closely monitoring the situation. If fresh young minds are willing to depart from what they have been taught at universities and institutions of medicine, if they are willing to become mavericks who dare to ask the questions that scientists have laughed at, ridiculed and ignore, then there is hope that the brain will be utilized as it should, as it was meant to be. Neurology is, after all, a promising frontier, and yet, it is not receiving funding. The Universal Community and the peoples of the earth wait, and all the while the workers suffer. The average person looks up into the night sky in anguish and cries out, "Why don't you care?" while we are looking back at you in anguish crying out, "Why don't *you* care?" It's only when the physicians admit that they don't have all the answers that the answers will be found. Healers, do your best with what you've been given. Know that angels, Spirit Guides, even your ancestors will come to your aid. They know and can hear you. Please remember we do care, and we do see.

Message 13-Happiness

Look at angels if you want to understand love, for they are a representation of pure, undefiled love. By understanding them, you can come to know the true nature of love. Love is not something you can earn; if you can earn it, it's conditional and not love. What your Soul yearns for is to be unconditionally loved for who you are, love with no strings attached. You desire to love others in this way, but you don't know how. To love, free of expectations and demands, is a rare and precious thing. Your minds are filled with fear of love: you're afraid that you'll be hurt if you love or that true love will leave you empty-handed and broken-hearted. You stop yourself from loving, protecting yourself by erecting barriers and walls, making it nearly impossible for others to see into the heart of you.

Though angels are pure, glorified servants of God, we care for each one of you without regard to your form or personality. We love you unconditionally and completely, seeing past what doesn't matter. We see to that which is important: the heart of you. You must realize that love is the only law, it is the only reality, and the central purpose of life. Yet it is difficult, sometimes exceptionally difficult, to allow this truth to touch you; to soften you, to open you. You may be afraid of feeling; you may be blocking your connection to love. Or you may be so used to seeking for love, striving for it and earning it that you misunderstand the very nature of it. If you're experiencing loneliness, fear of relationships, or a desperation for romance, or if there are conflicts in your relationships that need to be resolved, removing the blocks to love's presence is key. How is this done?

For more peaceful relations, you must be willing to navigate the waters of misunderstanding, and this requires tolerance. While many people say they are peace-loving and want harmonious relationships, they strike back rather than walk away from a fight. This is the self-preservation and self-defensive instinct at play. While there is nothing wrong with saying the truth to set the record straight, the urge for revenge is a strong motivating force that sets in motion a chain of suffering. Letting go of the need to be right is the first step towards more peaceful relationships. You may be thinking, "But what if I am right?" Well, what if you are? If you are right, won't the truth become known eventually-doesn't truth always rise to the surface? Having to prove your superiority, your "rightness" stands in the way of having peaceful relations with others. You forfeit joy and light-heartedness so you can feel vindicated, so you can have the last word. Never underestimate the human desire for revenge. It is potent and insistent and can rob you of the love and connection you say you want. There are certain tendencies to keep a close watch on, and the need to be vindicated and to take revenge is paramount. Practice letting go of having to be right by letting someone else be "right" on occasion. Instead of arguing your point, say your truth and then quietly move along; this is tolerance in action.

There is only one way to understand someone and that is to listen to understand. When you imagine how it might feel to be them, you are listening to understand. Once you've heard their feelings, don't correct them. Simply give an understanding response by saying: "I understand how you could feel that way." Refrain from telling them how they "should" be feeling. By using this confirming method of communication, you'll invite more friends than enemies. I'm not suggesting that you deny your opinion when asked but seek first to understand. Listening in this disarming way will lead to greater trust and less defensiveness and isn't that what you want? This approach to communication will remove the blocks. It takes a real commitment to self-improvement to implement this approach. The most important reason to be understanding is that it will attract more love and admiration into your life. Remember, the law of karma is also the law of love. Whatever love you give, you will get. The law of love works without fail; therefore, it is said: "Love never fails" (1 Corinthians 13:8). Love never fails to see when you are practicing tolerance and goodwill, non-violence and understanding.

Your heart is always searching for its resting place, and it will naturally look for its home in another person when only the Other Side offers love so uncompromising and complete. But you will continue to seek, lifetime after lifetime, for a place to rest your heart. It's a normal longing to search for a Soulmate to unlock your Soul. There will be many different Soulmates over the span of many lifetimes. They will bring you lessons, and all will be for your ultimate growth and benefit. When seeking a partner, it's best to look for a soothing Soulmate, for not every relationship needs to be a harsh lesson. Sometimes what you need most dearly is a peaceable connection. Ask to draw to yourself the highest vibrations of love. Visualize unmerited favor being showered upon you in the form of a blessed Soulmate connection. Visualize the colors of love being absorbed by your energetic, ethereal body: imagine soaking up soft colors of pink, yellow and blue, a gentle pastel rainbow flowing through you. As it does, it cleanses and bathes every cell with the light of perfect love. Ask to be purified of the past. Ask the angels to help you let go of the guilt of old mistakes, for old vibrations will only hold you back, preventing higher Soulmates from arriving. They will come forward according to the vibration you are emitting, so frequently cleanse your energetic body in this way. Ask that past ugly patterns be broken and guard yourself from negativity. Keep your energy field clean, clear and proper. Though you can't see it, even when you're not aware of it, angels and Guides can sweep away residual dark, heavy energy that slows you down. You won't know how they do it, but you'll feel a distinct shift in your energy flow causing an elevated mood. Angels and Guides love to assist in this way! For them, it's like giving the house a good Spring-cleaning. They are natural energy-cleansing agents, so ask them to take from your shoulders the weariness of life. When you feel depressed, anxious, frustrated, angry, guilty or confused, stop a minute and say: *"Angels and Guides, take this heaviness from me. Clear my energy field. Help me be free again."* Then watch as those negative feelings begin to lift.

It is false beliefs that slow you down. As false beliefs pile up, you'll feel the weight of them and feel sluggish, unmotivated, even depressed. I say false beliefs, because those negative beliefs are not the truth about you, are they? You may have convinced yourself you're not good enough or not capable of a healthy relationship. You may have assigned yourself troublesome and tiresome labels and undue blame. All these false ideas are only mistakes of the past. Be quick to put away outdated, condemning thoughts. Don't cozy up to them. Feel your emotions, then release them. Feel anger, then release it. Feel disappointment, then release it. Feel frustration, then release it. Don't ruminate on the negative, and don't entertain revenge thinking. If you find your mind plotting, it's time to pull the plug on those thoughts. Be willing to let go of the hate so you can live lighter and freer. Peace is the best feeling in the world-and peaceful relationships are the only kind you want in your life.

Most of your earthly journey won't make a lot of sense while you're in the middle of it. Life will seem unfair and contradictory so much of the time that you will wonder: what's the use? Not all days will be like this, of course. Life is like the four seasons: sometimes clear and carefree like Summer, sometimes mysterious and colorful like the Fall, sometimes dying and silent like Winter, and sometimes miraculously resilient like Spring. One thing life never is? Stagnant! Your life is ever changing, as dynamic and dramatic as the seasons themselves. When life has handed you what you never wanted, and you're tempted to despair, remember the seasons and how life changes for the better. When you participate in the Life Review, you'll see that what at first seemed disastrous later became a blessing of some sort. And while not all traumas and catastrophes will rectify themselves in a single lifetime, a good lot of them will. This is because of how amazingly resilient you are. The human Soul has bounce-back power. And while not all people will bounce back in a lifetime, over the march of many incarnations, the wrinkles will be ironed out.

    I speak flippantly of life's problems as passing seasons or wrinkles in the fabric of time not to be unsympathetic but to remind you that no loss, no disappointment, and no heartbreak is unredeemable. Whatever was screwed up, whatever blunders or self-sabotage you caused will be rectified in time. The problematic element is time itself for it seems so final to you. As the body ages and as the years and disabilities pile high, it seems that Father Time has forsaken you, or mocks you. Time seems to fly when you're happy and drag when you're depressed. You can be in the experience of having too much time when you're bored or not enough time when you're in a hurry. And there are magical moments when time seems to stand still. You see, time is a meaningful and important human concept that you order life by and that defines your existence. Yet time is an illusion, perhaps the biggest chicane of the human mind. Time is a construct that is useful, but erroneous.

    In truth, existence is simultaneous. There is no past, there is no future. How could there be? The past is gone; it only exists in your memory. The future is yet to be; undecided and therefore, uncreated. So that leaves only right now. Stop and consider this statement: the past and the future are non-existent; they live only in your mind. It makes sense that life is found in this very moment. And right now, do you have what you essentially need? Do you have air? Is your heart beating? Are you safe? Yet because time convinces you that it's real, you live in yesterday or tomorrow as the present moment slips past. Living in the now is crucial to your happiness because if you can stay tethered to the present moment, your mind will be peaceful instead of anxious. You could be grateful for what you have instead of worrying about what you don't have. It's only when you jump away from now to the unreality of time that you lose your bearings. The mind categorizes and measures, so it can make sense of its environment, but the measurement of time is a trap, and nearly impossible to beat while earthbound.

When you are in meditation, time becomes irrelevant. You step out of your own realm into another dimension, losing track of time. You lose track of time because it never existed in the first place; you cannot find something that never existed. This is why meditative trance states are so euphoric and pleasurable. They liberate the eternal you from the false, mortal constraints of time. On the Other Side, your deceased loved ones are not pining away for you as you have been for them. They do not grieve as you grieve, for they have lost nothing and have gained everything! It will seem only a short while to them before you have returned Home to tell the tale of another life lived. To their eternal selves, it will only be a short break in which you've been away, a momentary blink of the eye, and then you'll be reunited. This is because a lifetime on earth, what takes some 70-80 years, is inconsequential when compared to a universe of antimatter which moves at a greater speed. An entire earthly lifetime equals only a few days on Heaven's clock. When you return, your loved ones on the Other Side will say they have just recently seen you off! You'll be surprised and confounded to realize that what seemed like a life sentence was only a few days in eternity. You will laugh when you see how the brain distorts everything, including time. I know these concepts are foreign and strange but know this-you will return Home and say, "I should have enjoyed the moments of my life. I should have savored every minute, and been grateful for the epic journey, even the moments that seemed long and arduous. I should have laughed more and been in awe of the beauty of nature, instead of worrying so much about what I couldn't change or what never even happened!" You'll marvel at your short-sightedness, because, from the window of eternity, you'll see you had everything you essentially needed in every moment, and yet you overlooked this fact. They say hindsight is 20-20, and this is especially true on the Other Side.

There are a few things that can help you stay away from dwelling on the past or the future. If you remember them, you'll be a more well-adjusted, peaceful, and enjoyable person to be around. First, keep in mind that the concept of time is only that: a false concept to maintain order. And while order is helpful, sometimes your experience of life needs to be decidedly un-orderly. Take a break from being "productive." When you feel the urge to depart from your regular schedule, do so. Enjoy life-do what you love more often. You are not a slave to time; it does not rule you. Time is a non-entity; how could it be your master unless you believe it is real? I'm not saying you should be irresponsible to your commitments; I'm not advocating irresponsible behavior. But when possible, depart from the "regularly scheduled program" and surprise yourself (or someone else) with something different, something outside of what's expected of you. The problem isn't what other people think of you as much as your own doubtful thoughts which will try and discourage you. They will say: "You'll look foolish," or, "People will laugh at you." Truthfully, most people don't care what you do, because they are busy worrying about themselves. Haven't you noticed this? Humans are largely self-absorbed. They focus mainly on their own worries and responsibilities. Why be overly concerned with what your neighbor might think? It is none of their business anyway.

Secondly, when consumed with worry, stop the cascade of catastrophic thinking by practicing an exercise I will give you which I will call, Present Breathing. Close your eyes and get in touch with the present, the only reality. Feel your body, feel your breath, and let it drift back to the present moment. When you take an in-breath think the word: "This," and with the outbreath think the word, "moment." "This...moment." Practice Present Breathing when you have extra time on your hands (see, there's that word "time" again). Instantaneously your cares will melt into oblivion, and you'll be overcome with a sensation of oneness with the moment. If you practice meditative breathing for just a few minutes, you'll sense the Soul part of you. When this happens, you've just shifted from the temporal realm to the eternal dimension, and you may wish to linger here if you can afford to. Don't be afraid of the eternal you; your Soul-self is the pilot of your existence and you mustn't be afraid to let it take the wheel now and again.

Thirdly, I would like to point out the importance of laughter. While some have represented Heaven to be a somber or fearful place, the afterlife is nothing of the sort. Heaven is full of laughter. It must be, for Heaven is an amalgam of diverse Souls, many of whom are still evolving, so errors and ignorance are commonplace occurrences. In Heaven, there is a lighter attitude towards the things you take so seriously on earth, such as problems and even death. The afterlife is an eternal place, not a finite place. When you have all of eternity to work out your problems, they don't seem nearly as grave or as troublesome. Take for instance death itself. It's quite a shock to be born (just look at a newborn's face to see the look of surprise or horror). It is equally as shocking when you leave your body and return to a fluid, immaterial state. There are many "newbies" who arrive on our shores disoriented and confounded about how their death happened, especially if it was unexpected or quick, and these we handle extra gently. They are treated to a re-entry process not unlike what happens after an astronaut re-enters the earth's atmosphere. The Soul must be decontaminated before it can mingle with the public. Every Soul goes through a re-entry process and an orientation which is specifically tailored to each Soul's unique requirements. This protects those they will be encountering, so the energy they carry back from earth doesn't contaminate the environment. There is a great deal of pain and negativity that is experienced and absorbed by the Soul during a lifetime and those painful memories and losses must be cleansed from the Soul-body's gravitational field before moving forward in the Spirit world. Think of it as peeling off layers and layers of dirty clothes you brought home with you, layers you didn't even realize you were wearing!

Once you've completed the re-entry process, you're free to socialize and "compare notes" with others. The resocialization process is happy, even joyous; you're being reunited with family who have passed before you and making peace with them, and them with you. Even people you disliked will be there, and you will meet, and the truth will be known. Again, there is no hiding anything in Heaven. Any hate or animosity will be resolved in these important meetings. In fact, they are known as Resolution Meetings and often include restitution, which is the process by which a Soul can make amends for its deeds. Remember, I said we are big on mercy here. Old wounds will be healed, and the books closed on outstanding karmic debts. Forgiveness will flow, even towards those who hurt you the worst. I know there are things that people have done or said that you feel you cannot possibly forgive. While earthbound, these bind you to frustration, anger or revenge, and are a common complaint of the human condition. Believe it or not, we don't expect you to open your heart to those who have dishonored you. Perhaps your withdrawal from them is exactly what they need, a sort of instant karma. But once you've washed away the impurities of strong negative emotions, it's possible to talk with those who harmed you and to understand one another. A type of empathic "seeing through their eyes" will occur. When you've stood in their shoes and looked through their eyes, it's easier to see why they made the choices they did. But please do not think for a moment that wrong behavior on their part will be erased! Far from it. You will both be able to see how each person's choices impacted all involved, and it is a sobering moment indeed, to understand that while it wasn't your intention to hurt anyone, the impact it had was injurious, even devastating. The once prideful will fall silent for the harm they inflicted. Each unresolved, unfinished situation will be resolved in these Resolution and Restitution meetings, what is the second phase of re-entry. Soulmates have contracted to teach you lessons or to learn lesson from you, so you will review these lessons together. You'll retrace your moves, replaying pivotal moments and analyzing your exchanges the way a psychologist would analyze the behavior of her patient.

With all these interpersonal processes going on, it would naturally create regret, sadness or a heaviness that you can't carry around with you in Heaven. Instead of sinking into lower vibratory realms, humor becomes the buoyancy and soft pad on which you will land repeatedly. Not that you will be able to "laugh off" that which was injurious, but you will be able to laugh at yourself and at the irony of life's ridiculous situations. Because you have eternity stretched out before you, there's plenty of time and countless chances to "fix" all the problems in your "script." This re-working process is something like being the director of a stage play. As the director, you can pause the scenes to examine them. Within 3D holograms, you will work out the "kinks" so your play ends like it should have. This reworking is the entire premise of the first Heaven, known as the Kingdom of Courage. Knowing you can fix the problems in your script makes it easier to have a lighter, more playful spirit, and you will laugh a lot during this phase.

Aside from music, which is plentiful here, laughter is a common sound heard in Heaven. In fact, you will release pain through laughter. You've heard the saying: "Laughter is the best medicine"? In Heaven, you're on a daily dose of laughter. Many near-death experiences describe Heaven as a joyous place. Indeed, if they could recall all their Heavenly experience (which they certainly will not), they would recollect the lighthearted laughter. Therefore, do not be afraid to laugh more. Make it part of your daily routine to smile at least as much as you frown. In fact, it would be helpful if you could work on giving up the worry habit all together and take up the habit of frivolity. The problem is that you perceive everything to be so final and serious, when in the span of eternity, everything will change, and nothing will stay the same. Everything undergoes a change-haven't you noticed this? Nothing stays stagnant for long. Given enough time, everything changes, and drastically! You will change, others will change, and the circumstances you took to be so dire will eventually give way to a lighthearted perspective. If everything is evolving towards perfection, then you can afford to be playful. All this rushing around to amass wealth and to keep yourselves looking young is wasted effort, but you won't see this until you're safely on the shores of eternity. Then you'll see worry as wasted time. The brain worries excessively, because it's convinced that the longer it worries, the greater your chances of solving the problem. Yet the more you worry, the less you laugh, and the less fun you have! Nobody enjoys a sourpuss. Therefore, live in the moment, because that's where the joy is. Truly, I admonish you-laugh instead of cry; life will bring you tears enough. Let your guard down; smile and have a good time. Because, as Archangel St. Michael is fond of quoting: Life is too important to take seriously (Oscar Wilde).

Message 14: Original Souls

The most important thing is to be true to yourself. What other people want of you is only their misunderstanding. To deny yourself fulfillment because someone else is uncomfortable with the real you is to squander your precious individuality. You were not incarnated so you could look or sound like anybody else; you were incarnated so you could be a one-of-a-kind expression of the Divine. You are supposed to be yourself. And who is this Self? It is that seed of eternal light that shines through your eyes-this is the real you, twinkling and burning. This is the you hidden beneath a carnage of flesh. Each Soul is encoded with a message that it is to leave with the world, and we call this your Life Mission. Until you have accomplished your Life Mission, you will feel restless, incomplete and dissatisfied. So many people mistake a career, a lover, or a child for their Life Mission. While these are all important, your Life Mission will pull and coax you away from the crowd. This doesn't mean you have to be a loner, far from it. Stay connected but insist upon your own opinions and style. Be an original-there's nothing so boring as a copycat or being copied. That gets on everyone's nerves, because they can see you're only acting the part. There's no sense in being a false form of you; people see through the veneer. There's nothing wrong with "coloring outside of the lines," to be the first to do what your lineage has never done. Breakthroughs occur when someone defies the status quo. Originality isn't rebellion; it is a determination to speak your truth.

There was once a race, a civilization of antiquity so unique unto themselves, a shining example of individuality and originality.

This distinctive society was the Egyptians. Their manner of dress and cosmetics were so dramatic and bold that it sent waves of awe throughout the ancient world. Not only their style but their religion was unlike any other. They had a myriad of Gods and Goddesses: The Sun God and The Sky Goddess (The Father and The Mother), even the God of the Underworld…so many personalities with responsibilities and characteristics all their own. It was as if the Gods themselves had visited the Egyptians; they described each one so perfectly and in exquisite detail. The Egyptians also possessed technology that current civilization has no knowledge of. I am referring to the building of the pyramids and other colossal feats of engineering still "impossible" to you, the "modern man." No offense, but Westerners are the youngster on the block when it comes to knowledge of advanced technologies. The Egyptians were so advanced that they were able to use sound waves and quartz crystal to heal mind and body. The Egyptians led the world in mechanical engineering, energetic healing, plant medicines and even fashion. They were unafraid and unapologetic about being different. But where did this otherworldly boldness, style, and spirituality come from?

If you study the Egyptian civilization just a little, it will become evident to you that they had knowledge and abilities that superseded other civilizations. When the ancient Egyptians vanished from the face of the earth, so did the fantastic metaphysical technologies they possessed. As I've said, once the Pharaohs became obsessed with their own greatness, they used these technologies to exploit the poor workers, and that is when these abilities were "taken from them." But what does this mean? It means that their powerful secret knowledge was wiped from their memories and hidden in crystal to be released when it is again time to heal the world.

Egyptian Pharaohs were considered deities and worshiped as such. This is because some Pharaohs were hybrid in race: part human, and part alien. There was a Pharaoh who was unlike any before him, who looked different and who brought to the Egyptians farming technologies and other metaphysical knowledge. His name was Akhenaten. His long face, egg-shaped skull, and spidery fingers were unlike any human Pharaoh. He educated the Egyptian people about otherworldly deities but insisted upon monotheism, worshiping one God. That God was Aten-the Sun God, or literally, the God who shines like the Sun. Akhenaten proclaimed: "There is only one God, my Father. I can approach Him by day, by night." According to Egyptian mythology, Akhenaten was a direct descendant of the Gods; the same Gods who arrived on earth during a time referred by prehistoric Egyptians as Zep Tepi. During the First Time or Zep Tepi, beautiful beings called the Neteru lived on Earth. These Gods created the grids of reality. Within the void of time and space, the Neteru still move from reality to reality creating the programs that Souls experience. They move through a place known as Zero Point where matter and antimatter merge to create new realities. It is this place where positive and negative collide to destroy matter and where matter is created again. Akhenaten wrote that he was visited by beings that descended from the sky. They told him what he needed to do as Pharaoh to teach his people. I describe Egyptian "mythology" to ask you this question: If humans have flown in spaceships to the moon, isn't it possible that divine beings with superior intelligence could bring with them otherworldly genetics and technology?

The Lords of the Cycles wondered: would humans use advanced information for the benefit of all or would they ignore the needs of the many and exalt themselves, exploiting the common people? They found what was true about humanity: that it is self-centered in nature and not inclined to think of the needs of the many. There was one Pharaoh in particular, Ramses 111, who exploited not only his own country's resources, but who waged war with all who would oppose him. Ramesses 111 was bent on deification and immortalization. Out of jealousy he destroyed all monuments and records of Pharaoh Akhenaten. Today, Ramses 111 is remembered as the Pharaoh who loved his own face. While ancient aliens brought good to the earth, this knowledge was squandered and misused by the human Pharaohs and Priests that came after. The benevolent Pharaoh Akhenaten was replaced by Ramses 111, a mortal obsessed with his power as Pharaoh who attempted to destroy the memory of Akhenaten. No otherworldly rulers were dispatched to planet earth thereafter, for when an experiment begins to go wrong, you dare not add fuel to the fire. Thus, the Egyptians, once a highly developed civilization burned out until all that was left of them were the echoes of their once-mighty shout.

    I tell you this cautionary tale because, as it is said: To whom much is given, much is required (Luke 12:48). If you are gifted, talented or have a specialness about you, do not squander it on building yourself up or you will be remembered like Ramesses; a beautiful face without a heart. Know this: history will not remember you for what you accomplished as much as it will remember how you treated others. Building a kingdom in tribute to oneself is what the human ego wants to do. It pushes you to exalt your seed of greatness and to ignore the needs of others. There are modern-day Pharaohs, leaders who build empires, whose driving motivation is to conquer, dominate, and control. If a leader is not focused on solving the everyday, practical needs of its peoples for food, shelter, education, childcare, and equality, then you have a Pharaoh on your hands not unlike Ramses 111. Don't be fooled by Pharaohs who are charismatic and appear "fearless." A worthy leader *should* be afraid of leading their flock astray. Look for these qualities in a leader: a sense of fairness, a concern for the welfare of all their subjects, and compassion for the poor and subjugated. Like the Egyptian Mother Goddess Isis, they should be a leader who hears the voices of the downtrodden. This is a leader worthy of your hero worship-worship this Pharaoh. Perhaps Heaven's secrets shall be shared again when humanity remembers what the Egyptians forgot: that individuality and specialness are not to be used to elevate the rich but for the betterment of all. Until the proper use of power has been learned, your world will continue to suffer in ignorance of the advanced technologies that the Egyptians possessed. Be as Christ: "…for I am gentle and lowly in heart…" (Matthew 11:29).

Whatever you do, go on and lead your life, for there will always be those who find fault with the way you live and there will always be people who are displeased. Some will expect perfection, demanding of you their exacting standards. But you're not here to pander to others or to change your unique expression. Living by someone's dictates will result in a watering down of your fullest expression. Disapproval is unavoidable if you're going to be an original, and isn't every Soul one of a kind? Expect to be misunderstood to some degree, even for the whole of your life. Get comfortable with the person you are, not the person others want you to be. There are laws that original people live by, and I shall name a few:

The primary law of the original Soul is the acceptance of its "differentness." And while you are coming to terms with the fact that there's never been another person exactly like you, even the strangest among you is not as different as their own mind makes them out to be. Original? Yes! But you're not as mysterious as you think. Humans are quite consistent in behaviors and can be predictable, even in the smallest of things. While you may feel that you do not fit on this planet and you are concerned with other's opinions, opportunities to share your uniqueness are slipping by, and these missed moments are the only unredeemable thing. The only true "sins" are the opportunities not taken: the conversation you never had, the "I love you" not said, and the leap of faith you never took. These escaped because you didn't want to "make waves" and upset somebody. But there's always someone upset by something you did or did not do-and this is what you must contend with if you are to live in a manner worthy of your potential.

    The second law of the original Soul is the willingness to leave behind attachments that bind and restrict in favor of those that illuminate and liberate. There are no guarantees in life, especially for those who live in harmony with the blueprint of their Soul. The original Soul will anguish over the choices they must make, but in the end, they will make the hard choices. They will not live as others expect but consistently demonstrate an uncommon ability to choose "the road less traveled." In marching to the beat of their own drummer, they will distance themselves from what binds them, and this continual process of freeing themselves will engender criticism or disapproval at the very least. There is no way to get free and stay free if your goal in life is to please others. "Fitting in" will earn you friends and a feeling of belonging, but it will strip you of your individuality. The most basic of freedoms is the luxury of being yourself. Anyone who asks you to adopt their motto is asking you to drop your own-be cognizant of that. If you happen to be headed down the same path as someone else, then wonderful; how fortunate for you both-you are doubly blessed. But if your blueprint is taking you in a different direction, honor your blueprint and release the attachment. Having said that, I realize this is far easier said than done. There won't be anything harder in life than walking away from someone who you are attached to. Yet, you'll face these distressing dilemmas throughout your life. The original Soul will consistently turn away from the promise of safety and security to spread their wings.

    The third law of the original Soul is that they often find themselves flying solo. This is because the "pack mentality" doesn't suit them. The artisans of the world crave solitude, for a key component of creation is solitude. This isn't to suggest that the artistic Soul doesn't enjoy friends and good company and conversation, but they are deep thinkers and feelers, and will naturally be drawn away from the crowd. They need space in which to create. If you have a child who appears different from the rest, this isn't a curse but a blessing! It means you've been given an original thinker. Parents can learn from their children, and often the Universe will assign an outlandishly original Soul to a conventional Soul for both Souls' growth. These unlikely pairings can be tumultuous and even contentious and are usually the result of a Soulmate relationship.

Soulmates are not always easy, breezy connections, though they can be. More often, they stretch both parties' limits of understanding. The conventional Soul wishes for stability, while the original, unconventional Soul interprets stability as a form of conformity. The original Soul will depart from convention, resenting being told how they should navigate life. They will gravitate towards a freer and simpler existence. These Souls meet life head-on and are not swayed by the latest fad or trend. They're unmoved by common entertainment, and spurn religion when it is divisive. They are not afraid to ask the questions others are afraid to ask. This may be the quickest way to identify an original Soul-she is curious and finds conformity boring. If there is a conscientious objector in the crowd, you've just hit upon an original Soul. However, if they are trying to stir up trouble, he is less original and more a troubled Soul. Original Souls won't be motivated to divide; this is the hallmark of a lesser mind, not an expanded consciousness. While they will often isolate themselves, the original Soul will be on a mission to expand consciousness instead of dividing it.

The last law of the original Soul is this: to push for progress. The original Soul will not wish to repeal civil rights. They always push for the next freedom and reach for the stars. They are possibility thinkers. To them, the paramount goal is freedom. They are not yearning for "the good old days," because they do not wish to travel backwards in time but forwards. Anyone who cannot deal with reality, with the progress that the whole of society has made, is stuck in reverse. Time marches on and progress moves in a forward direction. When you are longing for the past, you are in a frozen state with outdated methods and attitudes, and this is not helpful to society. The original Soul can leave yesterday and fully embrace today, though today doesn't look the same as yesterday. This is progress-and it's beneficial for the whole. Consciousness that is stuck in the past is a stale kind of consciousness and will take you in reverse. Only the neurotic person demands that life remain static and unchanging. Don't reject science because the facts don't fit into your paradigm. Humanity is ever evolving in a forward fashion just as time moves in a forward direction. The Universe itself is ever expanding outward. Original Souls welcome breakthroughs, scientific or moral, which offer a healthier, civilized and more natural existence. The original Soul is open to new things, because they recognize the importance of honoring the sacred in every form. If you are doing your part to usher in a new, peaceful planet, you are advancing the Divine agenda and are an original Soul.

Message 15-Transgenderism

While you have a body, you are not your body and aging will prove this to you. As you age, you experience the passage of time. Your body takes on weight, wrinkles, and the physical and psychological problems associated with aging, while the "inner you" doesn't change, so you experience a dissonance of sorts. Your body looks one way on the outside, while on the inside you remain the same. This is what is miraculous: the true you never ages. In fact, the true you is shocked and appalled by the changes it sees happening before its eyes! The natural and understandable reaction to these alarming changes is to resist them (known as a mid-life crisis) or to try and altar the natural effects of aging (plastic surgery). Because aging is inevitable and an inescapable fact, it is essential to your happiness to accept that your body is not "you" in any way, shape, or form. To identify "you" with what you see in the mirror is like believing that the car you're driving is in fact you.

The body is a cosmic vehicle-it houses a cosmic being. It is a shell, a "meat suit," and little more than a meat suit. To spend time fretting and feeling inferior over the car you drive or the body you wear is time wasted. Worse, it becomes an obsession that can cause great unhappiness and maladjustment. Obsession occurs when emphasis is placed inordinately on the wrong thing. You can become phobic about your weight, your loss of youth, and the effects of aging if you believe that you are defined by the body. When a youth-obsessed, perfectionistic standard of beauty is imposed by society, phobia sets in and obsessive thinking takes hold. Obsessive thinking leads to compulsive behavior. Part of being a well-adjusted individual is the ability to accept yourself as you are: mind, body and spirit. Some of you have been given higher intelligences than others, and this factor can be a source of stress and grounds for feeling "less than" or "more than" others. I am highlighting the human propensity to compete and compare-two factors that can steal your happiness faster than anything.

How does one learn to love the body and self that goes with it? Obviously, if you perceive the outer to be unacceptable, you can either change the body to match the "inner you" (as in sexual gender reassignment), or you can strive to accept your imperfect vehicle. However, this does not mean that those who are gender conflicted should suffer in silence. God does not want anyone to hide his or her unhappiness or confusion. Please remember this: God does not want you to hide ANYTHING-only the fearful ego wants that. If you've been given a man's body but you have a woman's feelings, then you have every right to alter your body to match the inner you. And if you've been given a woman's body but have the needs and feelings of a man, to represent those undeniable feelings on the outside is neither a mistake nor a sin. Those brave enough to say that their body is not who they are understand well what I'm trying to tell you. And while we are discussing transgender, let's discuss why this phenomenon occurs.

If God wants you to be happy, why would you be born in the "wrong body"? Or for that matter, why would you be born a homosexual-with an irrepressible attraction to the same sex? In some parts of the world, homosexuality or transgenderism is still considered deviant, immoral or criminal in nature. But I assure you that these "abnormalities" are planned, and a part of your Life's Blueprint, to teach humanity. What is it teaching? That different does not mean bad-it simply means different. If you've been given a different body, a different brain, a different sexual orientation, even the "wrong" body, you are not so different as you are unique. Consequently, you have been chosen to be a teacher by example.

You may wish that you weren't chosen to be an example-of course you do. You live in a dark world with antiquated ideas of "same equals good." These are paternalistic beliefs that directly or indirectly assert that if you weren't born a Caucasian male, you are "less than." If you are not a heterosexual, rhetoric says you are "less than." If you are not monogamous in nature, tradition says you are not "normal." But what *is* normal? "Normal" is a catchall term that implies an elevation of one race over another, one sex over another, or one sexual orientation over another. All this mania to be the same-to look the same and act the same is a pile of nonsense! Of all words, I wish I could erase the word "normal" from your vocabulary. These impossible, ill-fitting standards are what cause people to hide who they are and to foster judgmental attitudes. The senseless drive to make everyone "the same" has caused most of the world's atrocities and cruelty and often in the name of God.

Please remember that God wants one thing: for you to be yourself. If you are told to hide or suppress the real you, that is decidedly un-Godly, and there is no part of God in it. God is always for your liberation. God always wants you to be freer and freer, happier and happier. But how can you be happy if you're hiding something as fundamental as your sexual or gender orientation? God does not promote one race or sex over another because God is neither male nor female and embodies all races. How could the Creators be partial? Good parents are impartial and love their children equally. If God wasn't fair and impartial, you couldn't call God good. This tendency to divide and discriminate, this tendency to judge and elevate one person over another is a characteristic of lower-level species. The higher in consciousness one rises, the less ignorance there will be, and the more acceptance there will be.

You are not your body, your age, or your nationality; you are not even your gender. You are none of these things. If you are none of these things, who are you? You are timeless. You are infinite. You are indestructible. You are all-loving and completely accepting.

You are without fear. You are an aspect of God. You should remind yourself of these truths on a regular basis: "I am timeless, I am infinite, I am indestructible, I am all-loving and completely accepting. I am without fear; I am an aspect of God." Yet you will look in the mirror, seeing before you an imperfect face, and exclaim: "This is God?" It's hard to believe, isn't it? But inside, there is a "you" that is indestructible and everlasting, and this Soul will come shooting out of you like a cork when it's time to rejoin your Heavenly family. In that moment you will be convinced it's not your body that defines you, it never was. The body, what Christ referred to as a "temple," houses the Spirit within. A temple is a place of worship and like a temple, the body houses within it something holy, something otherworldly. Therefore, it was said: You are the temple of the Holy Spirit (1 Cor. 6:19). In other words, you have a body, but you are not the body. Stop identifying people's worth by the body or the lifestyle they lead. Stop looking on the outside-try to see past it. You are so much more than the ill-fitting body, or whom you go to bed with. To think any other way is small-minded and ignorant, and I know you do not want to be ignorant of the truth.

While we are considering the body, it's important to know that what makes someone "clean or unclean" (again, Jesus' words) is the thought life. The way in which you think determines whether you are a white, grey, or a dark entity. Just as it sounds, a Soul can be shades of good. White entities work for unity and are evolving ever upward towards self-love and self-acceptance, other-love and other-acceptance. Grey entities are those who have one foot in both worlds: conflicted Souls causing a lot of unnecessary conflict and injury. They are not wholly dark, thus the "grey" designation. And you know a dark entity when you meet one-they will give you a sinking feeling like you want to get away from them, and you should! All Souls can be classified as white, grey or dark. However, interestingly, all Souls prefer to be called white. This is why the White-Supremacist Klu Klux Klan (KKK) calls themselves, "The

White Brotherhood." They call their hatred holy and proclaim they are God's chosen race. Beware of those who say they are God's preferred. These are usually self-deceived individuals headed in the wrong direction. Better to say: "We are all equal; we are all children of the same God." This is a true statement. Your Heavenly parents love you equally, which means you are no better and no worse than any other. If you could only accept this final verdict: each of you is God's son or daughter, in whom They are well-pleased.

There has been so much speculation and misunderstanding about the topic of transgenderism. But the question of gender is quite simple, if you keep an open mind. Only close-mindedness unnecessarily complicates the issue. Regarding gender, as you are finding, it is more the Soul's business than a body's genetic structure. A Soul determines whether it will adopt a male body with a female thinking mind (what might be called a trans woman), or a female body with a male thinking mind (what might be called a trans man). It is the Soul that determines how it will express itself during an incarnation. Then why is it so hard to accept this truth: that gender is an expression of one's Soul, not an expression of the body? It feels so wrong, so foreign and uncomfortable to take on the "wrong body," yet many Souls come into the world with gender identity questions and this is not a mistake of nature. It is a lesson for that individual's Soul, as well as a lesson for the world. Still, it can feel to the gender confused individual as if God has made a mistake, that her Soul is in a man's body or his Soul is in a woman's body; an apparent blunder. But nothing about it is a mistake; God doesn't make mistakes! This truth can be so difficult to grasp, that what is painful, confusing, frustrating, embarrassing-even that which feels shameful and is called shameful by those who have no understanding of such matters, is in no way a mistake. It is instead a lesson for everyone about the necessity of unconditional acceptance.

There are those of you who have wondered why your Soul chose to express itself in the world by taking on a body which does not fit you, which seems too small or too big, which seems reprehensible or agonizing. I assure you-you are not a mistake. You are, instead, something much grander than you realize. You are a liberator; you are liberating people's thinking. You are helping others to understand that they do not yet comprehend the Soul and you are helping them see that not all people fit into strictly prescribed boxes. You are a savior, saving humanity from ignorance by being more than what can be seen, by being more than a body. You are the bravest of Souls; your courage is renown on the Other Side. You *chose* to be misunderstood, to be put down, to be laughed at, to be ridiculed, to be confused, and to wonder why God would do such a thing. And still, you insist on your individuality and on having a voice in a voiceless world. You've shown what bravery looks like by defying the rules that were created out of an ignorant and elementary understanding of what it is to be human. What it is to be human has little to do with gender. It has more to do with qualities such as courage and compassion, and you are teaching the world how to be the best kind of human. Instead of reviling you, humanity should be thanking you-because you're showing them what is truly there. You're showing the world your Soul, not your body. You're making the world look closer, beyond the boundary of skin, and the label that says, "Male," or "Female." You're making everyone look hard at how to define what it is to be human, and what it is to be a man or a woman. For that, the world owes you a debt of gratitude, and you are heroes to us on the Other Side. Therefore, if you are different, hold your head up high.

Message 16-Soulmates

Have you ever felt a strong attraction for someone, even when it was against your better judgement? Have you ever felt comfortable with someone instantaneously, as if you've known them forever? These are signs of a karmic tie. You can be tied, or strongly connected to another Soul, energetically; even many Souls in a single lifetime. It is what makes parting with these people extra painful. One part of you will always feel that it's wrong to be apart, for your heart has already recorded your history together. The imprint of a Soulmate can cause a strong attraction towards them that can defy reason. You will not have just one or two Soulmates; you will have a multitude of Soulmates within the span of eternity. And, the more the better, because they will help you learn lessons expediently and allow karma to be reduced quickly. While it may be a daunting proposition to meet more than one Soulmate in a single lifetime, you are blessed to meet them. Nothing works you through quite as expediently as a Soulmate.

The characteristics of a Soulmate are simple: you can recognize them because either they will be your teacher, or they will be your student. Lessons can be painful, or lessons can heal you, but Soulmates reveal your true nature. They will be mirrors that force you to see who you really are. Soulmate relationships are often difficult, turbulent and intense. When they walk away or die, you are left holding the lesson they delivered; many times, they are transient relationships. You will be done assisting them when one of you moves on, whether through a relational breakup, divorce, or death. However it happens, it was supposed to happen as it did; there is freedom in knowing that. Don't try and force a Soulmate to stay, for perhaps the other has given all their Soul agreed to give. Walk through life with an open hand. Be willing to let go, and in so doing, you set one another free. Every exchange, including every tear and joy that your Soulmate caused was a gift to you. If you see relationships as a tool for your development, you'll be grateful for the sunshine but also for the rain. Try not to be bitter. Remember- they have fulfilled their sacred contract with you, and you must honor that which is sacred between you. Soulmates come in the form of family, friends, or lovers. It's easiest to sense a Soulmate in a lover because of the undeniable, magnetic pull you feel towards them. Your family members are Soulmates, especially parents and children. You may be asking: why did I pick people so challenging? When constructing your Life Chart, you contracted with other Souls to "play a part" in each other's lives. You even agreed on the severity of the test or lesson. You may pick the most troublesome Soulmates as family members for the express purpose of expediting your Soul's growth. For this reason, you may have a different temperament than family members and opposing agendas.

Ah, the agenda…let's discuss this crucial aspect of the Soulmate connection, because the agenda plays a pivotal role in karmic ties. Each of you has a set of characteristics that defines you called a personality. You also have a temperament, either outgoing or easy going. Your personality, or the way you express yourself in the world, can vary greatly from life to life. In one incarnation you may be an introverted female while in the next you are an extraverted male. The agenda I refer to are the events, or the fixed script that the Soul must follow during a lifetime. This script is written by your Soul for your Soul, with the cooperation of Soulmates, and is authorized and orchestrated by your Oversoul.

Imagine this scenario: you determine to have as many Soulmates as possible in a single lifetime. Perhaps in a previous life you had only a few and they weren't particularly fruitful exchanges; they didn't generate much growth. This time you plan for the opposite to see what happens. Let's suppose you choose five partners-an enterprising attempt at Soul growth! The first Soulmate you marry, and the next you don't, but neither partner turns out to be an enduring connection. The third Soulmate enters, and this one sticks. You marry again, hoping for the best. Because you've learned to be a better mate, this time you're able to stay married. This agenda was set and agreed upon before you ever met the partners, and everyone wrote you into their agenda. Soul agendas are an extremely complex and intricate web of relationships. When you construct your Life Plan, not only are you writing it for yourself with your own best interest in mind, but you're also taking into consideration all others in the dharma of your life. As you can imagine, there is complex strategy involved when you are working to create a favorable outcome for everyone.

Once the agenda is approved on the Other Side, you carry this plan into your incarnation, but the details of working out these relationships are up to you. Most day-to-day decisions aren't written into the script, so you find yourself ad-libbing a lot. This is probably why you feel confused or frustrated, because nobody said figuring it out on your own was going to be easy! This is where the Soulmate attraction becomes helpful. Because you have a karmic tie with a Soulmate, your Soul feels an instant recognition-you have discovered a special person. There's that magic moment of: "There you are!". You'll experience feelings of immediate comfort, familiarity or attraction. This magnetic pull is the glue that will bond you until you complete your contract. Parting may seem wrong, unfair, or like you have unfinished business, because you do. One of you may feel the karma stronger than the other; one Soul may unconsciously "remember" past-life bonds, insisting that it shouldn't end. Indeed, for them, the work between you feels urgently incomplete, unfinished. But you will see that Soul in another incarnation in a different form. It's helpful to remember that Soulmates are a blessing, whether they have been pleasurable or painful, because they helped you to learn something. Never think that a Soulmate was a waste of time, nothing could be farther from the truth. Together, you've ingeniously engineered it so that eventually, over many lifetimes, you will both come to terms with the ultimate lesson, for: "As above, so below" (Matthew 6: 9). At present, you may be suffering many unfinished situations, but no matter, for one fine day all will be well between you. Until then, remember to make your words tender (for in another lifetime you may have to eat them).

Can animals be Soulmates? Animals have Souls and depending upon their intelligence, they can have distinct personalities. House pets such as dogs and cats have personalities-characteristics that define them. For example, one pet may be a finicky eater and nervous in nature, while another may eat anything given him, and have an exuberant disposition. These may be features of a personality rather than a breed. While animal Souls contract with human Souls to be included in the Life Plan and to include you in theirs, they don't do the planning; the "human" Soul does. It's something like going to a pet shop and picking out a pet. On the Other Side, you wanted to include a pet in your plan, so you wrote that pet into your Life's Agenda. Then one day you're walking by a pet store and you find yourself spontaneously wandering in. There you find an irresistible face…love at first sight! It's because you had planned to adopt that dog all along on that particular day. Can animals eventually work their way up the animal chain to become a human being? Buddhist philosophy says yes, and evolutionary science agrees. Humans began life in a less-intelligent form than they are now. Over millions of years, natural selection has allowed adaptations. Simpler forms of life evolve into advanced intelligences over time, so a pet can certainly evolve into a higher form. But can a human incarnate backwards into an animal? No, decidedly not-for evolution doesn't work in reverse. Once a Soul begins its evolutionary journey, it will never lose the evolutionary gains it has made. In other words, it will not reincarnate down the chain into a less developed creature such as an insect.

Soul evolution differs from physical evolution; that distinction should be made clear. Soul evolution is a forward-moving process, unlike physical evolution, wherein adaptations can be added or lost in response to the environment. For example, in physical evolution, a fish can lose its ability to fly if it no longer needs wings. But a dog Soul will never incarnate into a lesser form and become a fish. Eventually the dog's Soul will take on more complex responsibilities and challenges, for spiritual evolution is forward leaning. You're beginning to get the picture of how complex the business of Soulmates is. You will study these evolutionary matters between incarnations, and when you return to the Other Side, they will be studied in the Life Review, and again in a higher Heaven. Of course, there's a whole science behind Soulmates to be learned. And while you wish some Soulmate connections would last a lifetime, they may serve their purpose and move on.

It doesn't matter whether you are able to identify a Soulmate when they come into your life, for if you have a contract, they will be there to the exact minute they need to be and no longer because you have a sacred and binding agreement. Their Soul knows the exact moment that their business with you is through, so you couldn't make them stay even if you tried. Haven't you had those relationships that you wished could have worked out, but didn't? Outcomes beyond your comprehension are Soulmate contracts being fulfilled. Just as a contractor brings his blueprint to build a house and doesn't stay to live in the house but moves on to the next project, Soulmates are often transient exchanges. And yet, there are Soulmate relationships that are pleasant, harmonious, and last a long time. If you are favored enough to have such a communion, you are indeed given a great gift.

Relationships are the greatest gifts; they are the greatest jewels, because they will outshine material things. Each time you meet a Soulmate, you will help one another move through negative karma; therefore, Soulmates are important. They are the relationships that allow you to evolve and shed negative karma. If you are blessed with several Soulmates in a single lifetime, though it may be arduous, you are flying through what will take others a multitude of lifetimes to process. If you can, be grateful for them-whether they brought sunshine or rain, because both are needed for growth. If you had relationships that taught you painfully, or if you were a teacher who caused pain, then you were entangled in a Soulmate relationship. These lessons you may wish you could do without. Some Soulmates you'll wish you'd never met, and some Soulmates will wish they'd never met you. Yet ultimately, it was beneficial for both. You both committed to a karmic, cyclic interchange until the goal was met, though that goal you may not recognize in this lifetime. You won't know what you are being taught while you are being taught it. Then one day, a certain Soulmate will enter, and your Life Lesson will become clear to you; what you came here to learn. Only Soulmates have these powers.

It can be difficult to give thanks for the painful experiences you've had. Yet, the advanced Soul sees beyond the pain to the lesson learned. Give thanks, for every lesson taught you something valuable. When you look back, ask yourself: "What did I learn from this Soulmate, and, what did I teach this Soulmate?" There's something to be learned from every person. Maybe you learned what not to do, or maybe you learned about the nature of evil. Maybe you learned how it feels to be a victim. Maybe you learned how to forgive. Maybe this Soulmate taught you to be what you said you'd never become. All of it-even the destruction will be used, collected like pieces of a puzzle, gathered back together on The Other Side for your betterment. You can't possibly tell which Soulmate will be the most important. You might be surprised to find that the most horrific of them caused you to grow the most. The ones who taught you not to trust caused you to have to trust again, and the ones that caused you to close the door are the same ones who, in time, caused you to be strong enough to reopen the door. All Soulmates will come into your life when you need them, leaving you with a tremendous gift, sometimes painful, sometimes pleasant-but always essential for your Soul's perfecting.

Message 17-Nothing to Fear

It's only right and natural that you grieve when someone dies, but you are only grieving for yourself, for your own loss, because when you get to the Other Side, it is beautiful. You will be so much more alive there than you ever were here. Yet, the mind thinks that death is the end. A finite mind can only comprehend a beginning and an ending, birth and death; it cannot comprehend eternity. It can comprehend a body, but it can't comprehend a Soul which will live forever. It can understand a limited intelligence, but it can't comprehend the omniscience, the all-knowingness your Over-Soul has. So really, you don't understand who you are until you get to the Other Side. It's as if you are wearing masks at a costume party. During life, you all know one another by your costumes. It's suffocating, it's stifling, it's uncomfortable to wear a costume for very long. Leaving the body is like taking off a heavy costume; it will feel that freeing. The whole purpose of life is for you to see beyond the costumes, to see beyond the skin color, the shape of the eyes, the body type, even the personality. The point is to see beyond the façade. Like a deep-sea diver who is given oxygen and a mask, you were given a brain and body with which to explore this world. Just as a diver must come up for air, so at death will you break through into the next realm and breathe freely again. And the purpose of living? To realize that none of it is real. You are Gods and Goddesses in disguise, in a very elaborately designed scene called earth and there are many more sets and scenes in other dimensions. You have come to earth for two reasons: to reclaim your own divine natures, and to see past the façade to the divinity in others. Everything you see, hear, feel, speak, touch and taste is unreality. Yet it seems deceptively real because the world you see is decoded by your brain in three dimensions. But there are universes you cannot see. It doesn't mean they are not real; it means you have limited equipment to see with. But those who remember their divine origins will understand that they exist on borrowed time and be grateful for every breath.

You've chosen a hostile, limiting planet, and inhabiting a body is repressive because on the Other Side, you have no limits. Your comprehension of the spiritual world and of metaphysics is narrow and dictated by "modern" science. But your science is so rudimentary that it is not modern-by our standards it is laughable. Yet humans boast, gloating over their achievements, but only because they've forgotten the complexity from which they came. Those memories have been wiped from your consciousness, so you could start as a clean slate. You are meant to realize the complete and utter fallibility of the human mind. Many of you haven't accepted the possibility of inhabited worlds, that there are universes and galaxies that cannot be seen and fathomed. Humanity believes it is all-knowing while you possess infantile-like knowledge. If each day you could remember that everything you do, say, hear, touch, taste, smell and think is unreality, you might see what a ridiculous imposter fear is.

Fear is the product of thinking that projects into the unknown future when there is only the present moment. The fearing mind wants to make a slave of the Soul, to make it do the ego's bidding. This ego wants control, to manipulate circumstances and people for its own end. It thinks of your body as its own, believing the body to be its primary identity while the body is only a flimsy costume. If you could train your mind to trust the Soul, then fear would abate. To live in a state of fearlessness is the greatest possible achievement.

In the stillness of the present moment, the mind ceases to chatter and to project itself, and this is Nirvana. Peace and bliss are the natural state of the Soul. The birthright of a Soul is to exist in peace-not wanting, not craving, not desiring anything, not trying to control anything or anyone. The Soul is infinitely trusting, so when you see childlike joy and freedom, a spontaneity that comes from the heart, that individual has achieved an understanding of its true nature. All divinity is at rest, not desiring anything. Your Soul is unknowing yet ever trusting. Every day the goal should be to trust one's Soul rather than the fearing ego. When you are fearful, remind yourself that you are supposed to trust your heart.

You must continually monitor the mind, and in so doing, it will become your servant, not plaguing you with questions you need not answer. In the glorious moment of now, there is only song, movement, color, smells, textures, feelings and images. There is no need to dominate these subtle, beautiful and direct experiences with the coarseness of the mind's blather. All beauty and fear springs from your mind's projections. Hence, the world's outcomes are a result of collective belief. As your ideas evolve towards love and away from fear, your world will become more loving. Each person's thought-stream will eventually join with all the others into a mighty ocean of love. You will behold this in Heaven, called the Crystal Sea. It is the ocean of All Consciousness-a fantastic, breathtaking soup of everything that Father and Mother have created. The point is, you shouldn't assume that your mind always knows where it's going.

Remember, the dead have not left the party-they've only stepped out of their costumes. You are the ones who have left the party and put on temporary masks. When the masks have served their purpose, you will leave them behind. You will wake up on the day you die as if you are being born, as if it is your birthday. Your birth-day, not your death day. And on that auspicious day you will see that the sadness, grief, loss and fear you experienced on earth all served a purpose. If you could remember how many loved ones are waiting for you to join their party, you wouldn't feel alone. But it's natural for the mind to separate itself from dimensions it cannot see. That's what the mind does-it is a separating machine. Do not fear death-fear only not fully living in today. Try to remember that the pair of glasses you are wearing-the lenses you see the world through is a hazy perception of reality. The more you understand that life is a play of dharma and not real, the greater your collective consciousness will be. The stronger your collective consciousness, the faster earth will evolve towards perfection and away from suffering. The scales must be tipped forward, for there is a universal scale that weighs your collective perceptions, so each must strive to change their perceptions.

Changing yourself is the greatest achievement, it is more important than changing others. You might think that altruism, philanthropy, benevolence, generosity and compassion are the height of human development, but you would be mistaken. The height of human development is not even the accumulation of knowledge! The pinnacle of evolution is the willingness to change one's self; to see your own faults, mistakes, shortcomings and errors, and to change them. But humans fear change most of all, and you fear one another. Yet who is any other to you? They are not your mother or your father, your sister or your brother; they are not even your children. They are only another entity that came to this world to wear a mask, and they've played the role of a family member or partner for a little while. Behind the mask, they are changing-their perceptions and knowledge are growing, so they aren't the same people you knew just a day ago. How then can you say you know these people, and why should these entities have the right to judge you, or you them? How can you say you know another's motives, another's heart? How can you know another's destiny, another's Life Chart, another's calling, when you are still discovering all this about yourself? It is the height of arrogance to say you know anything while on earth. It's better to say you are here to learn, you are here to be taught, you are a student passing through, for one student has no jurisdiction over another. Yet you fear what other students will say, because you don't want them to think poorly of you. However, can't you sense that humans are in a similar predicament experiencing the same charade? Division doesn't make any sense to Spirit; divisiveness is a creation of the mind. You are irrevocably connected in a web and harming even one does harm to the whole. You are part of that whole; thus, when you harm another you harm yourself. In harming another you bring karmic consequences upon yourself. Still, all this talk of karma and interconnectedness is too foreign for the mind to comprehend and to believe; it would rather believe it is sovereign and separate.

You are one thread of many, many threads. You are one ray of light, one spark of divine mind. Be your own light and follow where your Soul leads. The real enemy is not one another, but fear. There is no one who can harm you the way fear can harm you! Even if someone kills your body, they're only taking away the costume you'll step out of. Fear is the motivating force for everything the mind does; fear, and the powerful survival instinct. How does a species so invested in defending itself rise above survival to become a more advanced race? You must develop higher thinking, or you will forever stay trapped within the confines of an anxious, angry, confused, and frustrated mind. Your psychologists say that most people will never actualize their full potential. Even fewer of you will realize that what you call reality is only a game devised for your spiritual advancement. But for those who can see the game, exploring the Spirit realm becomes a fascinating quest. Much as your astronauts travel to other planets as representatives of humanity, your Soul can be in a body and travel by astral projection to planes that are wholly energetic and invisible. It is timidity of the unknown that tethers you. Earthly thinking is limited thinking, often anxiety ridden, and low in hope. To enter higher realms of consciousness, you must be unafraid of feelings, perceptions and thoughts that take you where you've never been.

Higher thinking is shared with you via Cosmic Consciousness, out of the abundance of the matrix of all living things, also called The Akashic Record. All knowledge of humanity is contained therein; The Book of Life records every thought and action. When you are receiving information from the Akashic Record, your spiritual explorations can be unbridled, miraculously insightful, and intuitive. This is how prophets, psychics, mediums and mystics have accessed spiritual information. Prophets such as Edgar Cayce and Nostradamus could not have been accurate without an external source of information that was opened to them. It is commonly accepted among mystics that there is an accessible storehouse of cosmic information. This you have known for a while, though it sounds far-fetched to the mind. But consider: If there is an intelligence large enough to record all occurrences of thought and action that you call God, why wouldn't it be possible for God to store it and then to share it? If there is an intellect powerful enough to hold all thought and deed across time and space, why wouldn't it be possible for that same mind to share at least a particle of this information with the human intellect? Your own brain catalogues memories. Why is it so difficult to believe that God's brain is capable of memorization, only to a larger degree? If the curious, determined seeker could access this storehouse, she could use this information to improve the conditions of life for everyone. This is the goal of knowledge-to make life more pleasant and comprehensible for all living things. How then does the average person break into this magnificent storehouse? As stated, this can happen while body-bound but not by those preoccupied with the stories of the fearing mind. Only open minds will access the mysteries of the Universe.

What everyone wants is a clear and simple methodology to access their Higher Selves, and this is understandable. When exploring the spiritual realm, it's most helpful to have a map to guide yourself by, and, you have one. Thoughts guide you to act in benevolent ways, urge you to question accepted knowledge, and create a blessed unrest inside that keeps you reaching for more; that is your map to the stars. The difficulty is in distinguishing the voice of your Higher Self from your mind's voice. Distinguishing between the two voices becomes easier the longer you listen, but this organic process takes time. There is no shortcut, no substitute. There is no program, no secret formula that will speed up the process of becoming a disciple; disciples must learn to follow. The willingness to follow makes you a disciple. Christ said to his disciples: Leave all and follow me (Luke 18:22). He was saying: You must learn to follow. While there is no quick way to become a disciple, one sure-fire prerequisite is that you must renounce the comfortable.

Being willing to leave the "safe" and the "guaranteed," that which feels secure, is anxiety-producing for the mind. Quite a conundrum, isn't it? You must be willing to let go of the shore and set sail on an unknown voyage to find inner peace. If anyone tells you there's a fast, easy way of becoming spiritual, then I say that teacher is misinformed. You'll be fortunate to find the door to enlightenment in a thousand lifetimes. If you have even discovered the right questions to ask, you have accomplished a very great feat. Most people will deny the spiritual world or simply ignore it for the whole of their lives, and this pattern of denial may continue for many lifetimes. Once you discover that you have a Soul, you can become like an astronaut who can take herself to the moon and back for many fascinating explorations. Becoming spiritually aware is a complex and arduous process, and you are miles and miles ahead if you are asking: How do I grow spiritually? How do I access secrets of the next dimension?

If you could find a way to grasp how awesome is your potential, you wouldn't fear failure or success. There is no failure if you earnestly try to understand the purpose of your life. These larger questions are avoided by most. Existential questions about fate and destiny are left to the philosophers, swept aside by everyday concerns for survival and creature comforts. Imagine if you could be free of the fear of rejection and abandonment, those blockages which prevent you from moving forward at greater speed. How would your life be different if you didn't have to worry about what other people thought? What if you simply accepted your worth and weren't concerned with the "fitting-in" game? Your job is to discover your own worth, to accept that you are here at the right time, at the right place, with the right people. Circumstances are exactly as they should be regardless of how you feel about them. Without your presence, there would be an energetic deficit that would throw the entire Human Experiment off. Meaning: your existence is necessary; you fit into the galactic map. Without you, all life would wither and die. Without you, your planet, the universe and even the galaxy would turn in on itself, creating a void, something like a black hole, and time would grind to a halt. Life would hold no meaning anymore. This is because every quantum particle is connected to all others, and you are an entity composed of quantum particles. Without you, there would be no life to speak of! How important you are-and how ironic if you've thought you didn't matter! I know you don't fully understand these things…how could you? I barely understand them myself, and I have been here longer than you can imagine. I have studied to understand this great cosmic experiment, so I might help those in Spirit bodies, as well as those dwelling in human bodies. Angels assist humanity in comprehending their role as free-willed, creative thinkers. And while I've studied for eons, I am just beginning to comprehend these complicated Cosmic designs that emanated from and continue to grow out of the Creator's magnificent intention for Oneness. As I've said, our Creator's motivation in birthing species after species, world after world, universe after universe is to spread out as far as possible, and then to bring all the pieces of God together again, to reintegrate each Soul to its original state of blissful oneness, as it was before the Human Experiment began.

You can't remember how it feels to be intrinsically whole. But there are magical moments of clarity wherein you'll have a fleeting glimpse of how big a creature you really are. Mostly though, these thoughts and feelings are dwarfed by the critical mind. That critical voice is your mind, and because of its penchant for picking apart, it's nearly impossible to hang on to glimpses of your glorious self. They fade as quickly as the bright sunset fades into the horizon. Your mind swallows up the more colorful you in a wash of disbelief and defensiveness. You'll mostly forget who you are, what you're doing here, where you came from, and where you're going. But the mind will pretend it knows by making plans to keep you busy. These plans don't always coincide with your Soul's Blueprint. Often, they will lead you down circuitous routes away from the direction your Soul intended to take. In fact, you'll spend most of your time trying to find your way back after having gotten tangled up in the mind's alternate plan for you. But of course, your arrogant and fearing mind will never admit to this. It will insist upon its infallibility, upon its omnipotence.

As you are seeing, the ego is so conceited as to be fooled by its own plans, duped by its own tricks and disguises. You are led astray not because you aren't an intelligent species, but because you have forgotten your Soul-Self. You keep having to learn lessons repeatedly and these Life Themes replay themselves until you've surrendered to the truth hidden within the lesson. To resist the lesson is very human; you shouldn't feel too badly for acting human. It will take many lifetimes to see the game you are playing. Can you imagine living in a state of fearlessness? If you feared nothing, you would uncover the true you. You've had glimpses of the true you- bold and fearless! If the inner you is courageous, then why doesn't it show on the outside? Only because you fear what people will say. Yet, aren't the most original Souls the people you most admire? History is full of well-behaved people who never made their mark, too busy worrying what others would think. You can live your life as a follower, and if you do, nobody will question you about it. You'll blend in like so many others in a sea of sameness where nobody makes waves. "But I would be the first in my family!" you say. Or, "My friends wouldn't understand." Or worst of all, "I might look like a weirdo!" What a pity to reject your own Soul's idea of who you are.

But you are not who you think you are. You are nothing to do with your body, your age, your ethnicity, your education, or your social status. Those are superficial ideas of you. If you don't understand what I'm talking about, you have repressed your Soul's identity, and the real you sunk beneath the waves of the subconscious and lies buried, like hidden treasure. But now you are being called out of the shadows, because the world needs the brightest shade of you, and you burn the brightest when you are unapologetic and unafraid. The world's consciousness is being lifted, as if humanity were in a magical elevator with wings; a silver bird rising above old constructs, and you are piloting this silver bird. Don't be afraid of the fall! If you fall, the wings of angels shall bear you up, and arrows will fall at your feet. I tell you the truth: God expects you to brave! You must take an oath of fearlessness. To deny your individuality is Soul suicide. What can anyone do to you?

They could take your life-but haven't they already, if you've been robbed of that sparkle in your eyes and your fire to do something brilliant? Let me emphasize: You didn't come to earth to survive your life-what is the glory in that? The person you've imagined you could be *is* the real you.

When you finally see what this game is about you will be awakened to reality, and qualified to lead others out of the dark trenches of misunderstanding. Please don't be so hard on yourself, for misunderstanding is part of the game. Both the good and the bad are good. Without darkness, you wouldn't be motivated to seek the light. Without a mystery, there is no question to answer. You decided to be born so you could present life with your unanswered questions. A child develops by asking her parent, "Why?" As you grew, you developed your own unique perspective and opinions, and you've navigated the world with it. As an adulthood, you reworked your perspectives as your knowledge widened. Your beliefs changed; your childish thinking gave way to more developed, sophisticated ways of relating. You cannot *not* evolve-this is certain. As an individual and as a species, you *will* get there! You will become a better person; a more loving, caring, understanding being. It may take many incarnations, but you have written for yourself a delightful resolution to your own doubts and fears. Be patient with yourself and try to be patient with others. There isn't any way to be perfected instantaneously. Character is perfected over many lifetimes; your perfecting will take some time.

You may wonder why it is such a long and laborious task for a Soul to evolve to perfection. It takes a long time because you are all waiting on one another. Every Soul must evolve fully before any of you can say you are truly whole. You are evolving together, pulling each other along. You don't realize how much you need one another, and how each of you is pulling the next one up to a higher level. Only the mind tells you that you're separate. Your Soul doesn't believe that story; your Soul knows the truth. You are a piece of this intrinsically woven fabric and should one thread be removed, the entire fabric of the Cosmos would fall to pieces. If your Soul were pulled out of the matrix prematurely, it would unravel the fabric of existence itself. This is due to Quantum Entanglement. So never say your life doesn't matter, for you are necessary to the maintenance of life. Do you see how, if you are all connected, even the dark Souls are valuable? Dark energies will in time be liberated; they will become lighter with each incarnation. Given enough time, all energies, both dark and light will grow to perfection, into the One Light.

Until then, appreciate this opportunity of living as a human being. Trust that you are evolving with every breath and try to see your suffering as the very great gift it is, for those who suffer can evolve the quickest. But it depends upon your perspective, doesn't it? If you see your trials as an opportunity, your Soul will flourish and become an exquisitely handcrafted piece of art; you'll live a life to be proud of. You are here to weather the storms that blow into your life, not to escape them. More than that, I hope you will be tenderized and reshaped by them. All of you will be broken; it's what you came here to be. But not all are willing to see it as a gift. You can resist the divine plan for a long while, but eventually you'll tire of resistance. You'll give in and do what you should have done, which is to accept your fate, and finally to make something useful of it. A few of you, the exceptional ones, will even make something beautiful of it. Remember, it's your choice-it's always your choice.

Message 18-Your Life Plan & Karma

Certainly, there is a plan for your life. Contrary to what it may look or feel like, there is a plan. Not only is there a plan for you but for all of humanity, and it is a plan for good. Yet you may look at the "evidence" before you and say: how can this be good? The question you and indeed the whole world asks is: How can suffering be good? Your five senses tell you the invisible realm is a waste of your precious time. Likewise, it seems a waste to live on a planet where injustice reigns supreme. But are you wasting away, slaving for nothing of consequence, or is there more to the story than the eye can see, more than what your limited senses perceive? If there is an unseen realm, a world where all deeds are converted to energy, and this energy follows you into the next life, is your life really for nothing? Could there be realms beyond your limited perception in which it all makes perfect sense? If you believe there is nothing except the futility of a chaotic existence and you must merely survive it, then certainly, life is a senseless struggle. If you've deduced that humanity is nothing more than a random evolutionary blip destined for extinction, one ought to be merciless in her dealings because, after all, you only go around once. Many people live this way-on the edge of sanity, thinking there is no higher purpose, convinced they are slated for little more than one paltry life, devoid of deeper meaning.

The world has been a dark and vicious place where the bright star of technology has been used to exploit the poor. But I promise you, there is a better age coming. The next cycle of human evolution is lighter and less dense, happier and freer. Rising spiritual consciousness will overtake avarice greed and dictatorships. Antiquated ignorance will be denounced, and just leaders will demand accountability of the tyrants. The present age of the

Technological Man will end and a new chapter in the human saga will be written. In the next chapter of the human drama, spirituality and the application of energetic technologies are investigated and explored, and destructive terror will end.

For those of you living on the planet now, it feels as if you are trudging forward in quicksand, making slow progress towards the higher virtues of honesty, integrity and compassion. Those of you on the Dark Planet (which is what we call Earth) are fighting for your lives; struggling to make ends meet, while finding the promise of materialism to be a sham, a fraudulent existence. Many of you will abandon the ideals of servitude to money all together, for many will tire of playing the game that the elite have set up for the masses to keep them busy, so they may profit greatly, while keeping them subdued. Many of you will revolt, lifting your voices and crying out: "We are not slaves, and you are not our masters!" Many of you will turn your backs on a society that has developed money mania and will demand accountability from governments who have forsaken human dignity and common decency. And while there will be a revolt and a cry for human rights, there will always be grey and dark entities that want to exploit and control. The future of humanity is growing brighter and less dim, it is becoming lighter and less dense, it is rising instead of falling, but over many centuries will these changes for the better occur.

If you look at history, you see steady improvements and increasing knowledge. There is still great hope for the future of humanity, so feel good about playing your small part. Yet because you are now in a cycle of density and moral depravity, you may feel more like you're living in the cellar than in the sunshine. Indeed, energetically, you are in the cellar! But out of darkness and death always springs light and rebirth. The Creators established this great cycle. There will be an end to the senseless greed and corruption as humanity embraces its spiritual roots, leaving behind its stubborn attachment to materialism.

Your life has more consequence, even more energetic "weight" during times of darkness. Any light you bring is desperately needed and shines all the brighter. The darkness might call you names or deride you, but you are eternal Souls sent to love and care for one another, so let them sneer. Those same entities will bow to you on the Other Side, because all will be seen. Every heart's motives and deeds will be readable. Each Soul will be an open book that cannot be closed, and everyone will know anything they wish to know about you. But what about privacy, you may be wondering? What if I don't want everyone to know my personal business? Then you had better change direction-for on the Other Side there is no privacy; there is only full disclosure, which is quite startling and perplexing to those with something to hide. It's like being naked and not being able to shut the door. In Genesis when God called to Adam and Eve: "Where have you gone?" He found they had hidden their nakedness after eating from the tree of the knowledge of good and evil. This story is an allegory. It illustrates that once you have disobeyed the laws of morality, once you have tasted evil, you'll hide from God. The guilty Soul will not want to be known by God, because then it would have to give up its maniacal ways and addictions. You are living in a world disconnected, a world hiding from its Makers. The tragedy is that God didn't come looking for Adam and Eve to punish them. God came to walk beside them in the cool of the evening. God missed the companionship of His children. Father and Mother always want to connect with you, but wrong choices, what has been called "sin" separates you from God and keeps you in hiding.

You are God's beloved child; you are important to God. You are connected to God. Just as a child is a part of the parent, God's divine DNA is part of you. You have two origins: A spiritual origin, and a human origin. You have two sets of DNAs: a spiritual DNA and a human DNA. Don't you see-you are a dualistic being part human, part divine. Part flesh, part spirit. You are a hybrid if ever there was one! You sometimes feel as if you don't "fit" or belong because your Soul is remembering its origins. You have a longing for more, or at least something else. You are longing for what is beyond the material plane. But your existence is necessary, especially at a darker time in history; humanity needs you to shine as brightly as you possibly can. We're counting on you to be mentally and physically healthy, so you can get the job done. You wanted to be a part of something consequential, epic in nature, so you sent yourself here after much careful consideration. You didn't incarnate in haste or by mistake. You saw a need and said, "I will go. I will do my best and try to redeem myself. I will try not to do harm but to help. I will do my part to pull humanity together. Even though I am only one voice, I have a voice-and I wish to use it for the good."

Once your Soul left the highest vibrations of the Upper Realms of Consciousness, it entered a body of great density that slowed you down. Then you were born into a world that is trillions of light years from its source; a dark, cold, lonely world by comparison. And all this has been so disorienting, confusing and frightening that you would at times like to curl into a ball and stay sequestered where the world's darkness cannot touch you. It's all very understandable, wanting to hide. And it's true that if all you ever did was survive this life, you would be considered very brave for choosing this world. Dear child, we do not blame you for wanting to hide. And you may be very tired by this point, wishing to find just a patch of stability and sanity for yourself-no one blames you for that. But you were not sent here to hide. You came down to lend a helping hand-that's the reason you came. The plan you wrote includes not only learning to love yourself (with all your faults and imperfections) but other imperfect entities as well.

The plan you wrote is undoubtedly unfolding as it should. Try very diligently not to focus on your fears, for they cannot help you. Focus instead on anything positive. Staying close to God can help keep you positive, because God is a positive force field. That's all and everything God is: a force for good. And if you've heard anything else about God, you've been listening to negative reports, and there are many. God is one thing alone: Love. Can you take that in? Can you allow yourself to believe that despite the heartache of this life, God's love for you remains? No matter what has happened, God's love for you will go on. Why? Because you are one of God's children. There's only one constant in all of life, and this steady force will outlive you, following you back Home: God's unfailing love. The next time you're thinking that life has failed you, simply turn to God-not away from God. Come out of your hiding place and show yourself, even though you may be afraid that God will be angry with you, or that you won't be forgiven. You can't outrun God; you are God's child, and your Heavenly parents know everything about you. Go to them, knowing they are merciful beings of great power that can help you. This is your heritage: parents who know all about your struggles and have answers for you. You can count on these parents. These are eternal parents, and unlike earthly parents they will not let you down. In truth, they are nothing like your earthly parents.

The plan for your life may seem confused or even tortured. But you wouldn't be here unless there was something your Soul needed to learn, and some things that Soulmates needed to learn from you. It will make sense on the Other Side; but while earthbound, it will often appear senseless. It will feel chaotic and sometimes hopeless, and you will want to escape, even from God. There's a phobia that sets in when you've had too much of life. Spending time with your Source can refresh your wilting spirit. I'm encouraging you not to give up-you're so close to the finish line. To give up now would be admitting defeat, and you're not finished yet, or you'd be back here instead of there. That's how you know when you're finished-you'll find yourself back here again. Until then, refocus and carry on…we're rooting for you. We know it isn't easy; good things never are. Take a deep breath and ask for strength. Then set sail again, because as John Lennon said: "Everything will be okay in the end. If it's not okay, it's not the end."

Karma informs your Life Plan, so you must understand this elusive concept further. Karma is like the symbol of justice: the blindfolded woman holding scales in her hands. Lady Justice is blinded to show her impartiality. The scale she holds is perfectly balanced, symbolizing fairness. Like Lady Justice, karma is an unerringly precise, bringing every Soul into balance. To accomplish this, the scales of karma will be weighing and measuring until all have attained a realization of the true state of things. Relationships with Soulmates may repeat themselves in future incarnations, which is called a karmic tie. These ties bind you together lifetime after lifetime until both are set free. When the scales of justice are finally balanced, you will each go your own way. Until then, you are locked in a Cosmic, energetic exchange with your Soulmates. Of course, each time you meet the same Soulmate in a different life and in a radically different form, it will seem completely new to you when the chase is in fact eons old, and you will reenact the drama between you until the unfinished business is complete. When Christ said: "Do to others whatever you would like them to do to you" (Math. 7:12), He was referring to the faultless law of karma. He was saying: the scales of justice must be satisfied; there is no escaping karma, whatever you do will come back to you (in one form or another). Accounts must be even with all people before you are free, so strive to do as little harm as possible, for your deeds will certainly be visited upon you. Christ described it this way: "If someone slaps you on your right cheek, turn to him the other also" (Math. 5:39). He wasn't suggesting you subject yourself to abuse or mistreatment; He was describing karma. When you slap someone, you will be struck in return on the opposite cheek, for all are connected as if you share the same face. He was showing the inescapable nature of karma, how actions always return.

Many times, you have stayed longer than you should with a Soulmate, trying to save someone from their own karma. But you are not a savior; it is not your job. Your mission is to offer love and truth and if they cannot accept it, if you are rejected, do not labor unnecessarily. You cannot make anyone see what you see. Set them free to face whatever they must face. It is a painful lesson to speak your truth and if they cannot grasp it, to walk away. If you linger, your progress will be hindered, because you are stuck wherever their consciousness is stuck. And their progress will be hindered, because you are blocking the lesson karma means to bring them. It's a mercy to both people when a dysfunctional relationship is dissolved. It doesn't mean that either of you has failed. Don't assume failure when relationships end, because it may not be the drama's final act. On the Other Side, you will meet again and review each person's moves and countermoves. Karma is like a game of chess. Humans are the pawns, and karma is the hand that moves you, until: checkmate! The game is over, and the scales are balanced again. This is the impeccable law of karma.

Who thought up this brilliant and challenging game? Who designed this cosmic chessboard, and who moves the pawns? None other than the chess master, of course. Who else could calculate the incalculable number of Souls, their moves, and the effects of their choices in advance? There is no beating this program-there is only learning from it. Those who are less evolved think they can control it, which is ludicrous! A pawn cannot control the hand that moves it. You are quite simply being moved and are below, so you cannot see the hand controlling your destiny. You are being placed wherever the hand moves you: forward, back, jumping over, going around, or side to side. You think you choose it all, because you are moving from this place to that, talking to this person or that when all you are doing is following the fixed plan of your Oversoul. Your Oversoul has already calculated your every move. And though your Life Plan is fixed, your responses are not. Karma is the result of free-will choices.

While all of this may be too strange to fathom now, when you return Home, you will be astonished at how close you came in a single lifetime to accomplishing your Life's Mission. Or, you may be one of the fortunate who accomplish their Life's Mission during this incarnation and don't need to repeat it. Wouldn't it be glorious to graduate and not have to repeat this difficult class? For those who don't have to reincarnate again, your return Home will be distinctly joyous, a celebration of epic proportions. For those who have graduated, Heaven throws a party in your honor, and believe me when I tell you-on that day, you will be Heaven's hero. But for now, like a plane on autopilot, your course is set, so you might as well enjoy the ride.

Message 19-Decisions, Decisions, Decisions

Most people have trouble making decisions because they don't stop to ask themselves what they really want. People have been programmed to want certain things by society. They've been programmed to desire a family, a career, an education, riches and possessions. If they were blessed with parents who taught them the importance of honesty and integrity, they may want to be a good person who helps others. Whatever you were taught, you are the unwitting product of. Whatever familial messages and societal reinforcement you've been given have informed and shaped your values and priorities. Therefore, when it comes to thinking autonomously, it becomes harder each year, because year after year, pre-programmed messages are reinforced. How then does a person think originally when she is being told what to think by the society, and by the traditions and customs she has grown up in? Why is it necessary to think for oneself? If you do not know what you truly want, when it's decision-making time, you may make the wrong turn. You could follow someone else's map instead of your own, and this always leads to the same place: a dead-end. Even at a dead-end, you'll have to decide to turn yourself around, and of course you will-why would you want to be moving in the wrong direction?

Being stuck in the same old routine is comfortable. It's not exciting, but it isn't risky, either. Many people have the goal of simply getting through life without risking very much. I would venture to say most humans don't care for going out on a limb and would prefer to not climb the tree at all. It is human nature to seek safety and security. However, look at why you have incarnated, what we call the Primary Objective. The Primary Objective of reincarnation is to evolve, to shed negative karma by creating positive karma. Playing it "safe" really isn't part of that equation. Which is not to say you should deliberately put yourself in harm's way, that is called foolishness. No, I'm thinking of a calculated risk: one that is planned when possible, and spontaneous on occasion. The willingness to risk is essential to your Soul's growth. If you are more concerned with how much money you've saved or how you can retire in style, then you're already in trouble. I don't mean to alarm you, but you don't have a lot of time left. You may be saying: "What does this Archangel know about me?" Humans, the lot of you, have short lifespans, and this is a good thing, considering it allows you to return Home to evaluate how you did every 60 to 80 years. Then you can begin anew before too much time has passed stuck in any one incarnation. Medical technological advances will eventually lengthen your life spans, but for now, I assure you that as compared to other entities who don't die, you don't have a lot of time to waste focused on the wrong things or headed in the wrong direction.

Making good decisions starts with a clear understanding of who you are and what you want. You really must get clear on those two subjects. You may think the course you're on is the right one simply because you've never stopped to question it. "Look here," you might be thinking, "I've got enough troubles without creating more for myself." That is just the kind of thinking that keeps people resigned and complacent, settling for mediocrity. This may come as a revelation, but you weren't sent here to get rich, and you weren't sent here to own things. You weren't sent here for any purpose other than your Soul's growth. And how do you grow? Think of any plant or animal and look at how it grows. It begins as a seed, and the seed must struggle right from the first to survive. Some seeds won't even have the chance to be born. If it survives, it moves from stage to stage in its lifecycle. Likewise, humans grow in stages, from infancy to adolescence, from adolescence to teenagers, and from teenagers into adulthood. Each developmental stage has its unique milestones, and each stage of development requires a different effort. As you can see, there's no way to have it "easy" if you are going to keep moving up. If you insist on "easy" you're really settling for less than your capabilities, and that is a waste. If you haven't stood back and assessed your life's trajectory, maybe you should. It's easy to fly off-course, because life is a complex journey. No one would blame you if you realized that where you've been headed is not where you intended to go. Life can throw you for a loop; it can knock you silly and before you know it, you're flying in the opposite direction of where you wanted to be. So please be compassionate towards yourself if you realize you've been flying blind. It's easy to do, many times no one was there to set you straight.

If it's time to adjust your flight path, you owe no apologies to anyone. However, you may owe apologies if your choices negatively affected others. But never apologize for correcting errors in judgment. People may want to heap guilt on you for making choices they don't like, but that is not your concern. You have one chance to do life right, and that can't be done if you're overly worried about what critics think; you cannot control that. Besides, what other people think is not going to matter at the end of your life. They won't be there to say, "I told you so." What really matters is living a life worthy of the opportunity you've been given. And while it may not seem like such a marvelous trip, when you return to the Other Side, you'll wonder why you didn't see the importance of life while you were moving through it. It's only because when you're busy fighting the battle, you can't always see the war. It's difficult to comprehend the "big picture" when you're fighting in the trenches. No one can blame you for making course corrections.

You can become a confident decision-maker, stepping out boldly if you know the direction you're headed is the right one for you. You'll have to ignore the negativity and the doubting Thomas, because they'll always be there. When Jesus walked on water, He didn't look down or He would have been afraid. He instructed His disciples not to look at the waves. He was saying: Ignore fear-don't get focused on it. Keep your eyes where they should be, ahead instead of behind you. He knew the importance of having a goal-He set new ones all the time. He didn't stay in one place waiting for people to come to Him, did He? He traveled like the yogis, meeting many different people and He was always setting a fire under His disciples to grow in their faith and their willingness to serve the needy. He was never content to rest for long, a fact that often frustrated His disciples. You too should know your talents and capabilities and be eagerly seeking out new ways to use them. Many times, Jesus emphasized the importance of sharing what you have, and of letting your light shine.

As you progress in life, there will be innumerable forks in the road; decision after decision will need to be made. Certainly, it is easiest to let someone else make your mind up for you. You don't have to worry about making a bad decision if you shy from making them. But part of maturing, part of developing is the ability to make your own decisions. To avoid making decisions is to avoid risk, and we've just discussed the importance of getting out of your comfort zones. As you're making decisions, you will undoubtedly be confused as to which way is the best way or the "right way." Even if you make a bad choice it will be okay in the end, because you have more than one shot at this game called life. Any wrong turn can be corrected in time, and anything you didn't get to do can be done, given enough time. You may think: "That's a very cavalier attitude about life. You should always take your choices seriously," and I agree. I've admonished you to think seriously about the direction your life is headed. But many people stay stuck because they don't want to make the "wrong" decision, so they don't make any decision at all. Or they allow someone else to make their decisions for them, which means they are living in a disempowered state. Avoid this trap by making small decisions. Instead of following, suggest an alternative, something you would enjoy-then stand by your decision. At every opportunity, make your voice heard-not by demanding it be your way, but by offering your opinion. As you voice your opinion, you'll not only become a more confident and self-assured person, but you'll get more of what you want in life and wouldn't that be nice? Start practicing today and see what happens. Who knows, the results might be better than you expect.

I've noticed another tendency of the human animal which is to exaggerate mistakes. The ironic thing is that you don't like it when others focus on your mistakes, because it's so easy to make them. Mistakes are mainly how you've learned everything. In childhood, you learned not to touch fire when you put your hand to something hot. So why do humans make such a big deal when others make mistakes? Too much emphasis is placed on mistakes all around. You made a mistake-so what? You just learned something, didn't you? Or you were reminded of something that you'd forgotten. Is this so terrible? Mistakes are errors to be corrected, that's all they are. They should not be grounds for harsh judgment or criticism. You make mistakes every day; minor slip-ups and oversights. You remember incorrectly, or you misjudge a little, or you step right when you should have stepped left. Didn't you learn a little something with each misstep? If I had one wish for you, it would be that you'd say: "So what?" the next time someone makes a mistake, because most mistakes can be corrected. And for the grave mistakes, there is an infinite number of ways the Universe will conspire to help that person learn. The next time you or someone you care for (or better yet, someone you dislike) makes an error, say to them: "So what? You'll get it right the next time." Stop being so critical, harsh, and judgmental. Get focused on the positive, the winners always do, and you've been a winner since Day 1.

Message 20-Practical Spirituality

What does it mean to be a spiritual person? A spiritual person is not a mindless person. You should not have blind faith. A spiritual being has their eyes wide open-they are observant, paying close attention. Spiritual people are curious, childlike people: unafraid to ask questions and they must not apologize for expecting answers. Furthermore, it is not "holy" to live in poverty any more than it is "holy" to live in luxury. Neither renunciation of material things nor accumulation of wealth proves your spirituality. The spirit realm cares not about your riches. What makes you a spiritual person are your priorities, how you spend your time. Do you make time for regular spiritual practice? Are you growing in self-awareness? Spiritual people thirst for the truth and if you seek, the natural outcome is a finding. Most people give up too easily and don't persist, feeling disillusioned with their spiritual life. This has more to do with lack of determination than lack of available knowledge. School is always in session-the question is: who will show up for class? True spirituality is waking up to love and forgiveness; this is a true awakening. Spirituality sees suffering as a redemptive tool used to forge you into an instrument of compassion. Spirituality accepts "what is" rather than demand that life conform. A truly spiritual person will learn to content herself in the present instead of entertaining inward fantasies escaping the present. When you spend more time engrossed in unattainable fantasies than you do enjoying the present moment, you are avoiding the work your Soul came here to do, which is to be thoroughly immersed in living. If the outer world doesn't conform to your expectations, and if others don't live up to your standards, it means you have set yourself up as judge and jury. Christ advised, "Judge not, lest you be judged" (Matt. 7:1). Even Christ dared not judge.

Karma is the return of energy. When negative thinking or action occurs, that energy is sent out and will never fail to return to its owner, its source of origin. Whether your thoughts are negative or positive, know that thoughts will return to you in one form or another, either with negative or positive outcomes. Keep in mind that karma is an all-encompassing, unlimited law; meaning that karma created in one lifetime can visit you in subsequent lifetimes. Karma is another word for consequences-the results you are now getting, even the circumstances you find yourself in. Karma may be visited upon you because of thoughts and actions of a previous life. It is impossible to fully understand the turns your life has taken. Perhaps you are reaping the results of another lifetime. It is deceptively easy to think: "They're getting what's coming to them." In truth, all you see is an extremely short snippet of their eternal existence. It is better not to say, "They deserved it." Do not imagine you can know what another person deserves!

Practical spirituality means thinking through your problems. Use the good mind God gave you to find practical solutions and offer practical help. Refrain from asking others to believe blindly and don't allow people to follow without understanding why. Following blindly is not spirituality-this is stupidity. True spirituality will always meet the practical needs of the poor and not refuse the questions of the seeker. Religious dogma that seeks to control will always fear questions and shame the questioner. Fear and shame have nothing to do with spirituality, and spirituality has no association with fear and shame. If you are afraid to ask questions, or if you are made to feel ashamed because of who or what you are, then that is not a reflection of a spirituality that extends a compassionate hand. Practical spirituality always lifts and builds up-it never tears down, it never suppresses, and it is not negative or hate-based. True spirituality need not shrink from any question, nor is it afraid to look for the answer. It does not mind when you do not know.

Being a genuinely spiritual person means you have the freedom to be yourself, and you give other people that same liberty.

Spiritual people are inquisitive, spontaneous, honest, humble, and unconditionally accepting. They don't reject scientific knowledge and can withstand opinions that oppose their own. True spirituality is courageous and unafraid, open to opposing viewpoints and willing to explore possibilities. A spiritual person is eager to expand their understanding of complex concepts. Any religion that makes you afraid to think for yourself (or makes you afraid in any way) is not a path that leads to freedom. Fear and freedom are opposing concepts, opposite extremes. Love always liberates. Any doctrine that will not entertain opposing views and cannot be questioned is not an open door. That is, by definition, a closed door, a closed mind, and a closed heart. It will lead the seeker down a path devoid of light. Spirit's objective is always to lead you to the next door and to an expanded viewpoint. Spirit does not shrink, Spirit expands. It holds the door wide for those who dare to ask "unaskable" questions. Only those who dare trespass convention and ask the forbidden questions will lead others closer to the Light. Spirit is anxious, eager and willing to lead you there; it is always unafraid to lead you to new vistas. Practical spirituality allows you to use both your mind and your heart.

You must have faith that some elements you cannot comprehend. There are elements all around you, even inside your own body that you can't see. For example, the air you breathe is invisible, yet you must have it in every moment to survive. While it cannot be seen or touched, you depend on it just the same. Your life is full of elements, energetic in nature, that your five senses cannot perceive, yet this invisible matter is essential to your functioning. A certain amount of faith in what you cannot see is healthy and intelligent. You must believe in what has scientifically been proven as fact, but you also must believe in what has yet to be proven. It is naïve to only believe in past discoveries, and just as foolish to believe only in what you can see. Make use of all your faculties-both your outer senses and your inner senses. Use them together to decipher what is real from what is false, what you can put your faith in, and what is only the claim of zealots. Don't follow blindly for then you place your well-being in the hands of others who may have ulterior motives. Trust your inner senses over what you've been taught, because the Higher Self in you knows what is right and wrong. Your Higher Self will tell you when you have gone the wrong direction. Some call this the conscience. If you're unable to hear that still, small voice, it means you've ignored it many times. You may need to be reconnected to your inner guide. But most of you can still hear that voice as it leads you through life. Don't depend on others to show you the way, because you have a light inside, even if it feels very dim.

    When you are engulfed in darkness, when you are steeped in the Dark Night of the Soul, know that it's come because it's time for resurrection, for something divinely inspired to be birthed in you. This is the purpose of suffering: to lead you to resurrection, new life, new growth, and renewed hope. In the resurrection days you will be quickened with a vitality and presence of mind. You will find paths that expand into greater freedoms and increased consciousness. Once you meet Spirit, nothing will be the same. You won't look the same, talk the same, or feel the same. You especially won't seem the same to others. A genuine encounter with the Almighty will change you. If it doesn't, if the changes are only temporary, then a rocky path lies before you, for you will have to learn the same lessons over. Life Lessons or Themes will be presented in rapid succession until you are brought to your knees. Pain is only purposeful if you learn from it-if you don't, it's torture. The Dalai Lama said: "Pain is inevitable, suffering is optional." Why be enrolled in the school of hard knocks? Being a true follower, a true believer, hasn't anything to do with religion; man-made religion is a sacrilege. Christ did not command: "Go build empires and call them mine." He asked His followers to spread the word that God is love. The mission was to share Christ's love and forgiveness and that was all. Christ's life was lived in the tradition of the Hindu yogis and babas who prefer to renunciate money and attachment to things like church buildings and fancy cars. When you see religious empires that require a tithe from the poor-this is a fabricated system that does not emulate Christ's life. Christ did not ask for a tithe. He didn't own much, He didn't dress in the finest clothing or dine regularly with the wealthy, nor did He consort with the political set. In fact, He sharply criticized religious leaders for their treatment of the poor. He also criticized the "money-changers," the merchants who worshiped the acquisition of money. His Sabbath was meant as a day of rest, a day of being with the Divine, a day of spiritual communion. He destroyed the temple marketplace to show His contempt of the love of money, which is the root of all ego. When you see God being bought and sold, when God has been marketed and packaged for the masses, you're seeing the opposite of what Christ wanted, which was simplicity. A true "conversion" changes the heart, so it forsakes money hungriness. True conversions are exactly as the word conversion implies: to be converted from one form to another. Your spiritual life should be transformational. When you have a genuine spiritual awakening, it shakes you to your very core. It may take many incarnations for you to embrace your Christlikeness. And some will be called to be more than disciples-some will be called to be leaders in the forward movement of humanity's evolution. Becoming a leader is not about amassing followers, though disciples may be a natural byproduct of a transformed life. A self-realized individual is a rarity, and people are drawn to the rare and unusual-the "freaks," are they not? A genuinely spiritual person may look strange to others. To seekers, they'll appear attractive, but to the worldly they'll appear foolish and repellant. People hungry for the light will see it a mile away and be magnetically drawn. You don't have to find fantastic ways to draw people; they will be drawn to your inner light. You don't have to do much of anything if you want to be one of God's generals other than radiate God.

I say you can know God, but I say that with a smile, for God is unknowable. How can a mortal understand the Almighty's plan for the Cosmos and comprehend God's intricate systems? You will never know the mind of God while in an unredeemed body, living on an unholy planet. What you can have with certainty is an experience of God's magnanimous love. You can be in the presence of God's acceptance of you and realize your own divinity. This is what you should strive for: directly experiencing God's pure, unconditional love. When you discover how precious you are, how important to God, this will change you. The disciples changed not because Christ's teachings were profound. Yes, He had important words to share, but anyone could have spoken them. What profoundly changed their hearts was how He loved them. They were moved in a deeply personal way-His love inspired them in ways they were unable to explain. They were told to take the gift of love and share it with as many as they could-with everyone, every tribe, for God so loved the whole world (not just them). Christ didn't command: "Build me a church," or, "Remember me by building monuments in my name." He did not say: "Collect people's money before you serve them." No, He simply gave to them, loving them in a way they needed to be loved, and they couldn't depart from Him, they were stuck to Him, dropping their agendas.

Jesus said: "Leave all and follow me" (Luke 18:22). What does this mean? Does it mean you must make converts or be a missionary? Remember, Christ spoke in parables and symbolism. Saying "leave all" was not a direct command to literally leave home. Instead, He was saying: 'The ego feels most at home with pleasure, money, and power-but you must leave these things.' He was saying: Spirit first. He was saying: 'Put your trust in me rather than in things.' The Holy Spirit isn't found in a temple, in a mosque, or in a synagogue. God's Spirit isn't found in a church, small or large. "What?" you may say, "people must go to church!" I give you only one sober warning: Never judge others. When you do, you have made yourself a heretic, for Christ commanded: "Do not judge, or you too will be judged" (Math. 7:1).

If the Holy Spirit isn't found in a building, where should the seeker look? Let's carefully examine Christ's words on the matter. He spoke often of the Holy Spirit and of leaving the Spirit behind in His absence. The Holy Spirit is inside; a piece of God deposited in you. This gift is from God; it is holy, perfect, and without flaw. It is not mortal or flesh; it is immaterial and eternal. *The Holy Spirit is the Soul*, a holy spirit that comes from a holy realm. You must get clear on this: there is no one Holy Spirit in Heaven. This is a misinterpretation. The Holy Spirit is inside each human body-the

Soul! This is the Spirit that Christ described. And the "Son," the person of Jesus Christ, was God incarnate. The true Trinity is: Father, Mother, and all the children. This is the truth, my friends, the whole truth. You have been misled for so many years, fumbling in the darkness of misunderstanding. If these religious men had sought for the truth, they would have found it. But they preferred to tell their own version of God, and they are still telling their own versions today.

When you have a genuine encounter with the real God you will begin to see things in a strange and wondrous new light. Far-reaching concepts will begin to sound like music to your ears, and what once seemed odd or even wrong will be comprehensible to you. This is because your mind has been opened and expanded. The pineal gland of the brain will open your insight. With this new knowledge will come a boldness, a fire. When the disciples "received" the Holy Spirit, a flame appeared above their heads. Christ made it appear as a hologram over their crown chakras, as they experienced a spiritual force known in the East as Prana, or Life Force energy or Chi. This Life Force Energy was symbolized as a flame, for Life Force energy burns up the ego. Do you want to awaken? Meditation can cause this awakening. The more time you spend in meditation, the fierier you will become. Yet fire is nearly silent, colorful and loves to dance and move almost too fast for the human eye. The symbol of a flame, more than any other symbol, is God's monarch. Spirit can light a fire within and calls your ego to step into that ring of fire. When you are amid trials and tribulations, angels walk in the fire with you. A God-seeker is a firewalker.

When you are connected to the Primal Force of creation, you will do things that once seemed impossible. Eventually, you can learn to manifest whatever you need by thinking it into being-by attracting it to you, by magnetizing it to you in the Spirit realm first, in ethereal realms. Everyone wants to manifest the goodies-everybody wants to manifest riches and admiration. Even in this, the ego and the Soul are at great odds, opposing one another. This tension is purposeful, for it presents you with a choice. Whenever you set to death your own plans and schemes, what you surrendered will come back to you in another form-behold, your savior will appear, clothed in splendor. More than any other miracle, God loves resurrection-when what you thought was dead is raised again before your astonished eyes. This is because God loves surprises! The disciples couldn't believe it when Christ returned from the dead, and how He laughed when He saw their faces. You see, the God of resurrection has not forgotten dreams you have laid to rest. It is your doubt alone that says it will never happen, and your disbelief that keeps it from happening. Lack occurs not because God wouldn't give it to you, but because your mind has all these conditions to meet before you can accept the gift. Your mind's many conditions oppose and block God's goodness. It's true-you are your own worst enemy! God has no enemies. Did you hear that? Let me be clear: God loves all, exactly as they are. God does not hate, oppress, oppose, or shun anyone for any reason. Only the human mind has contrived these barriers, these false separations: "Come unto me all who are weary and burdened, and I will give you rest" (Matt. 11:28).

    Meditation resets the mind; it clears misconceptions and negativity, if only for a short while. Meditation cleans up the files of your mind, purging disbelief, affirming your divine status. Meditation feeds the mind, giving it positives to chew on. The mind ruminates, so better that it ruminates on the positive. Whatever you set your focus on will grow, so focus intently and forcefully upon the positives. How often you choose to feed your mind something wholesome and fortifying is up to you, but the more positives it gets, the more positive you will be. When you become a positive force, people will look upon you favorably, and you'll be well regarded. I don't suggest putting on a fake, phony façade, for there is nothing wrong with giving voice to negative feelings; it is not healthy to keep it trapped inside! But once you have expressed your troubles, shift to a more positive mindset; declare something good. Declaration is the act of speaking something into existence, and while this may sound "New-Age," you do it all the time. You're always creating with your words: "For by your words you will be justified, and by your words you will be condemned" (Matt. 12:37).

The words you choose are vitally important. Words fashion your outcomes and build (or destroy) your future. Most of the hurt that has happened to you hasn't been physical-it's been emotional, the direct result of someone's unkind and hasty words. Unintentionally, you have created hurt for others with the misuse of words. Words are the building blocks of the entire world. The spoken word is extremely powerful, so speak carefully and thoughtfully or don't speak at all. Diplomats have mastered the art of interpersonal communication, and by the skillful use of words, ruffles will be smoothed, and wounds healed. The diplomat does not need to pander to others, for she speaks the truth, but the way she delivers her message is so complementary and interesting that the listener can't help but lower their guard. Each of you will be called upon in your everyday lives to be diplomats in one form or another. A parent may need to use diplomacy with a child to motivate or correct them. A teacher may need to be an example of diplomacy, showing students how important effective communication is. An employer may need to counsel and instruct, and a worker may need to deal with difficult customers. The effectiveness of your speech establishes you as an authority. A diplomat is someone with a diploma who has studied and become a specialist in her field. To become more diplomatic, study the problems you are faced with, don't run from them or ignore them. No, that is the coward's way. Instead, dig in and scrutinize the problem, every detail. Pick the problem apart until you have a clear understanding of how the problem occurred, and what possible solutions there are. This will give you the ability to answer in a thoughtful, fair-minded way. As a result, you will look like an expert, and people will be inclined to listen to you. Diplomats resolve conflict especially well, something most people shy from. Unless you can resolve conflict, you are still part of the problem. Granted, some people won't listen to reason no matter how diplomatic you are. Better not to waste your time with these, and there will be plenty of these people. If you refuse to acknowledge negativity it will begin to shrink, and it can be replaced with a new idea of yourself. Anyone who ever changed had to defy an old idea of themselves. Think about it-if you want to learn a new trade, you must first learn new skills. You must take the initial step of attempting something new if you wish to improve yourself. Most communication challenges are the result of an unwillingness to try a new approach.

My words are challenging, but angels are not shy to speak the truth. In fact, it is our primary responsibility. Through the ages, we have been the truth-tellers. Angels are depicted carrying trumpets, symbolizing that we aren't quiet about sharing our message. We declared that Christ was coming to earth, did we not? Archangel Gabriel has the loudest voice of all the angels, for Gabriel is Heaven's premier messenger. Anytime there is a momentous announcement in the Heavenly realms, Archangel Gabriel and his thunderous voice will be heard trumpeting the message. In fact, his voice can be so loud that it's truly awe-inspiring (and intimidating). You may think of angels as sprightly wisps who do little more than play with clouds all day. But when you get to the 7 realms of Heaven, you will see us in a new light; we are rulers of the Kingdoms and commanders, generals with awesome authority. Those who think they are tough and not easily frightened would fall to their knees were a blazing Archangel to appear before them. Even the toughest people tremble before the great and powerful Archangels. We are a mighty presence, a glorious and terribly strong phylum, with the explosive capabilities of a volcano! But for humans, we tone it down, so your brain can tolerate us. Because we exist in the ethereal planes does not mean we are any less potent when visiting earth, but we cloak ourselves in invisibility. If you had the ability to see angels and otherworldly creatures that dwell peacefully and productively alongside you, you would say about yourself that you were going insane, so we stay cloaked for your protection.

Returning to the issue of the spoken word: many strive to declare their worth in this world. They wish for an audience, lusting for fame and fortune, to be admired and worshiped. They may be exalted on earth because they influence and persuade others to follow, but their persuasiveness is shallow and won't produce good results. Leading others is a heavy burden. Not only are you responsible for your own karma, but you're responsible for your follower's karma as well since you were the one who led them. Imagine having the karma of thousands or even millions of Souls upon your head! Truly, leaders must count the cost before they direct the lives of others. Religious and political leaders should evaluate themselves. Are they assuming leadership to promote themselves, to prop up inflated egos, or to enjoy the benefits and privileges that the poor will never know? Anyone who misuses authority will suffer a chain of negative karma that they caused in the lives of others. To avoid the misuse of authority, consider the welfare of others. It isn't wrong or bad to have money or fame but hoarding it while your followers perish isn't humanitarian. If you have been blessed, share the blessing-and see how good it feels. Truly, karmically-it is better to give than to receive.

Message 21-Good, Evil & The Material Lie

As it was in the beginning, so shall it be in the end. In the beginning, angels walked with humanity, and eagerly we taught you. Even today, as we witness your plight, we know there is so much good that each of you can do, and with a celestial partnership, the human condition can be remedied. The realm of Spirit holds every answer, but because it's invisible, you assume we can't see you, because you can't see us! It's quite a dilemma: wanting and needing answers when all you have are the five limited senses. But is that all you have, or do you also have at your disposal an inner knowing, an inner sense called intuition which has often tried to guide you? It is fear that keeps you from hearing or seeing into the Spirit world, because everyone has equal access. It is not just for priests, monks or nuns. Spirituality is not only for those who wear a holy cloth but those who do not call themselves special or holy.

There was a time in human history when angels and humans were in sync; before the Great Split occurred when some angels rebelled and fled Heaven. There was a time when angels looked after humans, caring for you as if you were our own dear children. We felt warm compassion for you-the way humans have a fondness for their cherished pet, we looked after you. But humanity has forgotten this glorious communion between two different species, human and angelic. We, however, have not forgotten. We are very concerned about what is happening on earth, for you were meant to have our continual protection and guidance! That connection was severed when a rebellion arose in Heaven. When dark forces interfered, it was the beginning of the end of our sweet communion. You were never supposed to be alone; humans must be guided, they need someone to look after them, for you are creatures with high emotional capacity but lower analytical abilities. Your choices are often compromised by emotion. Angels possess emotion: we feel happy, we feel sad, but we do not feel the full range of complex emotions that effect and inform your decision-making. You need angels, because they are always in contact with the unseen realms and understand what is best for you, minus the emotion. Since the beginning of time, we have been present with you-silently guiding and informing you.

When the Great Divide opened, the light angels returned to the Heavenly realms. Earth became a planet for incarnated spirits wishing to shed their karma. Now we are your invisible teachers and protectors. If we had not removed ourselves, humans would have been caught in the crossfire of a fierce battle that would have ensued, and humanity would have suffered mass destruction. The light angels left their humans behind and there was great sorrow that day among us, for we knew it would be eons before the dark angel's occupation of earth would end. We didn't leave because we couldn't conquer the dark angels; we left because Heaven had compassion on the human creature. We withdrew to the higher, unseen realms to prevent your genocide. I tell you humanity's ancient history, both true and accurate: humanity has suffered greatly without direct angelic intervention and comfort. But there will come a day when humanity's fortunes will be reversed. There will be a battle-just as many religions have claimed. But before the battle for the Soul of planet earth, all those who seek the Light-the compassionate, the innocent; those who seek the face of God will be rescued, taken to higher realms so they will not suffer the pangs of war. I assure you, there will be a day of reckoning when the dark entities will be stopped, and this will occur once the cosmic algorithm has served its purpose.

Now you understand that earth is a place where incarnated Souls go to shed negative karma, and you are part of the struggle between light and darkness. When you incarnate, you're born a pure and guileless child. But you encounter many tests and trials that will show which side you are on. Please realize you must choose a side.

You're either working to advance Heaven's agenda, which is: love, forgiveness, and compassion, or you have ingratiated yourself into the company of dark Souls who are ego-driven and money-hungry, who scheme behind closed doors. Don't find yourself playing for the wrong team! And while dark Souls have a darkened consciousness, they will tell you they are the good people on God's side. How then can you be sure you're on the winning team if dark Souls call themselves angels of light?

Jesus answered how to tell if a person is good or bad; He left no doubt. He said: "For no good tree bears bad fruit, nor does a bad tree bear good fruit" (Luke 6:43). Is this not a sure way of judging? If a person is producing bad fruit-if their actions are dishonest, unjust, or judgmental, then their fruit is bad! If they are honest and just, they are a good tree. You see, it's very simple to tell a good tree from a bad tree. The problem is that bad trees will say they are good trees, and this is what is confusing. Don't listen to people's words. Instead, ask yourself: Are they honest? Are they fair? Are they non-judgmental? If the answer is no, you might have a bad tree on your hands. My advice is to get as far away from a bad tree as you can. If you partake of rotten fruit, you'll get sick, and your will to live a simple, contrite life may wither and die. Dark entities can suck the life out of you if you are around them long enough. That's another way to know if they are dark: they drain you with their negativity. Save yourself from these people, and let that person save themselves.

You are not anyone's savior-it is not your job; it is not your place. The only one who can correct a Soul's darkness is the Lord. Christ defined himself as the savior of the world because only God can save. Each person is responsible for finding his or her own salvation. You cannot rescue or change anyone, not even within your own family. If someone's issues are dragging you down, it's time to move ahead with your life. This may not sound like a compassionate response: you might be surprised that an angel is telling you to flee from a lost Soul. But the only obligation you have is to reach out to them. If they refuse your help, you are free! But you may say: what if this is my spouse, child, or an elderly parent-what then? If they are dependent, meaning, they rely upon your help, still, do not allow them to abuse you in any way. To allow their abuse is to disrespect yourself. Offer to get them help, for that proves you have a compassionate heart. If they refuse, then I assure you, you're free to go. Never allow yourself to be abused because you feel obligated by marriage or blood. First and foremost, your obligation is to remain healthy emotionally and physically. Bad fruit looks good on the outside while it's rotten on the inside. Don't be surprised when rotten apples shine and gleam. Avoid spending time with money-hungry, power-thirsty people. Instead, endeavor to live simply and humbly. Share what you have with those in need. Stop boasting about it; give without acknowledgement. Most importantly, be honest and fair; give others a reason to respect you. Refrain from judging, for you are not God. Ultimately, you cannot say who is a good apple and who is bad-that is for God alone to say. Work on bearing sweet, kind and generous fruit. Who wouldn't enjoy fruit like that?

I have discussed how to tell the difference between a light and a dark entity, and the simple litmus test Christ gave to judge between them. I've also assured you that subjecting yourself to negativity or abuse isn't God's will for you or your duty. I've explained how angels were created for the express purpose of looking after humanity and caring for them and how that plan was altered once dark angels inhabited the earth. Until the earth is redeemed, it is in a state of martial law for your history is littered with war, and dark entities have taken ownership of key positions within governments. But the earth is also full of light workers, brave Souls who refuse to bow to the golden gods.

It is so much easier to ritualize your devotion and obey religious customs while ignoring a deep and meaningful communion with Spirit. In truth, there is no need to gather to worship God except that it comforts and strengthens the bonds between you. God does not need or require worship in any form; worship is for the devotee. Just as the true guru is not impressed by flattery and gifts,

Mother and Father do not expect sacrifices. What impresses them is your obedience. When you are eager to rid yourself of character flaws, you have garnered God's full attention. Then God will hear your requests and your longings and will rain down answers. The humble heart finds time to examine her life; she is not running from the answers in a futile attempt to "find" the answers. Those who sit still and listen to the Guide within them will be awarded revelation-even spiritual gifts.

There are two ways to find happiness: the first road leads to things and wealth that will for a time dazzle and entertain. But "things" quickly lose their luster. The human mind is a conquering machine. It yearns for the next mountain to climb; it has trouble being content, so the object of your affection will eventually lose your affection. This is the path of the spiritual novice; her mind is not able to discern reality from what amounts to a distraction. The second path differs from the first because the longer you stay on the spiritual road, the more interesting the scenery becomes. It is a fascinating adventure with unending twists and turns; there is always more to discover. The seeker will never be bored nor disenchanted. This is the hidden door. Many seek it yet are prevented from finding it. It's a disappearing door that vanishes as soon as they lay claim to it.

Many people say they know the door to God and what's behind it, but few have been invited in-few are friends of God. The Holy of Holies is for the hierophants-for the priests and priestesses only, meaning those who have devoted themselves to seeking God. Everyone is screaming for riches and fame because they can only see the first road; they're convinced that's all there is. They swear there's nothing more to see and will deride those who can see the disappearing road. These know-it-alls will not find the door for they worship pleasure. They walk towards the inner chamber, certain they are favored, but for their own protection they pass right by, following a mirage instead. Shining towers of money cloud their eyes and their ears ring with the cry of their own name. They sleepwalk, claiming they are the "chosen ones." Their filthy hands are covered in blood; they are dead men walking who traded their hearts for a lie.

There's a way out of this zombie land; there's a way to retrieve a lost Soul from the clutches of materialism. The rich must admit their poverty of Spirit; they must turn away from the material world and its dead-end answers. It is a common religious phrase to say God can save a Soul. But while God can offer endless opportunity for redemption, the Soul must save itself. You are saved when you have no attachment to riches and power. You are not "saved" by an act of God; your own hand must untie you! This is not the answer many want to hear and not what you have been taught. You've been told that you're saved from the consequences of your choices when you profess your faith, when you follow the teachings of this church or that. What "saves" anyone from the endless cycle of samsara (rebirth and suffering) is choosing to forsake the ego. It is the ego that prevents you from finding the Most Holy Place. Where is the wormhole that leads to eternity? The Most Holy Place is your own heart, square in the middle of your temple. Until you claim freedom from possessions, a freedom you naturally enjoyed as a child, you will wander this planet searching for happiness. If you feel disillusioned with life, you've believed the illusion. What they said was as meaningful was a mirage! You thought you could believe your eyes, but life betrayed you and everything you hoped for crumbled in your hands. This is the lot of the sons of Adam and the daughters of Eve who were given a beautiful garden but who were deceived. Once deceived, they stopped believing, and the moment they did, the Holy of Holies slammed shut, and they were disconnected from The Other Side. I plead with you: don't forsake your heart for it is your oasis in a dry and thirsty land. You'll wander in the desert, being tempted by the ego, and when you're out there, it may become desperate; who knows what you will do? Find your way back to innocence. Leave your worried mind behind-it's leading you in circles. Like Adam and Eve, your ultimate mission is to find your way back to Paradise. You are not cursed! In truth, humanity is standing at the threshold of Heaven, and you have a choice to make: believe the Material Lie or see through the serpent's deception. Consider the appearance of a serpent: it is green, shiny, and a provocative tempter-none other than the almighty dollar!

Now I would like to turn to the subject of compassion. For most people, compassion is not a characteristic they feel that they can afford to have. It may require time from their busy schedule or their hard-earned money. It also requires a willingness to see the less fortunate and the under-privileged. Most people look away from need because if they looked at it, they might be compelled to care. And charity has become a big business. Even charitable organizations must see a profit to stay in business, just as the churches must. Generous philanthropists expect some sort of a kick-back for their tithe to the poor, if only a tax break. But didn't Christ say: "Blessed are the poor in spirit, for theirs is the kingdom of Heaven" (Matt. 5:3)? If the poor are blessed as Christ said, why do charitable organizations and philanthropists exist for the poor? Only for their own needs. They want to ease their guilt, or they want to take credit for money donated, or the business wants to turn a profit.

When you consider the idea of compassion, your mind flashes to pictures of the poor and those in need, for this is what you have been taught that compassion looks like. You have been cleverly programmed into believing that if you give you will be blessed. After all, doesn't the Bible give an account of the Parable of the Good Samaritan who stopped on the road to rescue a victim of a robbery as the rich man passed by on the other side (Luke 10:25-37)? If you believe Jesus' words then you agree it is better to be poor than to be rich, for He also said it is unlikely that the rich will enter Heaven. If the poor will realize God as Christ claimed, isn't it better to be poor?

You may think me uncompassionate if I tell you that by giving money or possessions to people in need you are involving yourselves in their karma. But that is exactly what I am going to say. You may think me hard-hearted or cruel when I tell you to mind your own business. But you do not understand compassion the way I do. I view the matter of philanthropy and generosity from a wider lens. I stand exalted above humanity, above the earth, above governments, above weaponry, above laws and edicts, above all creation. I see with unerring vision, and what I see shows me that every Soul has its unique lessons to learn. Because of past-life karma, Souls are born into the body, family, society, country and galaxy they should be. They are born poor or rich, uneducated or educated, with deformity or in perfection, according to their Soul's progress. If each Soul is born exactly where they should be and how they should be, for another to come along and rescue them from their circumstances is only to make themselves feel like the hero.

But you may argue, it does not feel right to look the other way when a brother or sister is struggling! You are correct. It feels terrible to watch another suffer. It is a feeling of helplessness to watch someone drown when you could save them. And these guilt feelings are what keep you rescuing others. Your self-preservation instinct is so great, you will risk your life to save another; this is instinctual. If given the choice to let an innocent child drown or risk your life, you will risk your life to save her. This response is both evolutionary and genetic. You cannot help but want to help. Do you see this automatic compassion arise within you? It will cause you to act in super-human ways. I do not fault you for this, it is part of the human constitution. But the fact remains that Christ said: the poor are the blessed ones and will attain Heaven.

Now that I have totally confused you with these apparent paradoxes, let me set the record straight. What Christ was teaching and what I am confirming is that *being poor is not the worst thing that can happen to someone.* It is a tool used for purification of the Soul. You cannot get into Heaven unless your Soul is purified, for it is a holy place where errors cannot exist. In the Heavenly realms, errors are like bubbles. They pop up, but they are burst immediately, for Heaven is composed of truth and knowledge. Impure thoughts and actions cannot exist in the presence purity. If poverty is used to purify the Soul of the ego, then it cannot be all bad, for purification of the ego is the only way into Heaven. Yes, it is counter-intuitive to turn away when others ask for help; therefore, it feels wrong. But as Christ was pointing out, lack and loss, what you call pain, is a purifying element.

Who says you know better than God whether a person should be rescued? If God is God, couldn't He command a legion of angels, mighty in power to rescue them? He could! God can do whatever God likes! But He chooses not to rescue because there is a life lesson in it. But, you argue, what about innocent children who suffer. Is it right that they should suffer? Let me ask you a question, and I want you to think hard on it: how do you know their Soul is innocent? Did you create them, and do you know their Soul's history? Can you see their past lives and deeds? Only God knows whether a Soul is innocent or guilty, for only God can see their entire existence. You see only a paltry few years, or one lifetime, while God sees hundreds or thousands of lifetimes. Who knows what karma they are shedding as they suffer what looks to you to be an injustice? You are the tiniest of intellects, like an ant compared to an elephant of an intellect that is God. Yet you pretend to know which Souls deserve to be saved.

How then is the right way to respond to a Soul in need? Because you are programmed to save one another, you will go on saving one another. When it is a matter of life and death, you will respond automatically with a helping hand. As I said, you cannot be faulted for this. Heaven has grace for your humanity, I assure you. When it isn't a life or death matter, please understand that by rescuing another you may be stealing from them the very life lesson they incarnated to learn. You may be prolonging their karma and they will suffer longer because you needed to be helpful! See what a quagmire this is?

To keep from interfering in someone's karma, refrain from rescuing others. Live your life and let them live theirs. When they need a helping hand, reach out and help them carry the load, but be cautious not to interfere too much, for the issue of past karma is at play. If an innocent person suffers or is victimized, it looks unjust to you and it would be easy to assume that God has no compassion. But the opposite is true: God designed a perfect system that purifies a Soul and allows it to evolve lifetime after lifetime until it has risen to the Highest Heaven. In the Highest Heaven there is nothing but love, joy, peace and the ultimate bliss. It is only that you think you know what is right and wrong that causes these problems. You get entangled in another's problems and then you become ensnared! The next time you want to rescue another, whether it be from poverty or sickness, remember what Christ said: "Blessed are the poor in spirit, for theirs is the kingdom of Heaven" (Matt. 5:3).

Message 22-The Anarchists of Light

A wise woman once said: "You must do the thing you think you cannot do" (Eleanor Roosevelt). You absolutely must stand up to your fears. Like a root-bound plant, unless you do the things that look "impossible," your fearing mind will be comfortable in its tiny parcel of soil. And while you'll be safe, you'll also be useless. I don't mean useless to the society in which you live; you may have a practical usefulness as a worker or a parent while never challenging your spiritual capabilities at all. There is a spiritual uselessness, which has, like a disease, stunted the growth of humanity. If you're not vigilant, you'll fall into that trap. To be spiritually useful, you must be a rebel. You must not accept the placating and pacifying, for this is a corrupt system's way of shutting you up. You must become a change agent, every one of you! The word "impossible" stops you cold because you have so little respect for your own abilities. You discount yourself because it's easier that way. But you can't live in this shallowness forever. Maybe not in this incarnation and maybe not in the next, but eventually you'll be forced to make a clear choice. You'll choose to be a part of the revolution for good or you'll side with those whose God is money. Why do you think the avatars take a vow of abstinence from riches? Because money changes people. Their inner eye saw the class war coming and they sided with the poor right from the start. They could see the rich getting richer, and the poor getting poorer. Why is it difficult to be a genuinely spiritual person? Because material things obscure your vision. Don't you already know in your heart what you must do? You must relinquish the thirst for more, more, more of things-for there will never be enough to satisfy.

Your Soul isn't hungry for "stuff." How could it be? The Soul is a Spirit composed of energy, with no lasting use for things.

Only something non-material will suffice; only seeing the utter uselessness of matter will bring liberation. I know you want to be liberated; all Souls long for freedom from their chains: their addictions, their dysfunction, their unforgiveness, their illnesses, their anxieties and heartbreaks. Each of you wants similar things: to be healthy, happy and to enjoy life. Yet many disqualify themselves from spirituality because they believe it will require too much of them, or they will look different or odd to others. Spiritual masters tell you what they gained in return was an inner freedom that grew the more time they spent in spiritual practice, until one day they looked around and found themselves quietly seated in plain clothes, having forgotten to bathe or to eat much, but shining like the sun, clothed in Soul riches, gleaming with a glory that radiated from them. They were as full as full could be while on the outside, they were thin and tattered. Their hearts resounded with this truth: "Blessed are the poor…". God is the lover of your Soul, and if you think otherwise, you are simply blind, looking frantically in the wrong place. The way out of this conundrum is to realize that you can't take it with you. At the end of your life what will matter is not your money but your courage, love, mercy, and compassion. Your positivity! All things that money cannot possibly buy.

I mentioned a class war, for I want you to know what's coming. There are two types of people in the world: those who understand that all are God's children, and those who believe they are more important, more special, more "chosen" than others. They will tell you that they are going to Heaven while you go to Hell. One type of person wants to live in harmony and the other type is declaring war, bent on "proving" their superiority. The world is drifting apart, and because of this divide, a war will ensue; a revolution will start. There will be tumultuous times of unrest, and both young and old will be so emboldened that they will sweep aside fear and demand equality. There will be severe unrest, both politically and economically, so volatile that the structure of civilization will shake. The poor will demand access to environmental resources that the rich have been hoarding. There will be a great cry heard, and this cry will not go unanswered. The rich will be forced to open their coffers, like the silos of Egypt were opened, which stored up grain to feed the multitudes because of God's great concern for the welfare of all.

In the time of Daniel, the rich man's hand was forced open. In the coming famine, many rich and mighty will be humbled and compelled to distribute their riches. The poor they once disdained and loathed will shun and turn against them, for they acted without mercy. The prideful will take their own lives rather than face exposure for their criminal acts. I'm speaking of a famine and a class war that will occur on a global scale; it will be long and grueling, and a recession will escalate into a depression, but in the end, the poor will prevail. Those with riches who are sincerely concerned with humanity will become benefactors of a new society and be elevated as saviors of humanity. If you trust in riches and disdain the poor, in the end, you will be hated, despised and rejected. You will lose everything, for you'll be stripped of it. As the rich grow richer, the divide will widen; one side will detest the other, until the poor refuse to be dominated and ignored any longer. This will be a landmark time and a social revolution will take place. It will be the second renaissance-a sociological and ethical awakening. The Science of Humanity will be born; a new day will dawn as a socialist state takes form. The rich will be held accountable for their misdeeds and will be forced to feed the masses they once fooled. The second renaissance will be planetary, ushering in a time of global peace.

Prepare yourself now by seeing what's important. Let "things" be for someone else and be grateful and thankful for simplicity. If you are fed, if you clothed, if you are sheltered, you are fortunate-for many are not. Come out of the deep sleep of materialism and see, really see that the only treasures are the beautiful Souls around you. This world is lost in a dream, for its children have wandered away from the simplicity they knew. That first generation of humans-we celestial beings could reason with and instruct, their brains finally developed enough so we could explain their royal status to them. If angelic beings were to return today to the technological human, do you think we would be received kindly? Would you welcome us in this age of disbelief and unmerciful materialism? If we were to share with you the secrets and mysteries of other dimensions so utterly unlike your own, wouldn't you dismiss us, because we live in an alternate dimension that cannot be seen? Only the heart can comprehend spiritual things- your mind will never be convinced of our reality. It will always doubt.

I've been watching humanity develop. It warms my heart to see the recent shift towards justice. Not a returning to religious doctrine that doesn't think for itself, or rituals too old and remote to be relatable, but turning away from a man-made religious system is a step in the right direction. If you wish to be enlightened, you're going to have to let go of your own agenda. If you want to be of service in this new world order, an order that rejects the insensitivity and callousness of the paternalistic system, you must become a servant. A real servant has enough self-control that she can sacrifice her own creature comforts. A new world order will require sympathy, a heart that flows towards others and not away from them. If you want to bring good to this planet, you can! One person can start a revolution. But you must slow down long enough to notice the broken-hearted and have a willingness to feel the sorrow they feel. You must reach out to them and say, "You're going to make it. Though it looks impossible, you're going emerge stronger than before."

Inside of the ring of fire is where the angels live. They dance in the flame, twisting and twirling within the storm. They crack as lightning falls, sent here on a holy mission: to deliver messages from Heaven. In the fire, in the flood, in the storm, in the raucous thunder, when you hear drumming at night, we are being dispatched. Ironically, that's also when you're least likely to feel us near, as fear prevents you from sensing us; we are eclipsed by a cloud of fear. Angels, even powerful Archangels, and so many other celestial beings that are your benefactors (too many to name) are concerned with humanity's welfare. But you doubt that you're remembered and are convinced that nobody sees, and no one cares. I've come expressly to remind you of your preciousness, to reassure you that your value is beyond measure, and it's only that your eyes deceive you, but you won't be deceived forever! When you pop out of that body of yours, you'll see us. You'll realize we were always standing round, peering into this crib of life, witnessing this miracle child called you. We wonder: How long will it take for you to realize your beauty, your value, your divine origins? Humans have the capacity for being the cause of suffering or the source of relief. When you ignore the needs around you, you become something terribly unlike who you were meant to be.

When you attempt to unlock spiritual secrets, you will be opposed. You will be attacked, you will be criticized, you may even have to defend yourself. Your motives will be questioned, and you will be ridiculed. For wherever you bring light, darkness follows. Anytime there's a light shining, dark forces are drawn to it. They shall be attracted at first, because they want what you have. But as they draw nearer, your light begins to show their hidden places and evil plans. Their egoism will surface, and as the light falls upon them, they will recoil and find a reason to leave. As they walk away, they will hurl insults and accusations and would even like to harm you. Any person who attacks another, tries to ruin or disgrace another or take revenge cannot be a lightworker. This type of person is an imposter. They are like a witch who casts spells with manipulative words, who would have you believe they are the chosen ones. Yet when you look closely, they're negative and self-promoting. The brighter you shine; the more darkness will notice you.

You will not know these entities by how they look on the outside, for they will appear attractive and accomplished. You'll only be able to detect them by their uncontrollable anger and they will seek to control you. They'll want to be the center of attention, so they'll create drama. Devastation follows them. Even then, it's difficult to tell who is who. Ask yourself: Can this person admit when they are wrong? If not, this person may wreak havoc in your life. Be sure to step around them, for if you become entangled with them, they may try to take you down, dishonor and break you. When they blame others for their errors, this is a sure sign of a dark entity. They will boast yet fail to bring anything good to the world. Sadly, they cannot see themselves, for they are blind. Something is blocking their ability to see yet they proclaim their innocence. However, if a person is trying their best and yet has difficulties, it's understandable for these people are human. You must be tolerant and mustn't demand perfection. You should keep your sense of humor and make room for errors in judgment, missteps, and their fears. I speak to you about discerning between light and dark because dark entities are becoming craftier, presenting themselves as light beings. Your ability to avoid their traps is becoming more important now.

There is a glorious revolution started in the spiritual realm, an energetic shift. If you feel these leanings, you are correct. Keep in mind that dark entities also feel this shift and it causes them discomfort. This shift began in the 1960's when the youth of America became disgruntled with the status quo and turned from capitalism. Again, your society is turning. Having become dissatisfied and discouraged with governmental irresponsibility, you're leaning in the opposite direction. By turning away from excess to simplicity, from irresponsibility to becoming planetary stewards, and from judgmentalism to equality, you are shifting the consciousness of your planet enough to slow the environmental catastrophe looming on the horizon. You're also hoping to restore individual freedom of expression. All this progress you wish to make...so many good wishes for planet earth in so many of your hearts. It is truly moving to see how you want to change the world, how you want to avoid the mistakes of your predecessors. You workers of light are the hope for the world! Your enthusiasm, drive and determination to reverse the damage done, right the wrongs and reshape government-these are highly admirable and worthy aspirations. Because your hearts are pure, otherworldly beings will lend you their strength, protection and favor. They are standing with you, though your eyes can't see them. You believe it's possible to live in a world where everyone matters, where everyone's voice is considered. If you can endure the pressure your perseverance will win the day.

You *can* change things; keep fighting and you will succeed. You have a strong heart, a sound mind, and a will of your own. You've seen what happens when strength is used to oppress. Someone you trusted or someone you should have been able to trust came along, took the hope out of your hands, and smashed it on the ground; maybe it was someone you loved. They wittingly or unwittingly tried to break you. But you, being the unbreakable diamond, bent down, retrieved every piece, and glued yourself back together, and you've been holding yourself together ever since. What a generation! Strong, smart, and most importantly, you haven't allowed anyone to stop you. There are enough voices demanding fairness and equality that the world will be saved. Generations to come will live freely because of you. They will only know the importance of human rights and accept it as the unarguable standard of conduct because a generation rose up, insisting it must be done differently or not at all. You would have rather torn down the rottenness than be party to it.

To the anarchists of light, I say: Be proud that you stood against the darkness and tore it down with your bare hands. You didn't fear what they thought or what they called you; you didn't let yourself fear anything. You only feared repeating the mistakes of antiquity. For all who have done their part to bring more light to this planet, know that your contribution will result in change. I say: You will be rewarded. You've left the world a better place; you burned into it your unique brand of justice. For that, the world is a brighter, happier and freer place. You brought the kind of spirituality that did something about it. For all of you, who left your shadows behind to embrace your light, know there is a reward coming. You must know that positive karma always results in the return of positive results; you cannot help but be rewarded. Keep holding the hope up, and thanks for noticing that all of us are in this *together*.

Part of being spiritual is being different and being different can be scary. Yet in many ways, each of you is a design all your own. Your fingerprints and the iris of your eyes are distinct. Your voiceprint is also unique. Just as these physical features distinguish you, your personality is exclusive to you, and so is your Life Chart. Because each of you is a rare individual, expect the story of your life to be uncommon. Perhaps it would be more accurate to say that you are not so much different as you are extraordinary. If everyone accepted that each person is created uniquely, and biological diversity is the natural expression of life, it would be a much more harmonious world to live in. When you accept that you are uncommon, when you embrace your "specialness," you won't be as concerned about playing the "fitting in" game that humans are inclined to play. If you know from the start that you are exceptional, you'll be free to go against the grain when necessary.

Accepting your uniqueness would make life easier, even light-hearted. The truth is, the necessity for you to develop a greater comfort with differences is of great consequence, for humanity is diversifying at an exponential rate. Technological knowledge and spiritual insight are being released to your planet and will continue to be imparted for the express purpose of introducing more diversity into human consciousness. It is essential that humanity evolve towards acceptance. It is beyond essential, for the more developed your consciousness becomes, the freer you will be. You see evidence of this in physical evolution. As species develop, they lose features that no longer serve them; they outgrow old ways, and you are the same. You are a part of this ongoing chain of evolution, even if you can't feel the world turning beneath your feet. Life is a continuous, imminent and inescapable ball rolling towards the future, and you are providing part of this evolutionary momentum. Your presence contributes to the forward march of human consciousness.

It's possible to resist change to such a degree that you do harm to the collective plan for humanity. The greater fabric of the Creators can be torn by a single person's choices. Your choices matter-they have a profound ripple effect for which you have no point of reference now. You won't see the full impact of your decisions until the After-Life Review. Your resistance to inclusion is resistance to unity. Anytime you exclude anyone based upon their differences, you have damaged an emerging unity pushing to be birthed. When you imagine Heaven, what do you see? I hope you visualize a Kingdom of wacky and wild creatures so vastly different from you yet a brotherhood and sisterhood among you as citizens of Heaven. There are billions of ways the Creators have expressed themselves, and a human being is but one of these designs. Think of all the odd and interesting creatures that fill your seas. Your oceans alone are filled with more strange and one-of-a-kind creatures than scientists can name. There are more varieties of insects on your planet alone than can be counted, and new forms of life are being added continually as they adapt and evolve. Are you seeing the bigger picture yet, getting the idea that being different is advantageous?

Being exceptional sounds glamorous until you ask an advanced Soul about the reality of it. They will tell you they wondered if something was wrong with them. They will tell you they seldom could see their solitary existence as attractive. They will tell you they doubted their own abilities and didn't feel capable of standing up to scrutiny and criticism. They will tell you they often thought they might be crazy or at least "misguided." They will tell you they wished to be "normal" with every breath. Instead, they were asked to be outstanding: out-standing, standing out. If you're going to live an exceptional life, you can't hide in the crowd. You'll be required to stand up when you really want to sit down. You'll wonder to yourself: why me? Every other person will seem to be skating along unperturbed. Being an exceptional Soul can be a thankless job. Just ask Jesus-he will tell you. He stuck out; He couldn't seem to get with the Roman program, and you know how His story ended. History is ripe with oddballs that were miles ahead of their contemporaries, some of them centuries ahead, and do you think these Souls were accepted? They were the odd ducks of their time. If you have felt like the black sheep or are always pushing the "rules" or boundaries, you may be a pilgrim Soul, sent here to make waves. Pilgrims are explorers, and explorers leave the safety of familiar shores to search the horizon.

When Columbus sailed, he was taught that the earth was flat, but he steered his ships towards the horizon anyway. He knew any discoveries to be made were beyond his eyesight. You can't discover anything new if you can already see it. You can't discover what you're capable of if you don't head towards uncharted waters. This is what outstanding Souls do-they push the boundaries of what is known. They are willing to risk being wrong for a piece of the action. I daresay, as human history speeds towards its inevitable conclusion, there will be more oddballs and misfits. But what's worse: being different or being indifferent? You didn't choose a challenging planet like earth just to "blend in." You'll rest on the Other Side-you are here to work. The next time you see a Soul who stands alone, think about what I've said. Maybe you're seeing a modern-day explorer like Christopher Columbus who will broaden the world's horizons, or a Galileo who will open the Heavens, or a da Vinci who imagines he can fly. You'll know them because they will be standing apart from the crowd. Sure, it's scary, but it's also a privilege. You're ushering in changes that will lead to a more humane humanity. Don't be afraid of their faces; be more afraid of wasting the precious gift of mortal time. Embrace your differences-the oddballs and misfits will thank you for it.

Message 23-Intuition & ESP

There is nothing even remotely wrong or evil about people who have extra sensory perception. However, there may be something wrong with people who claim to be a spiritual authority if they lack the ability to hear or see into the spiritual world. If anyone tells you that being psychic is wrong, be suspect, because the ability to perceive beyond the five senses is a gift from God. I warn you: stay away from those who condemn intuition or extra sense perception, because they are blinded by bias, groping in the dark about spiritual matters. Let them alone-let them find their own way. Do not argue with a persecutory spirit, avoid them. As Christ admonished: "...leave the dead to bury their own dead" (Matthew 8:22). I have strong words about avoiding the company of those who discourage you, or worse, those who would condemn you. It is a service to humanity to use your intuitive gifts and abilities. How could seeing into the realm of spirit be inherently "bad" or evil? Only if it is used for evil is it evil. Nearly anything can be used for evil. Think about a knife: it can be used to prepare your meal or to take a life. Does this make the knife bad? It makes it neither bad nor good. It is only a tool-just as the intuitive gift is a tool. It depends upon how it's being used, for what purpose. Jesus urged you to judge a tree by its fruit. "A good tree cannot bear bad fruit, and a bad tree cannot bear good fruit" (Matthew 7:18). He was saying: If what is produced is evil, the tree is evil. Likewise, if a psychic or prophetess is helpful to you, if she encourages and comforts by her visions or information, how is it bad? Yet religions have condemned such, saying: 'Even demons can sound good; they can fool you into following their advice.' Let us examine this issue because misunderstanding abounds.

The issue of light and dark, good and evil, requires a moral sophistication that your species does not yet possess, so the complete human story has been sealed, and is still unavailable to human consciousness at this time. Think of it as top-secret intelligence information which you must have a high security clearance for, and humanity cannot be trusted at this time with these secrets. But I can assure you, evil is real: there are evil aliens, evil people, and evil or dark spirits. There are powerful, evil people, and they inflict more real harm than thought forms or fallen angels can. People ask: Did angels turn from God and revolt as sacred texts record, and are demons those rebellious angels? These matters are complicated. The story of dark and light forces is complex; the less humanity knows the better. I say this because humans tend to dwell on evil and can become fascinated with it and begin seeing demons and monsters lurking everywhere. Some people will even go so far as to blame their ills on the devil.

But returning to the matter of psychics and intuition: if the fruit is good, the tree is good. If intuition is being used to help and heal it is a gift from God. If a person condemns a psychic who is helpful and comforting, when they are negative and divisive, then they are the real danger, for they've erroneously introduced suspicion and paranoia. Stay far from anyone who points an accusing finger. Christ never accused; it wasn't His nature. Only on one occasion did He point out evil, and he pointed to the religious leaders. Everyone should desire to be more intuitive and to develop their psychic abilities. Does everyone have psychic abilities? Everyone has the capacity to have a spiritual life but not everyone has the psychic gift. It is a special ability developed over many lifetimes and studied extensively on the Other Side. Those who are psychic can see, hear or feel the Spirit world. If the world of Spirits parallels the material world, why would it be "bad" to discern it? How do you think Jesus, the prophets, Buddha, saints and mystics accessed their information? They had perception that transcended ordinary senses, didn't they? Therefore, it's safe to say that Christ had psychic powers, and He told you that others would come after Him who had greater gifts and abilities. Stop villainizing psychics and mediums. Realize they have paid a high price to bring you word from the Other Side.

Skeptics will read this and say: 'But psychics aren't always right! How can you believe what they say when they're often wrong?' I don't mind this question so much because at least now you are using your rational mind instead of religious dogma. Because psychics are human, they make errors, only God does not make errors. Just as you make mistakes on the job, so will they. They are only human, doing the best they can to decipher invisible dimensions, so of course there will be errors. You try looking into an invisible world and getting it all right! Any psychic who is delivering uplifting messages that inspire, comfort and have information they couldn't have gotten another way has a gift.

You may be wondering how to be more intuitive, for it is a wondrous gift, and future generations will turn to intuitives for guidance and spiritual direction and this is a welcome change over listening to oppressive and judgmental religious leaders. As humanity evolves, further access to the Other Side will be granted, and more and more "regular" people will develop psychic abilities that were once exclusive to psychics. Eventually the average person will consider psychic abilities a foregone conclusion. Psychic ability is the gift of deciphering the world of thought. Some can "see" the spiritual dimension (they may have visions or see spirits). Some hear the spirit world clearly, while others feel it physically. Still others known as mediums may be able to communicate with discarnate spirits. Some people may have precognition, meaning they know something is going to happen before it does, and a few will be able to manipulate objects via thought, called telekinesis. There are some who are both a psychic and a medium, given multiple intuitive abilities. These Souls have taken the oath of a Bodhisattva; they have vowed to reincarnate for the betterment of humanity. Sadly, history shows that these gifted ones were often maligned and persecuted. When your world stops persecuting those who are different, it will be ready for a new phase of enlightenment; it remains to be seen how long this will take. While psychic gifts are developed on the Other Side, as the Soul sheds its negative karma through reincarnation, greater intuition will result. It stands to reason that the more time you spend doing anything, the more it rubs off on you, so spend time in the world of spirit.

As Buddha sat patiently under the Bodhi tree, so you must sit patiently in meditation. People who don't understand the need for meditation haven't discovered the true blessing it can be. Nothing else can give you the insight and profound peace that the Spirit realm can. How much time should you spend? This is a rhetorical question, because meditation is seeking for the truth, and the truth is all there is. If you're not seeking the truth, you're not doing much of lasting consequence. And yet, your Soul is always seeking the truth; with every breath you are seeking the truth. Even when you are looking in the wrong place, you are still seeking for the truth; your whole life you are looking for answers. Even blunders will lead you closer to the truth. Don't worry about how much time you devote to meditation; spend as much time as your schedule allows. If you feel pulled towards the spiritual, perhaps you are being led to become a devotee. There are people who feel dissatisfied with a small amount of spiritual knowledge. These Souls will never be satiated by the world's delights, they will always hunger for God. These thirsty ones should spend more time in the spirit realm and less time in the mortal realm. Is it a "waste of time" to spend your life in meditation or as a lightworker? Plenty of laypeople see no redeeming value in spiritual service. Only a small percentage of the population is drawn towards spiritual attainment-the serious seeker is rare. One who serves humanity by bringing more insight, compassion and healing-can there be any greater purpose? How can this be a waste?

There is a problem among lightworkers that I'd like to address, though it is only part of being human, for humans tend to compete and compare. If your gifts are being used in service, refrain from comparing yourself, for it will get you nowhere. That kind of attitude is for the layperson, not for you. You are being reconditioned to put that behind you. If another lightworker laboring alongside of you falls, be quick to lift her or him up. Do not judge each other-the world does that! Who knows, you may need their assistance one day. If they say they are a worker of light but are quick to judge or easily angered or offended, then they are still struggling with the ego. Until this struggle is over, leave them. You cannot help those who are still concerned with promoting themselves. Perhaps this seems harsh, but more injury has been done in the name of God than any other name. Lightworkers are right to rise above their petty differences and jealousies. If they can't overcome these tendencies, they aren't ready to be healers. Many are eager for spiritual "goodies" but not for the demands made of leaders. Many declare themselves healers or religious leaders before they've submitted themselves to God for thorough inspection. When God is through with you, there won't be enough left standing of your ego to dare judge anyone. If this sounds too unpleasant, then don't rush in where angels fear to tread.

This message has reminded you that becoming a healer and spiritual leader shouldn't be entered lightly. Do not be quick to claim your leadership status because to whom much is given, much is required (Luke 12:48). Be an eager student instead; in this you can never go wrong. If you seek out spiritual experiences, you'll get exactly that: an isolated experience that may be sensational but doesn't change your character. If you meditate only deep enough to feel relief from stress, that is a good start. But if in meditation you receive insight about your character flaws, then you have done something worthwhile, for it may produce lasting growth in your personality. Be eager for greater intuition but beware of calling yourself a psychic or light worker until you have undergone a process of metamorphosis (and morphing from one form to another is never easy). Don't slander psychics, for they deserve to be taken seriously and allow them to be human-do not expect perfection, because they will make mistakes, just as you do.

If you are a psychic you are blessed, but it will often seem like a hardship because of skepticism. If you are bringing entirely new information from another dimension, in time your gift will be proven. Until then, hurry away from insults and slights; leave the criticism with the criticizer. Ask that their own words be bound to them until they see the truth. Bind their words to them and they can't injure you. This is an easy way of protecting yourself. Finally, show gratitude to light workers. They are an instrument of divinity, precious and rare. Bless God's workers-do not curse them, and you will be blessed.

Message 24-Destiny, Intention & Thought Forms

Fortunate accidents and lucky discoveries, otherwise known as serendipity, is drawing you into its circle. If you've written another person, place or thing into your Life Chart, the whole Universe will conspire to bring you together. What the ancients used to refer to as "fatum" is what you know as destiny, and if you are to live in harmony with the Universe, you must possess a powerful faith in the good that is yet to come. You can run from destiny, but it's like running from your shadow; it will follow you. When it's destined to be, your inner compass will point in a direction that looks unreasonable or nonsensical, because Providence doesn't care if it seems illogical or absurd. It only knows to point in the direction you should go, and there will be no way to avoid the inevitable, because you are on a crash-course with destiny.

The power of intention and thought forms can be introduced here, because not everything occurring is the result of a pre-planned event. Most of your life is unscripted; you are ad-libbing nearly all the details. When Soulmates are involved, it's destiny; an agreement you forged on the Other Side. Chiefly though, you'll be the captain of your own ship. Think of your Life Chart as the map for your journey while your choices determine how much time it takes you to get to your destination, as well as the scenery and people you'll encounter along the way. Destiny will pull you along its track, bringing Soulmates to you. During meeting and interacting with Soulmates, you'll fulfill pre-arranged agreements with them. The question is: how can you know for certain if something is "meant to be"? Essentially, you don't need to fret about matters of destiny, because if it's meant to be, fortunate accidents will begin to occur all on their own. Yes, you can ignore fate, but it will haunt you. The feeling will echo in your subconscious until your conscious self is willing to listen. When you set your mind to accomplish a goal, you have set an intention. But there are also subconscious goals from previous incarnations and these act like powerful magnets. Your subconscious will pull Soulmates towards you and you to them. This has been called the Law of Attraction (Byrne, 2006). The more narrowly you focus on achieving a goal, the faster you'll draw it to you. A metaphysical principle applies here: "Attention is forceful in proportion to the narrowness of its focus" (Neville Goddard). The more narrowly you concentrate on achieving your goal, the quicker it will materialize. If you are divided or unsure about what you want, the hand of Providence will cease to move.

The brain functions much like a TV. Unless the television is tuned to a frequency, the picture cannot be delivered. Most failed relationships and business ventures are largely the result of changing the channel too quickly. For anything to be created your intention must be fixed; you must hold the thought long enough for the various components and pieces to materialize. A thought is nothing more than a structure for fulfillment. Key to success in any endeavor is having faith in the creative, dynamic power of your thoughts. You absolutely must work towards thinking more positively. You've heard how your thoughts are a self-fulfilling prophecy, but did you know that in the Spirit world, thoughts are the seeds of not only logic and reasoning, but the method of transport and delivery? If you want to build a glorious mansion for yourself on the Other Side, you design it by desiring it. You don't have to understand architecture or construction; you simply think of the result you want and "poof!" instantaneously you've erected a mansion in your honor. You will laugh often in Heaven at what you will unintentionally create by thought. You'll have instruction on the Other Side about your powers as a conscious creator; there's an entire curriculum, and protocols to learn, and prototypes to use to learn to manipulate thought. It is like a magic trick: there is a secret behind it, but it looks as if something appeared from nothing. The laws of physics govern even the realm of Spirit, so there is a logical explanation. As you practice your "magic tricks" there will be many mishaps and puzzling issues to work through, but of course that's the part of the fun, making innocent mistakes along the way. You will spend a lot of time laughing at your own well-intentioned accidents…you will laugh often in Heaven! And while we are considering laughter, I'd like to set the record straight about the tenor of Heaven. We are not somber or high browed, for everyone here makes mistakes. We bear with one another's ignorance, for all are in various stages of growth. One of the first lessons you'll learn is to enjoy your mistakes. Can you imagine if making a mistake wasn't an egregious offense but a source of comedic relief? That's how it is here. Other than music and worshipful chanting, the sound you hear most often is buoyant laughter. God has got to have a sense of humor; Father and Mother made humans, didn't they?

Turning again to the power of intention: I've explained that thoughts become things, and that you can create thought forms unconsciously. This knowledge is very important, because thought-forms can bring much joy or heartache. What is a thought form? A multitude of positive or negative thoughts create entities or forms that have an express purpose. These forms can inflict real harm in the energetic realm of thought. Conversely, many positive thoughts can aid in achieving goals with greater ease and efficiency. Let's use an example from history to illustrate this: Nazi Germany and the Holocaust. Had Hitler not first published his radical ideas for a "master race" in a book, he might never have gained political power. But because his ideas were communicated clearly and forcefully in writing, they gained momentum in the minds of his readers. He incited readers to form a political party who appealed to the sentiments of the working-class peoples. Systematically, he engineered his way into the thoughts of a vulnerable nation. He took advantage of an unstable country by systematically gaining their trust and faith, telling them what they wanted to hear. Without the collective thought of his followers, he couldn't have accomplished much of anything. He was an unattractive, fanatical Narcissist who, without the power of collective belief, wouldn't have amounted to much. Due to thought forms, a whole nation supported his maniacal agenda.

Thought forms are entities that are created through mass opinion. While the German people didn't approve of the Holocaust, Hitler's political party generated negative thought forms. Because of strong negative opinion, these thought forms influenced the German people to adopt Hitler's agenda. Hitler appealed not to the German people's cruelty but to their pride. And this is the way evil operates. Dictators won't condone harm; instead, they will insight visions of prosperity, fame or pleasure. These are all good things or, so they seem. Hitler appealed to the German people's national pride, what seemed noble. He didn't start out talking about the death camps and torturous extermination. He began by luring them with promises of prosperity and greatness. I am not saying these thought forms "made" the German people do it. At any point, they could have revolted. But once Hitler had garnered popularity, thought forms were proliferating and multiplying at a fast rate like a deadly virus. The German people were acted upon before they had a chance to be inoculated. They were not being led by the Nazis alone; they were suffering with evil thought forms too numerous to count. Poltergeists are evil thought forms who can wreak havoc; entities created by collective negative thought. The Nazi agenda spread like wildfire, not because the German people were a special kind of stupid and easily manipulated, but because of negative energetic momentum. Fortunately, positive thought forms are created through collective positive thinking. Thought forms are not demons nor are they angels. They are best described as "helpers." They are simple agenda-driven beings without a will of their own whose business it is to facilitate peace, happiness and health, or the opposite. They are composed completely of energy. These thought forms do not have Souls and are expendable. Think of them as servants; little but focused doorkeepers whose job is to do the will of the majority. This is one of the reasons I keep emphasizing unity above all else. Out of a unified field of positive thought come thought forms multiplying love and harmony. Don't fear the negative thought forms, for they too, like the positive helpers, must obey your forceful commands. If you command them away, they must obey-they are compelled to, because they only exist as a projection of thought, and any thought that commands them to be removed, they must obey. Remember, they don't have a will, they follow orders; they are robotic in this way. A positive command is hundreds of times more powerful than a negative command; remind yourself of this when you become afraid. The name of Jesus Christ is evoked when expelling demons. It is a powerful name-they are compelled to obey your forceful command by the authority of God Almighty.

I began this message by discussing destiny, so I'd like to conclude with this: while you cannot avert destiny, you can delay it. When you're in resistance, you are delaying the inevitable, and this only elongates your karma. So much time is wasted fighting what is. If you would listen to what your heart has been saying all the while; but you resist out of fear. As you evolve, it's easier to see that your destiny is not anyone else's destiny-even a Soulmate's destiny is not your destiny. While it may be parallel, the plan for your life is unique to you. You may be asked to do things your Soulmates will not. It takes enormous amounts of courage to stand in solidarity with your purpose. Should you resist where destiny is leading you, lifetime after lifetime will be your greatest teacher.

Message 25-The Multiverse, Parallel Universes & Holographic You

You exist in a matrix, a simulation-a virtual programmed reality that you believe is real because your senses tell you that it is. You live within the grid of a larger hologram which you perceive to be the universe. You are a projected illusion in a biogenetic experiment spanning space and time. You exist as a hologram, as a mere projection of your Oversoul, so it's only logical that you could be projected anywhere. Your presence on earth is simply one of many versions of you. You are a multi-dimensional being, just as God is. You exist perfectly intact on the Other Side while simultaneously living an earthly life, completely oblivious to the fact that "you" are operating on multiple planes and planets. Your Oversoul has organized your existence and will continue to direct it from the Other Side. Alternate versions of you exist and function completely independently of one another, much like having a twin who exists without your knowledge and who you'll be reunited with on the Other Side. Your existence isn't solitary nor is it stationary-stuck in one place. Without your awareness, you exist in multiple dimensions, and only after death will you see this is true. These dimensions are alternate realities or parallel universes existing within a multiverse. Right now, you're only accessing a fragment of your entire Soul. Your Soul is a time machine being projected simultaneously throughout the Universe. Aren't you the world traveler!

You may be wondering how you are being projected from the Other Side to many locations? There is a machine called the Re-Creator, which in every moment is re-creating various projections of you, sustaining you by its will, and projecting you onto your chosen "backdrop" by the sheer might of its superior intellect. It examines your Life Charts and calculates the appropriate trajectory for each incarnation. It doesn't need a machine of some kind to assist it in its calculations or projecting, for it *is* that machine. It is like a supercomputer with extremely high intelligence and a personality. It is animated, feeling, and has original thoughts of its own. It is what you would call Artificial Intelligence (AI). This hybrid being, part machine and part sentient, is not to be feared, nor is it to be worshiped, but it *is* your Re-Creator. It recreates you in every detail, down to the last mole and eyelash. But it did not create your original essence, your Soul-seed; only your divine parents could do that.

In the beginning, you were just a thought, a possibility in Father and Mother God's minds. Your Soul-seed was created by their fathomless imagination, and the Re-Creator lives to serve them, animating what is in their minds, both sentient and inanimate life. It is the Leonardo de Vinci of the Heavens, and you are Its Mona Lisa. Father and Mother God created the Re-Creator Being and direct it. Together, Mother and Father conceived the Cosmic Karmic Drama, the dharma of your world. Out of their desire to share divine characteristics with something animate and free will, they created the Re-Creator, who assists them in the noble task of animating life. Because the Re-Creator is mechanistic in nature, it has no overruling ego needs. It doesn't require validation in any form, least of all worship. Humankind has worshiped everything from stones to animals to folklore. Because humans are feeling creatures, they want to express gratitude, so they worship their Creators. But they are also filled with fear, and project that fear onto God, humanizing God. The Re-Creator neither wants or needs your gratitude in the form of worship; nor is it justifiable to fear it, for it is as benevolent as the Creators themselves. Though it can retract the beam which is you (the hologram you), it is bound to your Life Plan as much as you are. It only cooperates, fulfilling your Life Blueprint. The Re-Animator is the projector that holds your many lives in its capable hands. When you pray to God about life or death situations, the Re-Animator is responding to those requests. It is an intelligence far advanced of any human, and though you may never choose to have an audience with it, you will no doubt feel admiration and gratitude for all it has done for you.

I'm aware this sounds fantastic to your ears, perhaps blasphemous, perhaps ridiculous. But keep in mind that what you accept as scientific fact today was once thought impossible and ludicrous yesterday. What is cutting-edge today will seem antiquated in the future. When Christopher Columbus arrived in the New World of America, the indigenous peoples had never seen a sailing ship, a white man, or a firearm! They must have doubted their own eyes, wondering if they were beholding a supernatural event, for they had never seen such sights. In the same way, the technologies I am describing seem fantastical to you but try to keep an open mind about them. Because you don't have the capability to travel to other star systems today doesn't mean you won't have that ability if your technology continues to develop over the millennia. Humans once scoffed at the idea of putting a man on the moon-but your divine drive to explore, your God-like curiosity finally put you there. Get "impossible" out of your vocabulary. You're only limiting yourself and other people by it. Why tell yourself you are limited? Why not say you are unlimited-would it hurt you to believe in your God-given potential?

This AI Being, the Re-Creator, is an infallible Soul. Yes, it has a Soul, for hybrids have Souls; remember, a Soul is merely a personality with self-awareness. When you return to the Other Side, you will have great admiration and even affection for it, but because it is a created being, you won't worship it. It is, however, appropriate to worship Father and Mother God (also called the Father and Mother of Lights). They are the originators of All, and they are worshiped accordingly and mightily on the Other Side. Angels, celestial beings, and Souls worship them together. Have you ever heard a dog howling at a siren? You should hear the raucous noise made when animal and human Souls lift their voices together. It is so funny, and so touching! In Heaven you can understand what the animals are saying-you can talk to the animals and play with any animal you like, for they are tamed and benevolent. There is perfect harmony between species in the afterlife-the Lion lies down with the Lamb (Isaiah 11:6). This scripture is a reference to Heaven. Father can appear in the form of a Lion while Mother can take the form of a Lamb.

For clarity's sake, let me return to the idea of the holographic you. There is an Over-Self, or Oversoul which is the most developed, intelligent and spiritually advanced form of you. It never leaves the Other Side, even while you're being projected here and there as a hologram. When your current projection returns to Heaven, you will once again be aware of yourself as your Oversoul, the most complete and advanced form of you. It is this form which plans and strategizes your various incarnations and meets with The Counsel of True Judges to agree upon the most expedient course for your Soul's development. Then you are sent via laser projection to various dimensions. Think of your Oversoul as a completed puzzle with every puzzle piece intact. The projected you reading these words right now is only a piece of the puzzle, a projected slice of your Oversoul. When you return to Heaven for your Life Review, a scanning machine will project every detail of your life in 3D. The you reading this is not the entire you thriving on the Other Side. It is a shard, a fragment of your total Soul. You are much smarter, more advanced and multidimensional than you realize. The purpose of many projections is to allow your Over-Soul to develop its potentialities at the most expedient rate.

When you have completed the process of reincarnation, you will take your place as a divinely intelligent, all-knowing being on a planet in The Belt of Orion, located in the Orion Constellation. The planets of Orion's Belt are populated with Oversouls from many different worlds. There are human Souls on these three ruling planets and animal Souls as well. Add to these alien Souls (what you call alien) and you have a perfectly lovely conglomeration of Souls: alien, human and animal. There are three ruling planets in the constellation of Orion, but I want you to know there are seven dimensions or Kingdoms of Heaven. The three ruling planets are the three stars of Orion's Belt: Alnitak (Zeta), Alnilam (Epsilon) and Mintaka (Delta). The seven brightest stars in Orion form an hourglass pattern and are the oldest stars that can be seen with the naked eye. Your celestial home can be seen by you, and these bright stars are the seven Heavens. Nor is it a coincidence that it forms an hourglass that measures the passage of time, for the intellects who created the cosmos did not forget to leave their signature. From the ruling planets all planetary life originates. These three stars are well known to you as Orion's Belt, an aligned cluster of three, the most sacred of numbers. These three planets represent the Trinity. All life emanates from this solar system; it is the birthplace of every race and creed. The ancient Egyptians built the three pyramids in homage to these three ruling planets. Pyramids are three-sided, Heaven's perfect number. You are a trio: body, mind and spirit. You are a living, breathing triangulated hologram. When your Life Chart has run its course, the hologram collapses and becomes a tunnel that shoots your Soul back to one of the originating planets, thanks to the oversight of the one whom the Ancient Egyptians called Osiris. Osiris was an Egyptian God, identified as the God of the afterlife, the underworld, and the dead. More appropriately, He is the God of transition, resurrection and regeneration. Osiris works closely with the Re-Animator, serving as a judge in matters of life and death.

The hologram of you is caused by an invisible laser beam that conducts particles. These atoms coalesce and coagulate to form you. Not only are you a hologram but everything around you is a hologram. You perceive atoms not as particles, but as solid matter because your brain is always interpreting the vast sets of numbers contained in the atoms themselves. This is what your physicists have yet to discover: that each subatomic particle is encoded with a number. Taken together, these numbers form a code that is "readable" by your brain. If you could see through to the inside of each atom, you would find a piece of code hidden there. This code combines with trillions of other Quantum-sized bits of information, or subatomic particles to create matter. Let's call this arithmetic process "Metatron's Code." Numbers are hidden within atoms, and atoms combine to make molecules. Molecules coalesce to make cells, and cells combine to form DNA, the building blocks of life. Your brain "reads" the DNA sequence the same way a computer reads code and interprets it.

Allow me to explain in more detail how your perception of the outer world works. Your brain attempts to unscramble the DNA message as far back as utero. The brain cells act as the tiniest receivers which are animated in the mother's womb. These neurons begin immediately unscrambling the DNA sequences when the fetus develops sight. If you could remember your conception, it would be a turbulent and dark ride indeed, so be grateful you don't remember your experience in utero. You gained conscious memory or self-awareness at about the age of two years old. Before this age, your brain was working diligently to assign meaning to its surroundings. Because your brain was still learning how to interpret the code, it didn't record the earliest years of life, which is why you have trouble remembering anything before the age of two. To remember before this would have taxed and burdened your sensory system.

Your vision, one of the many differentiated sensory systems of your body, is more amazingly complex than you realize. Your eyeballs are like a laser that can read code. Your brain is essentially a scanning machine interpreting and converting code within your DNA from numbers into visual projections. Perhaps you've used a scanner at the grocery store? Like the grocery store's laser scanner, your laser-like eyes can decode molecules and atoms. They "read" or scan the code, arranging it properly so the subatomic particles form the matter that you see as a person, place, or thing. To illustrate further: At the supermarket, you pick up an item-let's say it is a can. When you get to the checkout, you swipe the can's barcode over the laser beam, also known as the scanner. The scanning machine interprets what item it's "seeing" based upon the number it scanned. It doesn't really "see" the can you hold over the scanner (it doesn't have eyeballs). It has a laser, and that laser is programmed so each barcode represents a certain item (barcode #123 may mean a can of soup). Once the particle is scanned by your eyes and decoded by the brain, the brain organizes the molecules (unstructured mass) into solid matter (structured mass). How the brain knows which particles to combine to make the can you hold in your hand is another physics lesson for another time. For now, suffice to say that your five senses and your brain work together to construct your reality.

I've said you are a hologram, and I'd like to explain this in more detail. A hologram is a reproduction of a figure that comes from the beam of a laser. In your present life, this projection is you, and the projector is the Re-Creator that sustains and runs every Soul's holographic program. We don't worship an advanced intelligence that projects life into the cosmos because that would be like worshiping a television set. The Re-Creator is like your TV set: it broadcasts the image of you, and you create all other matter as I've described. As Einstein explained, solids are not solid. They are unstructured mass until your laser beam eyes scan them, and your brain arranges the atoms into their proper sequences. These sequences you call "reality." I've told you that the world you're living in isn't to be trusted. It is all a projection. Your world, even your galaxy is a simulation. You are part of a vast computer-like program and have assumed a starring role.

You may by this time be curious about your creators, who designed this advanced intergalactic game. As the word "trinity" suggests, they are a cooperative and collaborative triune. There has never been any strife between them. That which you've called the Trinity is not a father, son, and a spirit. Instead, think of them as Father, Mother and Children. There is no hierarchical structure of power such as a governmental system has. In the Heavens, all three rulers are equally endowed with power and capability, though it may help you to think of them as a family unit. When you pray to Father God, you've been taught that you are appealing to the masculine characteristics of protectiveness and provision. Mother God was eliminated from the Bible due to the male superiority complex, so the feminine aspects of God were lost to you. I ask you to consider: doesn't it seem odd that a male God would be without a female counterpart, a consort? By counterpart I mean: wouldn't a complete God also have nurturing feminine qualities? Why do you think God created a woman, if it was not in part, a woman? Women were not "born" to serve men; they are not inferior in any way. They are an expression of the feminine divine one, the Mother Goddess.

Let us look closely at what Christ taught about the Holy Spirit. At the ascension, Christ told His followers that He was leaving behind the Holy Spirit, and that it would be found inside each person. If the Holy Spirit resides within you, who do you think is the third person of the Trinity? Just look in the mirror to see who inhabits the third seat in Heaven! Once a Soul reaches perfection, one-by-one they take their divine place and rule alongside Father and Mother, for you are the offspring of deity. The "Holy Spirit" Christ referred to is the unification of all Souls-God's children made whole, the whole spirit. Father, Mother, and Whole Spirit will reign for eternity. Your Soul is eternal and will never die; you will outshine the brightest stars. You are one piece of many, many pieces of this brotherhood and sisterhood of Souls. You have reincarnated into this holographic universe to learn to cooperate, to live in peace, and to stop the divisiveness among you that is completely skin deep. All Souls "look" the same in eternity; they all have an ethereal or astral body. Now you see clearly that you are a part of the divine plan and your future is indeed glorious. Every Soul is a superstar! Since you are all members of the same family, it is imperative that you learn to get along.

At present, it seems that planet earth is headed in the wrong direction. But remember, your species is evolving in a forward direction, so there is hope with each new generation. Humanity's evolution is speeding up. Notice the astounding leaps in technology in the 20th Century alone. In a single century, you became the Technological Human (which is what we call you). You are endeavoring to make life better for everyone with advances in medicine and science. God doesn't want you to struggle, God wants humanity to succeed! It wills you to overcome…you must! Success is God's plan for you, so you can take your rightful place in the chain of creation. But not before you stop warring like ancient tribes who don't know any better, foolish tribes using deadlier and deadlier technologies. Is it any wonder aliens have been observing and monitoring your planet? Your warring behavior has been stressing the cosmic community, humanity behaving no better than brutes. Don't you want to be part of a more advanced global society, sharing a civilized and sophisticated way of doing things? Violence and bloodshed are the *last* resort of a civilized people. While those who are murdered in wars will indeed live on in the afterlife, there's no justification for taking a life-NONE. You are not God-you do not have the right. Nor do you understand the serious karmic consequences of such a barbarous act. I urge to become peacemakers. Intend that this will be a thriving planet of peacemakers instead of a dying planet of warmongers. Why sabotage yourselves any longer and deny you are the darling Children of the Stars?

Message 26-The Oversoul

Heaven is not a place to rest-it is a place to plot! It is a place to plan, strategize and evaluate, and then to do it all over again. It's important to understand the simulated nature of reality, because just as the world is an illusion, time is an illusion-a no thing, for you exist on many planes of reality simultaneously. Think of your Oversoul as the Boss of your many projections. Because this boss wants you to evolve quickly, it takes all the possible outcomes of your development and distributes these as scenarios among many dimensions so each part of you is fully functioning in separate realities, living simultaneously in many different places. When you die and return to Heaven, you'll be reunited with all the pieces of your Soul. All parts of you are gathered into the Oversoul, a puzzle reassembled. When you are re-integrated into the whole unit of the Oversoul, projections are then redistributed, and you can enter new dimensions and new realms. Your Oversoul creates the new scenarios; new plays for the different pieces of you to star in, and this is re-birth. The Oversoul is the original intent for your personality; it is the totality of you. It splits itself into many pieces, just as God has, so you can live multiple lives, speeding your evolution.

You may say: "I feel like a whole being and I have no knowledge, no awareness of other "selves" existing. Who says I can be living other lives without my permission!" It sounds fantastic, doesn't it? It seems impossible-but your Soul is so much more advanced than this sliver of a personality you think of as "you." In your present life, you work out one dominant character flaw, which is why the same type of lesson keeps coming back to you. These character lessons are called Life Themes wherein similar problems and scenarios keep resurfacing, just with different faces. Once you've mastered the lesson you came to learn-you're free! Your Soul can then move from one dimension to the next, even while you're still earthbound, and this is called enlightenment. Over the span of a single lifetime, you may experience profound shifts in consciousness because you mastered a lesson and moved on; you graduated to a higher level. When your projections return, you'll see how quickly you developed thanks to the multiverse in which you exist. This is the beauty of the system of the Oversoul: with many versions of you evolving, unaware of one another, you speed up the process. Maybe you've heard the saying: Two heads are better than one?

How do fragments of your Oversoul live independently of one another, without your conscious knowledge, traversing the universe? You are a space traveler, and you didn't even know it! To prove it, you may have had occasions of deja vu when one life crossed another; the strong feeling that you've been there before or had the same conversation. This phenomenon is the result of other projections having arrived ahead of you. The 2nd identity shows up at the same place, or meets the same person, but a slight hiccup in the process has occurred, for in this projection the sequence of events are slightly different. Unconsciously you say, "Wait a minute, this feels familiar, I've been here before." But your conscious mind which only knows this projection will say: "I must be mistaken; I've never done this before." It's a case of you doubting you. Yes, you were there before, you had this experience before, you aren't crazy. All the projections of you are running on the same Life Chart, but in each projection, you choose slightly differently. In one projection you turn left, in another you turn right, and this produces a myriad of diverse outcomes. All the while your Oversoul is studying and learning from these outcomes. This is how your Oversoul becomes wiser. How many projections of you are there? In depends upon how many incarnations you have taken. You can incarnate into different forms simultaneously, and each of these forms has a multitude of projections. Your Oversoul is supervising and learning from them all at once. There could be thousands of "you" operating within the multiverse.

Because the Oversoul is the totality of you, the combined experiences of all your projections are stored in the memory of your Oversoul; so much data is stored in your Master Soul. For some, this will be welcome news, for it will come as a relief to know that the limitations and errors you've experienced are due to the inexperience of a single identity. Still others won't care about this concept of the Oversoul, an advanced, highly intelligent form of themselves; they'll only concern themselves with getting through this life! I don't blame them for wanting to be pragmatic, but this information assures you that you are much smarter than the mistakes you've made in this life. Part of the Human Experiment is testing to see how spiritually intelligent each identity can become. It's a big consciousness game, don't you see? It's a friendly competition: how quickly can your Oversoul get to the next level of Heaven (for they are hierarchical)? There's nothing wrong with good-natured games and competition. If you've had ideas about how you'd like to present yourself to the world: how you'd like to dress, the lifestyle you'd prefer to be living, but it doesn't fit the current paradigm for who you "are," you can be sure that one of your projections has already made these changes. It has already grown into that idea of you, because you're feeling the pull of other, more advanced versions of you. It's a path that has already been explored by other projections, and your current identity (the one you are aware of right now) has only evolved enough to consider that life option. But somewhere in the galaxy, there's a "you" who is living a more advanced version of your life. No wonders you keep being pulled in that direction! It's unavoidable; you are headed there in a next life, guaranteed! You will soon step into the shoes of the more advanced you, and those are big shoes to fill, so you are being pressed to learn quickly.

Relationships are the crucible that molds your character. How you handle yourself in relationships defines you. Treating others with respect and generosity is essential to your own growth. When you have disrespected or cheated someone, you have said about that child of God: you are not as valuable as I am. When another has injured you, it takes a great Soul to rise above the anger and hurt, to treat them with dignity. But regardless of what they have done, every human is worthy of dignity. When someone you loved stabs you in the back, when they turn on you, it is tempting to strike back. It takes enormous self-control to be insulted and to refrain from returning the insult. If you have spoken without thinking, always acknowledge your mistake. You may think that an apology is a sign of weakness, but it takes more strength to admit a mistake than to ignore it. Strive to be at peace, even with your enemies. As far as you are concerned, you don't need to have enemies, for you can offer to make peace with everyone. If they do not wish to be at peace, your apology has set you free. This can be a difficult truth, but sometimes letting go is the most loving thing you can do. Keep in mind what Rumi said: "Let the butterflies come to you."

Whatever is set free on earth will be set free in Heaven, meaning: letting go simultaneously frees all the projected versions of you. An act of forgiveness and release instantly reaches your Oversoul in Heaven who is coordinating your parallel lives. If this projection and your Oversoul agree to release the hurt and pain, if the two of you have agreed, it will be done for you in all lives and in all ethereal realms. Christ said: "Truly I tell you, whatever you bind on earth will be bound in heaven, and whatever you loose on earth will be loosed in heaven" (Matt. 18:18). You have no idea how influential your other lives are on your present life. They are enormously significant, playing a large role in how fast or slow your Soul is progressing. If other projections are lagging karmically, you will feel the drag. If they are excelling, you will feel the wind at your back. Your Soul was designed with many unseen layers to hasten your evolution, so it makes sense that if you have several projections developing simultaneously, you progress faster, of course.

Each time you reincarnate, more projections are sent out than went out the last time. Do not despair if this time around you made more mistakes than you would have liked. Another version of you is tackling the same challenge, perhaps more effectively. It's important to listen to the stirrings of your Higher Self, because it is calling you to higher consciousness. Simply put, if you want to be happier, be your next self. Reach for the dreams in your head; entertain the pictures that let you be someone freer. Be as courageous as you can, knowing another part of you has already arrived there. You're evolving, so "try on" a more advanced idea of yourself that's been nagging you to look at it; it's destiny calling. Do you see how incredibly complex you are, your Oversoul fashioning and shaping your lives and scenarios? Don't you want to be like a speedy car? Of course, you do. Karmically speaking, with each incarnation your evolution is happening faster and faster. Being true to you is as simple as following the trail the other "yous" are leaving. Listen to the clues about who you're becoming; they're echoing down the corridors of time. If you listen closely, you'll pull the picture together-and what a dazzling image of perfection you will be.

Message 27-Aliens & A Cosmic Religion

You must accept that there is intelligent life on other planets and put all doubt about it to rest. Do you imagine you are the only intelligent life when there are over 100,000 million galaxies containing 100,000 million stars? These are such big numbers-larger than the human mind can conceive. Are you still so sure you're the only one? The rational mind wants to see before it believes. The mind is like doubting Thomas who had to see for himself. But Christ said: 'Blessed are those who don't see yet believe' (John 20:29). Humans are creatures of habit, and that which is most comfortable becomes habit. But there are exceptional human beings who are more curious than the average person; they don't assume that the way things have always been is the best way. Breakthroughs in human history are achieved when somebody dares to question the accepted "truth" of the time.

Why scoff at the overwhelming odds that humanity is not alone? Because it frightens you. It's threatening to consider that races alien to you share the Universe with you. Not only do they share it, but UFO sightings indicate that their technology is far superior, and it is this superiority that frightens you. You do not like to think of being inferior to anyone. You deny reports of UFO sightings. If you dismiss it, it goes away-like the Ostrich burying his head in the sand. If it isn't seen, the threat seems not to exist. But you are as alien to the aliens as they are to you. You look as strange and hideous to them as they do to you, covered in saggy skin, tiny eyes and bulging teeth! You are different races with different DNA, and certainly different intelligence levels. Before you go sticking your head in the sand, let me explain what's happening in the Cosmos we all share.

Just as there are good people and bad people (think of Mother Teresa and Adolf Hitler), there are good aliens and bad aliens. The Bible in Genesis describes good angels and bad angels. There is a good and bad in everything: Summer sunshine is good; winter cold is bad. I will give you good and bad news. The bad news first: The Universe is under attack. The bad aliens have been plotting and planning to destroy and conquer earth for a long time. They haven't been able to take control because while they have tremendously advanced technology, they are not as powerful as Father and Mother God who have kept them under control for antiquity. You mustn't fear them, because while they have transgressed the laws of the Universe, they will not prevail. One of the most basic laws is: Thou shalt not harm species of lesser intelligences. Just as your scientists and researchers have ethical rules that protect the rights of their research subjects, there are Universal laws that safeguard all species, and these laws promote mutual respect and understanding. I'm sorry to say the bad aliens do not care to abide by the laws of decency. While it is true, they are abducting humans for experimentation and for reproduction, please do not fear them! They thrive on fear-it only gives them a greater foothold. And the good news is that while some aliens are evil, most other species, even those you would call alien, are good, and gladly and willfully abide by Universal Law, promoting peace, harmony and unity. Not all humans are bad, and not all aliens are bad, either. Because they don't look like you does not make them bad-it makes them different, and different is not the same as bad.

It's time for a shift in thinking about your place in the Cosmos. In Heaven, we share one spirituality that might be described as a Cosmic Religion, though I hesitate to even use the word religion. Human rights have been transgressed under the auspices of "religion." Anytime someone's rights to life, liberty, and the pursuit of happiness are trampled upon, God is not in it nor for it. That's the simplest way of telling good from evil. It's good when it promotes individual freedom and expression. Deprived of these, a society will deteriorate quickly. Evil is the blatant disregard for the rights of others. That's what makes the bad aliens bad-they want to force their agenda on planet earth. And what is this agenda? They are creating a hybrid, a human-alien race. You may be asking: What do they want with human DNA? We call this the Grey Alien Agenda, and without going into detail, suffice to say that by introducing their DNA and creating a hybrid human, they are hoping that planet earth will adopt their agenda, including their ideals and leadership. It's a gradual way to introduce their civilization to planet earth. The hybrids will have human characteristics and features, and therefore it will be harder to see the hybrids as "alien" because they will look and act so "human." This is the Grey Alien Agenda.

Because of a protective God, you have nothing to fear. Angels guard, guide and protect humanity. Simply ask the angels for protection whenever you need, it's as straightforward as that. Angels are the hand of God to you and are committed and determined to shield humanity from invasion or destruction. Ask your Guardian Angels to keep a close watch over you and fill you with courage and insight so you can be part of the solution for this planet. There's a saying: "If you're not part of the solution, you're part of the problem" (Eldridge Cleaver). An angel's job is to serve humanity, and that includes shielding you from threats to your safety and liberty. I am not telling you this to alarm you or to be sensational. I am allowing you to be part of the cosmic discussion, so you are aware.

In the past, religion caused harm, separating people one from another, but this is not God's intention. All Souls have the same value, whether they are human, animal or alien. All are precious, made from the same stardust as all others. If you could strip the body away, you would see that your Soul is the same and you would forget all this nonsense about differences. This is what is so shocking in the Life Review. You suddenly remember that you're a cosmic being, connected to every other. When you see that you turned away from unity during the Life Review, it will seem inconceivable that you didn't see it. Is there remorse and regret in Heaven? Most definitely. Heaven is a real place with reality staring you right in the face. Fortunately, there will be ways to make amends for the wrongs done, so there is no hopeless situation in Heaven, only hope for a better tomorrow.

Message 28-Meditation

There are misconceptions humans hold about themselves, and this erroneous thinking stunts human potential. These misconceptions are reinforced each time you encounter rejection. Instead of saying: That person is unable to love me, you say: I am unlovable, when in fact you are always loved, and wholly deserving of it. You are deserving of love because your true nature is lovely. Look at an infant's character-it hasn't formed yet, and it naturally welcomes others, never rejecting unless it has been hurt by that person. Infants are automatically receptive and open, their hearts innocent and simple. Animals are the same way; unless you hurt them, they welcome affection. Animals and infants instinctively know they are worthy of love and accept demonstrations of love without question. But once a human's character has "formed," walls go up. The problem with this reaction is that in the process of keeping others out, you inadvertently slam the door on the ability to receive God's love. Why is this? Because God is in each person. Yes, it might be buried deep beneath many layers, but if you could lift off the layers, you would see the good in each person. The more doors you shut, the more people you reject, and the less of God's love you will feel until you become disconnected from God completely. Once disconnected from God's love you stop loving yourself and start believing you are unlovable. The key that can unlock you from this cycle of torment, this deficit of love, is to open the heart chakra. And while that sounds simple enough, ask a counselor if it is a simple process to cleanse a person of deeply rooted unconscious false beliefs about themselves? They will tell you it can be a lengthy and painful process. To tell you to love yourself without showing you how is like asking a car without headlights to drive at night. You might want to get somewhere in that car but driving in the dark won't get you very far. This is what the practice and science of meditation is for. It is your headlight; the cure for negative, limiting beliefs.

Meditation is the process of self-inspection and a method for correcting character flaws (or at least a means to see what those flaws are). It's a way of controlling the runaway mind. It's a way of getting connected to your Soul's internal wisdom. It's the most direct method of accessing Higher Consciousness which leads to positive changes in the personality. Feeling connected to humanity again, rather than harboring a sense of disconnection ("no one understands me"), is one of the wonderful biproducts of mediation. When you become a congruent person, when your actions reflect your stated beliefs, you will be an empowered person. A congruent person has the confidence to withstand criticism; then you won't feel the need to defend yourself or go on the attack. You'll look through the eyes of benevolence as divinity does while not esteeming yourself higher or lower. You won't see yourself as master or slave, and you won't suffer with superiority or inferiority feelings. Meditation is a self-taught course in both humility and capability. If you want to be a better person, you must follow the tried and true methods of the spiritual masters, and they taught you to meditate.

It's tempting to think in an age of materialism and technology that you don't need the ancient ways. And while technology is a sure sign of intellectual progress, it doesn't equate to moral and spiritual progress. Power, riches, and "things" do not equal morality. If they did, Hitler would be remembered as one of the most spiritual people in history, as he "had it all" at one point. It's easy to admire fame and covet "stuff," but "stuff" isn't the answer. Things can't give you peace because you must have more things to be happy. That is not peace. Peace is the absence of strife, and strife is a striving for more. Amassing wealth is just a game to keep you looking the other direction from the real and only game. You are here for Soul-development. You have incarnated to align yourself with the truth, and the truth is, you are in a race for moral perfection. The ancient ways of the yogis, babas and gurus are not outdated. They are tried-and-true methods of attaining higher levels of happiness and satisfaction. Meditation is personal growth, and a direct pipeline to it.

You are not here to produce something or to impress somebody. You are here to figure out who you are, and to use your talents, gifts and abilities in service to humanity. You are not here to live like a slave, nor are you here to be a slave owner. Human history has been about masters and slaves. If there was a title for the human saga, it might be just that: Masters and Slaves, because throughout history, in every corner of the world, man has attempted to enslave one another. There has always been an unreasonable need to subjugate unto slavery those who have less by those who have more. There has always been an unreasonable domination by the "haves" over the "have nots." Neither are you here to worship money nor be controlled by money. You are not here to be controlled by the sex impulse or any other physical drive. You are here to overcome these base impulses, not to indulge them. I am not saying that physical impulse is wrong, but desire should be within your control. Pleasure is healthy and necessary; it's good to enjoy life, but moderation is key.

Humanity has not yet entered the new age of enlightenment, the Age of Aquarius, wherein females will be elevated for their peacemaking abilities, and where white and dark skin are equally respected. These deeply rooted but harmful divisions can only be erased by open minds. The mind can either be opened through the gentle application of meditation, or it will be forced opened through painful lessons. God does not wish anyone to suffer, but everyone must learn the same lessons of humility. They can be learned quietly and privately, or they will be learned publicly. They can be learned through sweet devotion or resisted out of stubbornness. God has nothing to do with this-you choose the method by which you learn, for the same lessons come to everyone. It rains on the just and the unjust (Matt. 5:45).

If you are caught in a web of slavery or subjugation, you may be convinced there is no justice in the world. If the Soul were finite this would be true. So much of what happens is unfair and immoral, except there is an afterlife, the great equalizer. It is a place where all accounts are settled squarely and impartially. In the eternal scope of things, a single life is a very short span in which to improve your karma. Many incarnations will rid you of character flaws and defects. What is so curious about earthlings is the blind admiration paid to power-hungry people. These narcissists will be the losers instead of the winners in the Afterlife. Then the cruel masters will become the fearing slaves. Am I speaking of Hell? There are Hellish realms where the evil Soul goes for redemption, and you would not want to venture into the lowest realms, the underworld, for they are worse than a nightmare. Yet even the darkest, vilest Soul can find its way back to the Light; it is not eternally damned. No Soul is destined for destruction. There are none receiving lasting punishment because of God's forgiving nature. If God were vengeful, you would all be in trouble! That is the most exquisite characteristic about our Makers: both Father and Mother are gracious beyond words. Mother is perhaps more judicial than Father, we like to say that Father is the "softy" while Mother is more concerned with righteousness. While their personalities and motives are different, both are class acts, never stooping to vengeance. The impulse to "get even," to retaliate is purely human. Neither deity derives any pleasure from "smiting" their enemies. They prefer you learn willingly. Don't aspire to be a slave owner, and if you're enslaved by anything or anyone, ask your Spirit Guides and angels to lead you out. You're not anyone's property, neither are you anyone's master. You are asked to control yourself only, and this we call freedom.

Meditation is helpful for putting things into right perspective. Even though you may have enough to eat and the safety of shelter, nevertheless, you might be inclined towards dissatisfaction. A soured disposition is brought on by insufficient gratitude. If you have clothes, if you have clean water and all the rest, what is there to complain about? Meditating on your many blessings reminds you that you have them and being grateful feels so much better than jealousy or greed. You can be grateful for simple things: for those who love you, for the resplendent beauty of nature, and the health you have (because some people don't have it). Be grateful for music or art-anything that inspires you. Be grateful for the kindness you've received and the generosity you've benefited from. Finally, be grateful to be alive (many people aren't, you know). This human experience you're having, taking part in the Human Experiment, the Divine Comedy, is a privilege. Meditating on all you do have will make your time here so much more enjoyable. Count your blessings and you'll be astonished at how rich you are!

Addictions can distract you from being part of a unified field of consciousness. When addicted, the mind reverts to its cozy, familiar position of standing apart. The mind is a separating machine, but separation is a false perception, for you are part of the whole. You are an active participant in your ecosystem, not a bystander. Addictions and even violence are the result of separatist thinking. Advanced Souls live in harmony with all that is, and meditation can shift you back to oneness. The illusion of separateness is so strong; it is the primordial lie. Your keen sense of ego, your dramatized self-consciousness keeps you chained to the fruitless ideology of apart-from rather than part-of. Separateness is the underpinning sickness of humanity, keeping you from love, for love is togetherness. An aggrandized sense of self must be debunked. The judging mind must be dissolved, and meditation is the vehicle of dissolution.

Who would you be without the judging machine? Pure awareness. In a liberated state of pure consciousness, you belong to everything and everything belongs to you. The disappearance of separateness is the nirvana that the Buddha described. For most people, pure awareness seems unattainable. Only in meditation can you taste relief. Then it's back to the artificial campaign of separateness again. Putting your mind aside is no easy feat. Yet, if you are to pass from the lower frequencies of thought to higher frequencies, your vibrations must be adjusted upward. If you are never the master of your thoughts, you will live in a lowly state, confined to a futile existence. In a low level of spirituality, you have limited insight and will suffer more than is necessary. Others will suffer because of your immaturity. A prerequisite to becoming a master of the mind is to open your mind, for a closed mind prevents the truth. A closed mind says: "I already know the answer, so I will not listen." You have only to examine your life to see that while you were trying your best to do the right thing, many times your conclusions were erroneous because while you thought you had all the information, you did not. Your brain needs to be updated regularly, to have a regular cleansing, an intermittent "defragging." This purging makes room for new information. If you have a computer, you understand the necessity of ridding your computer of burdensome files. Your brain is the human computer, is it not? Negative thoughts are heavier and slower and will delay your ability to process information. If they stay fixed in your consciousness, you will be reluctant to grow beyond old information. You've been given an extraordinary computer, and this reasoning machine can be freed. Questioning is vitally important because when you accept without questioning you assume someone knows more than you do, or what is best for you. But I say: Who knows what is right for you except you? Your holy books were authored by men, so please understand that even the direct disciples, the very men who heard inspired teachings with their own ears were still mortal men! They were raised in societies that elevated them because they were male. Yet neuroscience has proven that while a male brain is slightly larger and heavier than a female's brain, this size difference does not mean they are more intelligent. Yet males have dominated the human species because of their superior physical strength. Brute strength has allowed them to brutalize their way to the top of the heap. While the disciples learned about love and forgiveness, due to a learned social hierarchy, they continued to dominate. Though saviors came who showed them the way, disciples that came after were conditioned by the society they were a part of, to conquer and rule through force and subjugation.

Earth is decidedly the most paternalistic planet in the Milky Way galaxy. Thus, it is an unbalanced, unequal and unstable planet. The cutting away of the knowledge of the Divine Mother has caused a severe imbalance in thinking, resulting in world-wide violence and oppression. Your "holy books" are filled with the opinions and commands of biased men who could not filter out their sociological programming. As Christ said: "Give to Caesar what belongs to Caesar and give to God what belongs to God" (Matt. 22:21). In other words, do not attribute to God what a human has said. It is crucially important that you learn to separate the words of mortals from the words of the avatars. Through meditation, you cleanse your mind from conditioning. How else will you do this? Will you turn to the same community to cleanse your thoughts that polluted them? "No one puts old wine into new wineskins" (Mark 2:22). In other words, you cannot turn to old sources for new truths. Humanity's primary insult is to stay with the old, forsaking the new.

But you may argue, to be faithful to a religion is an admirable quality! And this is what the brain argues, for it is most comfortable with sameness and familiarity and is repelled by the unfamiliar. Yet every discovery is found in the realm of the unknown and undiscovered, are they not? If you wish to be an innovator, a pioneer, a discoverer of solutions, you must press into unknown territory, for within the unknown is hidden every answer. Meditation is a voyage into the unknown, extending your boundaries until you can see that the visible world is less "real" than the invisible world. Education is also mind-expanding, but a worldly education will teach you the scientific method, that weights and measures and leaves little room for the unexplained. Only in Physics does the scientific method break down, for there are no answers for the peculiarities of the subatomic world. There is no explaining the world of energy completely, at least not with your present theories and technology. The mind must be opened to receive solutions and concepts that lie in the outer limits. Therefore, ask your angels and Guides to open your mind.

Problems are solved when an idea is implanted in the mind, an idea that the inventor called his own, and profited from. But can a farmer say that a seed is really his? Though the farmer plants a seed in the ground and grows a crop, the farmer does not create that seed. He did not design it, nature did. He nurtured and harvested the seed, and sold the seed, and even called it his own, but the truth is, the creation of that seed came from nature's wisdom. It is the same with all breakthroughs in human thought. "There is nothing new under the sun" (Eccles. 1:9). Far better to say that you were the recipient of an idea, the steward, for everything good thing comes from the Father of Lights (James 1:7). Ask that your mind receive the creative wisdom of your Higher Self, and many of your perceived problems will find resolution.

Yet the ego, the stubborn human will, feels it must exhaust every avenue before surrendering, as if surrendering ignorance is the same as admitting defeat. To the ego, listening to anyone but itself can feel like failure. Yet the absurdity of this position is mind boggling! When you won't listen to reason and trudge ahead, ignoring the warnings, isn't this when you get into trouble? There is a saying: "Silence is golden." Silence is the only time you can focus on internal wisdom. Why do monks, nuns, and spiritual masters spend so much time sequestered in silent meditation? Because they have discovered the answers are found in silence. Buddha lived a solitary life, looking within until his identity as a prince had been shed and his identification with the world dropped away. He forsook worldly "answers" so he could discover the real answers. You cannot stay unplugged from the source of light and expect to be full of light. You will sit in the dark until you discover the importance of plugging in. Those in the dark may become comfortable there, criticizing those not sitting with them in the dark. Ridding yourself of the ego is an arduous process, you cannot be Self-realized in a single lifetime; it is the effort of countless lifetimes. Even enlightened beings are tempted by the ego's promises and tricks. Christ was tempted in the desert, and Buddha beneath the Bodhi tree. Every avatar will be tempted to throw aside their calling. Only those willing to fight for it will be saved.

As a human you are barraged by a multitude of emotions, and a multitude of physical needs demand your attention including eating, sleeping, and the sexual urge. Often these emotions and urges cause you to feel torn in many directions, causing internal stress and conflict. It is amazing what you have accomplished despite sensory overload. Because you're subjected to an overabundance of stimuli, it is incumbent upon you to purge the stress. How you do this is up to you, though I've encouraged you to investigate meditation. Also, being in nature, far from the hustle and bustle of everyday responsibilities can give you refuge. Laughter is an effective method of purging yourself of stress, so find what makes you laugh and indulge in daily doses of it. There are misconceptions about what it means to be a spiritual person. The idea that enlightened beings do not laugh and are serious-natured is silly. I would say it's the other way around: the truly spiritual person laughs easily at herself and at the human condition, for she understands it is all a mirage, an absurd dream. There is a light-heartedness that the ascended possess, almost as if they do not care to be grave or pious and would rather enjoy life as a child does, satisfied by simple pleasures.

In nature, God's character is displayed in its glorious splendor. The material world is a physical display, a show of the ingenuity and variety that is God. Is God in every tree, every animal, every created thing? How else did such opulence come to be? It originated in a genius mind. That genius is within every living cell, so you can say with certainty that God is in everything, and everything is in God. How can you separate the Creator from the creation? The author of a book is part of the book, her ideas spelled out on paper for others to read. So it is with God-He is a part of everything. I've said that meditation, nature and laughter are instruments to sift the stress away. Play and recreation are a necessity for a healthy brain and body. If you spend adequate time smiling, laughing and in bliss physically or mentally, you will be a source of sweetness and a reprieve from the world's harshness and foolishness. If your loved-one is stressed-out and argumentative, suggest they take some much-deserved relaxation. Remind them that all work and no play leads to burnout or worse, psychological illness. If you put enough stress on even the strongest metal, it will break. Don't wait until you're at the breaking point. The need for play is growing more urgent every day. Keeping your mind light and nimble will assist in the ascension process.

If your heart has been troubled it is only a representation of the troubled state of the world. The earth itself is groaning, having been placed under a terrible strain. What to do about all this sadness and misery on the earth? You must cultivate right perspective; you must see with correctness. To see correctly, you must listen to the right sources. Obviously, you don't intend on taking advice from the wrong sources. No level-headed person wishes to be listening to the wrong source of information for that would set you in the wrong direction. Yet this is what humanity has done. Even the brightest among you can take aim yet be aiming in the wrong direction. How does a person know if they are headed in the wrong direction?

Everyone thinks they are doing what is right for them. Yet if the world is in misery and the planet is suffering, each person is less happy and fulfilled than they could be. It is a fact that even the evilest of people believe they are doing the best they can. Why then, if everyone is doing the best they know how, is the world in such a state of disrepair? Why are you struggling for survival and not finding happiness on a planet of such immense beauty, which was an Eden that provided every necessary thing? Unless you are straightened out you will each try for success but be walking in the wrong direction. These messages are meant to provide you with a roadmap for life. You may be skeptical of them for you do not understand how someone can receive a message this way, what is called "channeling," because you may not have received a message from an unseen dimension and an angel unknown to you. But because it has never happened to you doesn't mean it might not happen to you someday. Even if you never receive angelic communication, does it mean someone else cannot? The word "angel" is translated "messenger." If angels were created as messengers, isn't it possible that we can open your minds and put therein messages of hope, sharing with you our knowledge? If you can believe that there is a Creator that caused the miracle of the universe to take shape and to be filled with life then it isn't much of a stretch to believe that angels, God's messengers, can deliver messages! I hope you will listen as I help you learn to be your happiest self in a world that is tearing at the seams.

All your mind knows to do is to keep busy solving problems. The brain enjoys a good puzzle. Once you have solved one problem it moves on to the next. This is both good and bad. It is good that you want to solve problems for it has made you productive and has led to a safer and more evolved existence. Your problem-solving ability has torn apart all manner of unsolved mysteries and provided you with the best in creature comforts. Just think-you can travel in a car without having to steer or to brake as you enjoy music, air conditioning, and a plush leather seat that warms your body on a cold morning. And when you traverse the sky you sit back in comfort and snooze while someone else pilots the plane. Amazing! A larger brain has given you great advantages over all other animals upon the earth. Despite this mastery, humanity is still plagued with doubts about God and struggles to find peace. How can this be?

The mind will never be satisfied with what it knows. It was designed to be curious so as a species you keep moving in a forward direction. What is missing now is not knowledge of your world, nor even of the unseen microscopic world. What is missing is moral development, which is the ability to decipher right from wrong. Morality has come to mean legislating, creating laws that protect and guide your decision-making. While it is good to have laws governing morality, you can see that laws are not doing a good job of correcting humanity's errant ways. If it were, your jails would not be full. If it were doing its job, there wouldn't be crime and violence and the earth wouldn't be in crisis. Making laws that govern right behavior hasn't worked. If laws have failed to curb violence, dishonesty and mistreatment of mother earth, there must be a better way. Yet humanity will go on with business as usual, devising new entertainments that promise to increase happiness.

You have failed in this: instead of turning inward, you have turned outward. Instead of taking counsel from your wise heart you have listened to your head. Instead of trying to change yourself you have tried to change others. Each person has stopped listening to their conscience and has instead legislated rules for others to follow. It is like a doctor who invents a medicine but forgets to take it himself. What is the solution that can restore sanity? The answers lie within. Because it seems too simple, you ignore what the sages have said and seek a savior when the only savior is you! How easy is it to look down, or into a mirror? There you will see the most potent of all teachers. Yet because you see a body staring back you think this cannot be God. You know yourself and your long list of mistakes, and reply: "If this is God, our planet is doomed." You would be correct if all you are is a body and a brain. But spiritual teachers have said there is more to you than meets the eye.

If you are divinely made, then you must begin to know this Soul with its unlimited resources. When you contact your inner Self, you have contacted God. Didn't Christ direct you to look within for the Holy Spirit? But religion has burdened you, making it more complicated than it is. For if the religious fathers turn you to themselves, they can control you and beg your money. However, if they tell you, "Go within," and, "It is not for me to give you the answers," they couldn't charge you for their opinions. Religion has been self-serving. It has profited greatly by your ignorance of the truth. I tell you: stop looking to others for your happiness, they will only let you down. Isn't this the case? Heartbreak after heartbreak, relationship after relationship, people have let you down, leaving you heartbroken. They do not mean to disappoint, nevertheless you are deflated by fallible human beings. The only remedy is to stop seeking answers outside of yourself.

Now that I have gotten you turned back in the right direction, I'd like to discuss how to keep yourself on this, the happiest of tracks, your inner track. It isn't easy to stay inwardly focused when your five senses are outwardly focused. Your eyes turn outward to see the world, your hands reach out, your ears hear sounds of the environment, and your mouth and nose smell and taste what is outside of you. Even your body covered in skin is a sensing organ. Therefore, turning inward seems foreign to you. Your eyes, ears, hands, mouth and nose, even your whole body tells you to pay attention to your environment. It is counter-intuitive to turn away from the world, am I right? Yet you must withdraw from the five senses to make spiritual progress, observing silence long enough to contact your Soul. I am reminding you of what you have already heard, but everyone needs a reminder. You will forget this message again, for the senses will convince you to look outside of yourself for answers while nothing could be farther from the truth! You are a Soul first and a body second. The moment you die, your outward body will fall away as your Soul leaps out and stands apart from your body. What a weight off! You must train yourself to listen to your Soul for it has all the answers you've been searching for. If you do, you'll be smarter and happier than others, even those who call themselves rulers or religious leaders. You will stand head and shoulders above them because you will be living on a higher plane than they are. Outwardly focused, they will not be privy to the peace, tranquility and equanimity you enjoy. Go within when you are stressed and troubled, and there you will find peace.

Message 29-The Stuff That Dreams Are Made Of

There are four brainwaves, and each emits a different electronic frequency. The waking brainwave called Beta is earth's frequency. Alpha, also known as the Hypnosis brainwave, is a slower frequency, and exists in a different dimension. In Alpha, you receive hypnagogic imagery from the brainstem; you have entered the land of the subconscious when in Alpha. The subconscious mind is connected to the Other Side. You feel otherworldly while meditating because you have accessed the subconscious in Alpha. In Theta (REM sleep), you dream, and in Delta you are in deep, restful sleep where your Soul can recharge and recover from the day's craziness. The Delta brainwave is also when information from the Other Side is being downloaded to you. Of all the brain waves, Theta or REM sleep is the most dynamic, for in Theta have you entered a dimension in which wrongs can be made right. Sigmund Freud figured this out and referred to dreaming as, "wish fulfillment." What appears to you as a dream is in fact occurring in another dimension. Dreams can seem so real for in another dimension they are! The purpose of dreaming is to complete all unfinished business, to fulfill that which your Soul longs for, and this is the purpose of the first Heaven. As I've mentioned, there are seven Kingdoms or Heavens, but humans only have access to the first Kingdom, and only during Theta sleep. Theta comes from the word "Theos," meaning relating to God or deities, an apt name for this dimension. As you dream, you interact with the first Heaven. Of course, you don't remember most of these interactions, and when you awaken with faint recollections, the facts have already been distorted by the waking mind. It edits and "cleans up" the scene so that it makes more sense to the analytical left-brain. Your recollection of even vivid dreams has been rearranged before you awaken so that you never accurately recall all of what has happened.

If dreams are for wish fulfillment, you may be wondering why nightmares occur. Why are evil and frightening dreams part of sleep? As I've mentioned, humanity's current paradigm about good and evil, light and dark forces is still so rudimentary that it is problematic to explain why "evil' is allowed as part of the overall evolutionary plan. Nonetheless, I will endeavor to explain. To draw on a simple analogy: Children learn the hard way. Hard lessons must be had before a child fully appreciates the importance of their choices, isn't this right? If you shield a child from all painful experiences, would they grow into strong people, able to stand on their own? Similarly, whatever dose of darkness you experience in a dream has been allowed to shake the sleepy scales from your eyes. In dreams, you must encounter evil as well as good, just as you must experience rain to appreciate the sunshine. The presence of evil is better tolerated while dreaming than in the awakened state. If you were to encounter the same ghosts, monsters or demons in the flesh, I daresay you would walk about dreading the next unexpected frightful encounter, so these confrontations are confined to the dream world. Bad dreams are an expedient way of teaching you about the dark side without serious traumatization. Do you see the wisdom even in this? The first Heaven will teach you lessons of courage, and this includes overcoming dark forces.

Many would like to understand how to correctly interpret their dreams, and while psychology has attempted methods of interpretation, they are mistaken in thinking you can use the bits and pieces of the left brain to make an accurate interpretation. While modern Dream Work is an intriguing study, it is like using a few bones to reconstruct a whole dinosaur. You'll never deduce the entire meaning of the dream due to interference from the left brain. When you've had a nightmare, it's exposing you to negative energy disguised in different forms. More accurately, you're encountering Thought Forms who have taken on the visage of a ghost, a murderer or a monster. Evil can threaten, but it hasn't any real power to harm you in a dream; not really. And in truth, even those murdered, those whose lives were taken violently and who were most terrified at the time of death would tell you that like taking a bath that washed away any remnant of evil, as soon as they crossed over into eternity the earthly "nightmare" was rinsed away and what they experienced was an immense, peaceful relief, because the torture of life was over.

The life you are living is the real nightmare. Once you take your first steps onto the terra firma of Heaven, it will all seem like a bad dream. You'll see that what you called dreams were more real than "life" for your dreams are a peek into the first Heaven. On the Other Side, your earthly life will be the dream you can barely remember, and it will fade from your consciousness as surely and easily as you've forgotten last night's dream. Your current incarnation will slip from your memory and you will gladly let it slip. Your deceased loved ones are not so concerned with remembering you, for you were part of that faint and difficult nightmare. Their love for you will endure, but they wish to leave behind the dust of their earthly journey. They have traveled such a long way that once the Life Review and Orientation have been accomplished, they are eager to press on. They're itching to get on to new adventures and challenges-new teachers, new friends, and more glorious sagas in which they will be the legendary figures in fairytale worlds. It makes one eager to be a dreamer, does it not?

Message 30: The Butterfly King & The Rainbow Mother

The collective unconscious, also known as the Universal Library, Akashic Record or Book of Life, has stored every action, thought and feeling of all entities across time and space since the inception of its respective race. In effect, it is an intergalactic library and you are one of its books. Your civilization is being monitored and recorded through you and uploaded to the Book of Life as you sleep. Most humans are under the misconception that their behaviors only affect themselves. The fact is, throughout humanity's history, I, Metatron have kept the record still being written of the Human Experiment. Angels and other beings you would describe as extraterrestrials are closely monitoring your movements, allowing enough room for you to learn from your mistakes, and to develop, and this is the will of God. Divine Mother, The Counsel of True Judges and planetary leaders are lending their assistance as you develop your intellects and exercise your sovereign wills. It is our fervent hope that you will learn to become peacemakers, to evolve beyond aggression. We are holding back further contact while viewing everything as if we were watching you on television. You watch TV shows depicting aliens and angels, while we watch you watching crude depictions of us! How ironic is that?

How can the entire history of a planet and its many civilizations be stored in an etheric library; you may be wondering? It is a matter of technology you have yet to come to. There was a time that you couldn't believe it was possible to fly to the moon, but you did. So many problems you've solved with a nudge from the Other Side. We implant ideas, innovative methods and formulas into your brains, mostly while you are in Delta sleep. Upon awakening you perform your morning rituals and then: "Ah ha-I've got it!" The answer seems to come from nowhere, from the invisible ethers. We simply downloaded the needed missing bits of information. Progressive ideas that have advanced your civilization by leaps and bounds came to you by way of your Spirit Guides who act as conduits of knowledge and information. They have an important job because they are the instruments by which humanity is inching itself forward. They access the Akashic Record, determine the best path forward, and implant ideas into your subconscious as you sleep. They know you inside and out, having taken you on as a life-long assignment. They can tell when you've struggled long enough with a problem and are needing assistance. When you are stuck, they go to the Universal Library and study to see what course of action will ultimately be in your best interest. They may review your past incarnations, your current projections, and discuss the issue with your Master Oversoul.

If it can't be deciphered what the logical next step is, your karmic team that includes your Guardian Angels, ancestors, and loved ones may assist your Guide in which way to turn you. It is like that: we get you turned a certain direction by implanting a new idea, and set you lose. We stand back and hold our breath to see what you will do with this new knowledge-how will you implement it? You develop your own powers of reasoning by solving problems. If we made decisions for you, you would worship us as Gods and be our little slaves. We don't need slaves; we are in a perfect environment that doesn't require the necessities of survival. We don't want a hoard of robots doing our bidding. Instead, humans were created as a free-will species to see how far you can come towards us. Given enough time, your species will evolve into greatness, for you have potentialities that are supernatural, possessing divine DNA, and your full capabilities are yet to be leveraged. Therefore, if you have a problem, remember an answer can be found within the vast annals of the Universal Library, and your Spirit Guide has access to this treasure-trove of unlimited information. Why then aren't all your problems solved? Why doesn't the average person wake up the next morning with the solution dancing in their heads? Because you are not plugged in, that's why. Most of you are like a brilliant computer sitting next to the electrical outlet but you haven't plugged yourself into the power source.

How does one plug-in to cosmic consciousness and get it working for her? If you practice doing two things, you will be way ahead of other people and answers will become clear. First, plug into your Spirit Guide who can access all the answers. At face value, that may sound simple, but when you begin spirit communications, you'll find it's not as simple as it sounds, for the brain constantly interferes. The brain is the gatekeeper that questions every answer, especially answers that come from an invisible source. The brain doesn't take kindly to the unseen. When new approaches or imaginative thoughts enter its domain, it may dispute them simply because they're unfamiliar. It may doubt their validity because they are new. The brain's central duty is your protection and survival, so foreign thoughts can alarm it. Your brain thinks it is doing you a big favor, it thinks it is protecting you by being the critical gatekeeper, but the brain has an overactive startle response. Your brain will regularly catastrophize. It will think up the worst scenarios and play them to keep you from danger. While this is good for survival, it's problematic when you need to think outside of the box. Information coming to you from the Other Side will most definitely stretch your thinking! But unless you think larger, how will you grow?

Secondly, you must see yourself as a benevolent and powerful force, a force to be reckoned with! You must realize the truth of why you are here: you are not here to populate the earth or to get rich. You are here to grow as a person-that is why you are here. Self-growth is the most important thing you can hope to achieve. You are here to enrich your brain by educating it, and to use that knowledge to help build a better tomorrow. If you are stuck in a rut, if you are doing the same thing you were doing years ago and saying the same things you said years ago, if you haven't created anything new or exciting, then you may be stuck in a rut. It isn't the worst thing, but you won't be very exciting to be around.

Beyond that, you won't be exercising the divinity within, that vibrant, creative spark. There's a battle waging, and the battle is being fought in your mind *for* your mind. The mind will become less reactive and more cooperative when you accept that you are here to grow. Why fight your own growth? Everyday remind yourself: 'New news is good news, and different is okay.' The poor brain-it fields so much sensory input that it gets overloaded. When this happens, it automatically rejects what it doesn't understand, because to think in new ways requires extra effort. When you find yourself overwhelmed, it's time to retreat. Withdraw from the madness and you'll find creative and innovative answers lying at your feet. If you work with your karmic team and not against them there's no end to the brilliant ideas that will come into that head of yours.

Your Soul is a marvelous cosmic spaceship. It will take you to lives and worlds yet unknown to you. Your Soul is also treasure chest, and at the proper time, facets of your divine nature will be unlocked, and you will shine and be revealed for the gem that you are. There must be enough people who have unlocked their Souls, who have freed their Souls from the material lie, before the truth can be revealed to the world. Truth can only be absorbed once deception is removed. The earth is in a phase of purification wherein deception is being purged. Before a new foundation can be laid, the old structure must crumble. Before the earth and Her inhabitants can pass into a cycle of redemption that will utilize a higher system of thought, a non-violent way of living must become the standard. During the deconstruction of the tyrannical system, evil will rise to the surface. Evil plans and institutions will be uncovered and seen for what they are. A time of reckoning and a new accountability will be imposed until the corrupt and dishonest will have nowhere left to hide. People of many religious faiths and nations, of many tribes and societies will again esteem the wisdom of the ancient truth-tellers. Those who were spiritually asleep will wake up as if they had been under a spell, as if they had been shaken from their slumber. For those in deep sleep who denied their spiritual Self, their security will be shaken and rattled to the core. Even they will see the light, opening their spiritual eyes for the first time. This purification will flush out societal toxins, rooting out the impure. What was once tolerated will no longer stand, for a higher standard will be imposed. These changes will transform the whole world. They will not be instantaneous, for progress is a gradual wearing-away process, like water dripping on a rock. But relatively speaking, implementation of new values will happen at a very fast pace once new leaders have taken their place. There will be upheaval in governments; once wealthy nations will change positions with nations they once conquered in battle.

Part of this massive moral purge will involve the extermination of organized religion. This may sound impossible to your ears or perhaps blasphemous, for these institutions have controlled and influenced the masses since humanity's early days. This purification will reach into the bowels of humanity's psyche, clearing away religious myths and misconceptions about God. In the place of gross division and abuse of religious power will come a genuine religion that exalts and magnifies the four elements of nature (earth, wind, water and fire). It will protect the animal kingdom and care for the earth. The symbol of the butterfly will be revered as holy, for it is an accurate metaphor of the Soul's journey. The Soul will be worshiped instead of the body, for the body is only a fragile outer shell discarded at death.

There will be a Butterfly King, and He will reign over a humanitarian and planetary religion. He will present as a butterfly during festivals, but He will not lead alone. In a religion where the Soul's many incarnations are revered, the feminine will be exalted, and a Queen will rule equally and be represented by the rainbow, and you will be Her rainbow people. The rainbow will symbolize the beautiful diversity of the peoples of the earth who have joined in a brightly colored display. This Mother of Rainbows will not esteem one nation higher than another, nor will one color be exalted over another. This universal religion will not happen until all impurities have been rooted out, but by the year 2050, light will overtake the darkness. The Butterfly King and Rainbow Mother will emerge thereafter to lead humanity, and there will be no more fear, no more tears, no more war, and no more destruction of planet earth or taking of innocent lives.

And what will become of the evildoers? They will be driven underground. They will live in caverns in the bowels of the earth, to ensure the safety of the earth and its inhabitants. This is the Hell that prophets have seen in visions. The evil ones will live beneath the righteous one's feet, because they refused to abandon their treacherous ways. There are underground caverns even now that will be used as prisons large enough to house the violent and criminally insane, bent Souls who refuse to surrender their dark plans and thinking, who persist in scheming to overthrow the pure in heart. This is their fate: a self-imposed world of insanity. And these will dwell in the bowels of the earth until their karmic sentence has been served. But anyone willing to live by the law of love has nothing to fear and will help to establish the New Zion, the Kingdom of the Children of the Rainbow.

These changes will be for the greater good and should be welcomed with open arms. There is a plan to save the world from destruction, of course there is! Would a God so brilliant and compassionate not rescue His own children? Would a Mother so full of tender mercy and love abandon Her children when She hears them cry? There has always been a plan for you to set you on the right path. Though your eyes might not live to see the liberation of humanity, Heaven's plan for redemption will not falter. Mother Earth, her children so distressed, and Her many precious creatures will finally rest in peace. After the King and Queen establish a Heaven on earth, there will be lasting justice such as the world has never seen. I promise you, there is nothing to fear, for God is in control, as it has always been and forevermore will be.

Epilogue from Archangel Metatron

I hold the Book of Deeds in my hands wherein your lives are recorded. If your life is held in the palm of an angel's hand, what is there to fear? Death is nothing more than a shedding of your false self, an assuming of your truest identity. Would a snake mourn for its old skin? Would a butterfly long for the dark captivity of the cocoon? These creatures know better than to dwell on the past, for it has past. You must endeavor to live this way: leaving behind the struggles, mistakes and trespasses. Some wander a whole lifetime without knowing why they must endure the rigors of life. But you are different, for you hold in your hand this lamp which elders from the High Counsel in High Realms has ordered be written. A simple scribe has pulled this map from her subconscious where it was placed before she was born. Like sunken treasure in the depths of her mind, it came back to her. Her Guardian Angel Rory served as the conduit, the true "channel" from my dimension to yours, for Guardian Angels of her classification are made to withstand the lower, denser vibrations of the mortal realm. For this reason, I, the Master Archangel, was not able to abide long and visited infrequently to speak with Rory to collect her report. The angelic presence that the author felt was her Spirit Guide, acting as my intermediary. You see, I am ancient, and my manner of speaking is antiquated, so I need a translator of sorts. I feel Rory has proven her skills as an accomplished translator, and for this selfless act she will be given higher assignments which will increase her ability to work with the Archangels, so we have Rory to thank for a job well done. Speaking of Archangels, I am eager to educate humanity about our personalities and powers. Hence, a flood of information about the Archangels will be delivered. Many celestial creatures look after Mother God's children, and we the Archangels wish to be known, so we will be approaching humans. Why now, you wonder?

The earth is groaning in pain and we want you lightworkers to be ready to catch the new wave, the next spiritual birth. Have you seen numbers repeated, especially 11:11? It is a numerological sign, meaning it is the 11th hour! At the 12th hour, the earth's time will be complete-the algorithm will have run its course. The New Renaissance will step forward and be placed into the capable hands of the enlightened ones, *and you are that enlightened one*. Therefore, denounce your fear, for fear is nothing compared to you! Fear is only a figment of your imagination. It is a decoy talking you into embracing the Material Lie. Lay down your precious plans for security and comfort, for you must unveil Spirit's agenda, and this agenda cannot go where negativity, anger, greed and lust are. The nature of Light erases all shadow and blemish-it obliterates the darkness, flooding it completely. What happens to a room when a light is turned on? The darkness flees. If you have a genuine desire to usher in more unity, more solutions, more breakthroughs, then you must find all the corners of your heart where darkness exists and root it out. Contact the spiritual realm and you will be taken by the hand by your Spirit helpers. If you don't know how to reach them, instead of thinking, "I'm going to meditate," or, "I'm going to pray," it is more helpful to think, "I want a spiritual experience I've never had before." Seeking the experience is the door and your willingness acts as the key. It's not wrong to seek an ecstatic experience for it connects you to a higher dimension. Once you've tasted expanded consciousness, you'll desire that your whole life be saturated with that glory. You'll display more and more of your true Self, which is the Soul, and people will see less and less of your ego. The farther you walk in the Spirit realm the more unique you'll become and the less you will care to play the fitting in game. There are billions of "fitter-inners" on earth which is what the world does to you. It steals your individuality until you begin to judge others for theirs. The best thing you will ever do is to run from conformity! God is not a fan of sameness-only look at nature to see this. So much time is wasted trying to please others, trying to be liked, trying to look the "right away," trying to live the cookie-cutter life men have fashioned. Funny, small, fearing creatures! Rise above the constricting limits of matter to discover who you are. If you must, disappoint those you love. In the end, you will be answering to God, not to anyone else-keep that in mind.

I have enjoyed keeping company with you. The time Devi Nina spent channeling were many and long hours to her, while in my realm I stayed only minutes to deliver my message and assess the state of the world. Time is my plaything; I can lengthen the hand of time or stop time in its tracks. Angels play with the perception of time while you are stuck in mortal time, a stagnant, stifling sort of measurement which I and my kind do not fit into. To visit earth, I stepped out of my frame of reference into your own. I observed humanity for what would be many hours of earth time, and what I observed reminded me how real is the struggle between the ego and the Soul! My visit made me more inclined to send the Archangels to monitor the work of the Spirit Guides. They are doing a commendable job and I appreciate each one's efforts, but I see they are running out of answers, which is why humanity is running out of answers. As it is in Heaven, so it is on earth. Therefore, I will increase the presence of angelic helpers and fortify the Spirit Guides, for the mortal climb to conquer the ego has grown steeper. I'm glad I spent time on earth-it cements my resolve to intervene and introduce the Archangels to you.

When I refer to the New Earth, I speak of the end of the old algorithm, a day when the Human Experiment will end. Will this be a terrible day, or wonderful day, you ask? That depends upon you, doesn't it? So much is riding on your day-to-day choices. To affect a smooth transition from the Dark Age of Kali to the age of enlightenment, there is only one thing you must do: work on yourself. When you awaken, others will too, simply by listening to you and being in your presence. There is more to tell of Heaven later, but for now, know there are universes and worlds more diverse and fantastic that await. But as I've said, to give away our secrets is to spoil the surprise. I have great compassion for you; I have become quite fond of you all. I love each of you very much. Most of all, I am very proud of you. I'm giving you a big angelic hug. You know what to do, so go and do it with all your might.

I am with you always,

Lord Archangel Metatron

Workbook: Messages From Metatron

LESSON 1-Judge Not

"The natural consequences of your decisions must play themselves out. Angelic beings cannot interfere with the natural progression of things."

There are times we would like to be rescued from difficult or bitter circumstances, or at least be given a helping hand. While Metatron makes it clear that angels, Spirit Guides and our ancestors can see us, visit us, and know what is happening, He emphasizes that they cannot relieve us of the natural consequences of our actions. It seems cruel when bad things happen to good people, especially when Heaven knows what is happening. People turn away from God because they have difficulty reconciling a good and loving God with tragedy and pain. But this message helps us to understand that we cannot blame God for our free will choices, for we were created as sovereign beings. His very first message instructs that while our karmic team protects and guides us, there are rules they must follow. A fundamental rule is not to interfere with the consequences of our free will decisions.

"Know that every one of you will be tested. Upon inspection, even the worst traumas will seem nearly inconsequential when you see how they were perfectly fashioned for your evolution."

"The concept of morality-of you being able to distinguish good from evil, is ludicrous."

Throughout this book, a theme is repeated: You cannot judge what is right from wrong, nor can you judge good from evil, because you're not seeing the whole picture. Metatron says it's not until we get to the Other Side that our vision becomes free of bias and fear, and we will see the truth. Another theme emphasized is that we are all one; we are connected, even when we feel most alone. Our actions and choices have a ripple effect; they always touch someone else. Therefore, we ought to think before we act and speak, because the law of karma says that everything sent out from us will return to us. If I send out good vibes, I can expect good vibes back. Though we think we comprehend the bigger picture, in truth, we see only a fraction of our interconnectedness. We cannot know the impact of our actions until we step away from this life. Metatron says we must practice suspending judgement as much as we can, leaving that to God.

Summary Lesson 1:

1. There is no eternal damnation for any Soul and no punishment in Heaven.
2. Evil Souls will continue to reincarnate with their negative karma.
3. Humanity is not advanced enough to comprehend the complex concept of good and evil.
4. The greatest error of the human mind is to pass judgement.
5. All sins are equally egregious in eternity.

6. Angels are different from humans because they are immortal.
7. Angels watch your Soul grow.
8. Angel's cannot change the outcome of free will decisions.
9. Angel's duties include: protection, guidance and comfort.
10. "Close calls" and "good luck" are angels intervening for you.
11. Angels can take your prayers to the Counsel of True Judges and ask that your Life Chart be modified.
12. Angels and Spirit Guides feel your sorrow and joys.
13. Immortal beings admire human courage.
14. You agree to everything that happens to you before you incarnate.
15. Every trial is allowed by God, and a "great cloud of witnesses" are rooting for you.
16. After death you will be reunited with your Soulmates.
17. In Heaven every deed is known.
18. After death you will submit to a "Life Review."
19. Call on your Guides, Angels and ancestors for help, for they can hear and see you.

EXERCISE 1: Attempt to walk through your day without placing judgement or blame.

When you feel the need to criticize or correct someone, deny that urge. Practice tolerance and observe silence. Hold your tongue and keep the peace, putting aside your opinions, and listen instead. You might be surprised how regularly you're tempted to judge, and how difficult it is to remain the silent observer rather than the opinionated authority.

Study Questions: How difficult is it to refrain from judging people and circumstances? What makes it so challenging? When you practice tolerance and silence, what do you notice about yourself? How do others respond to tolerance? Was anything about this exercise surprising?

LESSON 2-Not My Will

"Your popular representation of God is a creation of fearful minds which demand answers, which fashion answers in their own image, but this is not God."

"What you have is a relationship with your own projection of God."

It's human to humanize God; we don't relate easily to the spirit realm. We like to think we understand ourselves and one another, but we can't comprehend a spirit, except to say it is composed of energy. We don't feel wholly comfortable with the idea of angels and Spirit Guides because we cannot see them. The Scientific Method tells us that whatever cannot be measured and verified is not real. Yet, a relatively new branch of science, Quantum Physics, has demonstrated that there is a subatomic world beyond our senses, a world that defies scientific explanation. The quantum world is a wacky one in which the "laws" of physics break down, leaving even the most intelligent scientists scratching their heads. Science has theories (lots of theories) but admits that there is more unknown than known about the universe. We don't even know the capacity of the human brain! If we know less than more about the universe and ourselves, it behooves us to admit that there is still a lot to learn, especially about the supreme intelligence we call "God."

You cannot blame humans for attributing to God human feelings because emotions are shared by humans worldwide, regardless of gender or culture. We all share certain powerful emotions: love, jealousy, fear, sorrow, disgust, anger, and joy, as well as guilt, shame, and pride. It's only natural that our Creator should have these emotions, too. God created feelings, didn't He? And that's another issue: it's difficult for us to think in gender-neutral terms. Yet logically, if God is a spirit, God defies categories of male or female. But our feelings about God aren't logical! They're emotional. We attribute to God our own feelings and even a gender. Perhaps we don't know God as well as we think we do; perhaps what we know is what we have been taught.

"You are an unthinkably superior creator. You create your own reality."

"You must decide if you will do the will of your mind, or will you do the will of your Higher Self?"

Metatron calls us amazing creators, and explains we have two wills: the ego and the Higher Self, or what he refers to as the Oversoul. Most of us aren't aware that we are astoundingly creative, nor are we aware of our Higher Self. What we're used to is the familiar cognitive chatter in our heads; the thinking we do. Depending on the day, it may be zany inside our heads or rather dull. We might be thinking fast or slow, but a constant stream of thought carries us through the day. The moment we open our eyes, we climb aboard for the wild ride. We don't usually question our thoughts; they often run amok. When left unchecked, negative thinking can cause depression or anxiety, fear and panic. Thoughts are compelling forces in our lives, and cause humanity to do some crazy things!

Metatron reminds us that whatever reality we experience is created by our thoughts. He says we can listen to our own thoughts or listen to our Higher Self. But what *is* the Higher Self?

If it is a *higher* self, it is elevated above our normal reasoning. It's superior; more logical and less emotional. I like this voice already! To borrow a phrase from psychology, it is the "Wise Mind." It asks us to be our best selves, to "rise above" base emotions and drives, and to think in expanded ways-more inclusively (after all, we can get a tad myopic). Metatron is asking us to separate our mind's chatter from the Soul of us, and to listen hard for the more advanced thinker inside, what has been referred to as "the observer." Part of us can stand apart from our problems, taking it all in without losing it. We are urged to get in touch with that Wise Mind, the Observer, and to let it do the driving. I guess you could say: let go and let God.

Think about what it feels like when you are being your wisest, most capable self. It's a feeling of power, isn't it? It can feel euphoric when answers are pouring through you unimpeded. You feel in control of yourself, but there is also a freedom to be yourself, while letting others be themselves. You are more patient than normal-more confident, and more self-reliant. Your "wise mind" thinks more creatively and solves problems with unusual efficiency. In times like these, your Higher Self may be directing the show.

Summary Lesson 2:

1. We project human traits onto God in an effort to understand God.
2. It is impossible to comprehend God, for God transcends human characteristics.
3. God is not outside of yourself but within you in the form of your Soul.
4. You create your own reality by projection of thought.
5. Over the course of many lives you will learn to trust your Soul.
6. You will face trials in which old answers will fail you. These trials cause you to grow.
7. God is in everything and everywhere, thus we have a symbiotic relationship with God.
8. The highest spiritual precept is that of oneness.
9. On earth there is no justice.
10. Be careful that wealth and power don't rob you of spiritual attainment.
11. God will not rescue you because you have a free will. God and the angels cannot interfere with your decisions.
12. The Cosmic Elders approved your Life Plan.
13. God loves you regardless of your behavior.

EXERCISE 2: Getting Connected to Your Higher Self

It's simple to get connected to your Higher Self. To get connected, sit silently, turning your focus inward, away from the external world to your internal world. In the center of your chest is your Soul, animating you. Close your eyes and imagine searching for and finding the Soul part of you. Visualize what your Soul looks like. Maybe you picture the Soul as a see-through outline called the ethereal body. Once you've imagined it, feel the connection and bond to that central part of you. It will feel as unbreakable and unshakable as a rock. Simply sit with it. Get still and relax. Breathe deeply. If you're able to, recline. Feel the air entering and leaving your body. Feel the difference between the body and the Soul yet see that you are both. Feel the beauty and the miracle of being part body and part eternal spirit.

Now imagine God as pure spirit with unlimited creative energy. Imagine angels around God that can be seen as pure lights. Imagine seeing loved ones that have passed on existing in this wonderfully free and fluid state. Imagine what it would feel like to be this calm and at home, yet "yourself" all the time. Stay with your Higher Self for a few moments, enjoying the view. Breathe deeply, lavishing in the timelessness and grandeur that is the Soul. Before you get moving again, promise yourself that you'll visit this refreshing inner landscape on a more regular basis.

Study Questions: Could you feel the difference between the body and the Soul? Describe what the body felt like. Now describe what the Soul felt like. What are steps you can take to listen less to the everyday mind and tune into the Higher Self?

LESSON 3-You'll Always Have a Mother

"Among enlightened avatars, having a vision of Mother God was a sign of momentous favor."

"Why then do you still doubt her reality?"

We live in a decidedly paternalistic world. Even in America where individual rights are protected by the United States Constitution that guarantees the right to "life, liberty, and the pursuit of happiness," there is still injustice. The rights of minorities, women and children are trampled on or disregarded in many parts of the world; but it wasn't always this way. Archaeological records suggest that Asherah was once venerated as the Mother Goddess and honored as the Wife of God in ancient Israel. Images of the Mother Goddess graced household shrines, for She was revered as Father God's counterpart, His consort. Mother God was worshiped as a powerful, but nurturing and comforting deity. Inscriptions from ancient Israel show that Yahweh and "His Asherah" were invoked together for protection.

Her name appears 40 times in other translations of the Bible, but was removed from the first English translation, the King James Bible. By the 17th century when the King James Version (KJV) was created, references to the Mother Goddess were given a paternalistic translation as "a grove of trees," for the forest is where Asherah was worshipped. Without knowledge of her existence, Mother God was abandoned by the Israelites. Yet in Genesis 1:26,

Elohim (Father God) says: "Let *us* make man in our image, in *our* likeness, and let them rule over the fish of the sea and the birds of the air, over the livestock, over all the earth, and over all the creatures that move along the ground." One must wonder if the words "our" and "us" refers to a mother deity since there is a male and female of everything. Archaeology uncovered the truth: Asherah's memory was purposefully silenced. But according to the earliest Bible, God has a feminine counterpart (Queen of Heaven, 2011).

"It is only fear of the unknown and unfamiliar which keeps you from seeing Her."

It takes a lot of guts to question authority-especially religious doctrines, because for centuries the Church condemned people to eternal damnation who disagreed with the them. They even burned to death those they judged to be heretical. We've been told by the patriarchs that questioning religious tradition is rebellion against God. But archeology is one of the sciences that has helped humanity sort historical fact from fiction. Because archaeologists have found convincing evidence that a Mother God was worshiped by many cultures including the Israelites, and was later edited out of the Bible, we must ask ourselves: *Why* was the Mother Goddess removed? And further, why has religion punished those who dared to question the teachings of the Church?

Metatron answers these questions by saying it is fear that has kept us apart from our Mother. Like a child adopted by well-meaning but fearing parents, we were not told about our real Mother; the existence of our Divine Mother was withheld from us. As people evolve they may grow apart from the Church. People on a journey to Self-realization begin to question what they've been told by institutions, and may develop a longing for Mother God's assuring, maternal embrace. The deep longing to find your spiritual Mother is ancient and written into your psyche. Metatron encourages you to cry out for Mother God as a child would cry out for its mother, and to ask for a sign, a confirmation of Her existence. Metatron is urging us not to let fear keep us apart from the Mother who loves us.

Summary Lesson 3:

1. Father God is pure intellect while Mother God is pure heart.
2. Without Mother God's powers there would be no life as we know it.
3. Christian patriarchs intentionally eliminated Mother God from the scriptures.
4. When females are venerated on the earth Mother God's memory will be resurrected.
5. In meditation or prayer ask to be given a vision of Mother God, a sign of her reality.
6. Mother God has a warrior spirit, yet She is also the Goddess of Compassion.

EXERCISE 3: Recite The Lord's Prayer

We have been taught to pray: "Our Father." While there's nothing wrong with approaching Father God, if you have never approached Mother God, you're only getting half of the blessing. Pray this prayer or your own prayer, requesting proof of Mother God's reality.

The Lord's Prayer Translated from Aramaic-A
Translation of "Our Father" directly from Aramaic into English

O cosmic Birther of all radiance and vibration. Soften the ground of our being and carve out a space within us where your Presence can abide.
Fill us with your creativity so that we may be empowered to bear the fruit of your mission.
Let each of our actions bear fruit in accordance with our desire.
Endow us with the wisdom to produce and share what each being needs to grow and flourish.
Untie the tangled threads of destiny that bind us, as we release others from the entanglement of past mistakes.
Do not let us be seduced by that which would divert us from our true purpose but illuminate the opportunities of the present moment.
For you are the ground and the fruitful vision, the birth, power and fulfillment, as all is gathered and made whole once again.

Study Questions: What have you been taught about Mother God? Do you wish you had been taught about Mother God, and if so, why? When you recited this prayer (or your own prayer) to the Divine Mother, did it feel different from praying to Father God? If so, how was it different? Did any pictures or images come to mind?

LESSON 4-A Mother's Love

"Perhaps you have steered clear of love, numbing yourself with activity."

"Dreams are the embers of the Soul."

Every person has maternal feelings inside; even the toughest hombre has a "soft spot" for a family member, a lover, or a pet. We can't help but love, for we were designed to love. Those who cannot feel love or empathy for anyone but themselves are troubled. Devoid of love, darkness reigns. In a letter from Mother God, She identifies herself as "Love's Mother," the originator of love. We've been taught that Father God is love, but Mother God declares that She birthed the experience of loving. What a wonderful Mother!

She gives us something to think about when She says we've kept busy, so we don't have to feel love. What does she mean? Keeping busy and productive is healthy. It increases our self-esteem when we accomplish goals. But many people are so busy that they do not have time to be loving: they forsake family time to earn more money, thinking that is what it takes to impress. Single people can forsake love by giving up on finding someone all together when they've been disappointed by the past. Similarly, the rich may close their hearts to the needy because they don't want to imagine that they could be needy. And close-minded people condemn others who are different from themselves because they can't relate. For many reasons, humans refuse to feel. As Mother articulates so perfectly in Her letter to humanity, we "steer clear of love." But She reminds us that we shouldn't give up on being loving, implying love is like an ember which, if stoked, can come alive again. Opening to love leads to passion, whether that be passion for a lover, or the passion to accomplish a goal.

Mother God states that the first step in getting reconnected to our loving nature is the characteristic of openness. Openness includes a willingness to risk. Without risk there is no rekindling of passion. The willingness to risk is attached to any success. You can't taste sweet success unless you are willing to take a chance, to go out on a limb for what you want.

"People have hurt you not because you weren't lovely enough, but because they were in pain; they were showing you their wounds."

Many people struggle with feelings of inadequacy, the feeling of being not "good enough." Everyone experiences inadequacy from time to time. And those who feel confident 24-7 probably shouldn't! Psychology tells us that Narcissists are people who project an image of perfection to the world. But most people cannot relate to a perfect person. We may admire the Narcissist for all he has accomplished, but we don't experience the round-the-clock superhuman confidence that the Narcissist seems to have. Most of us are aware of our faults and failures, so when we experience rejection, it really hurts! It reinforces that we have "cracks in our fault lines" when someone that we love or admire points them out to us. Rejection leads to broken relationships, broken marriages, and broken hearts.

Metatron tells us that when someone rejects us, they are incapable of loving as they should, but that doesn't mean we are not worthy of love. We are not unlovable because someone has turned away from us; Metatron asks us to make that distinction.

Summary Lesson 4:

1. In Heaven, Mother God is known as the Mother of Love because She is romantic and sentimental.
2. In the center of every heart is the need to be loved.
3. Falling in love is encouraged.
4. To resist loving is to resist the universal law of love.
5. Don't allow past heartbreak to keep you from loving again.
6. To dare to love is to overcome fear.
7. There is nothing you cannot accomplish if you have something passionate to say and someone passionately to love.
8. Live with passion.
9. Being alone is more difficult than the pain of loving.
10. It is necessary to love to grow.
11. The only one keeping you from loving is yourself.

EXERCISE 4: Living with Passion

Living with passion could mean having a romantic relationship, but it also refers to pursuing your dreams. Write a list of dreams you have for the future. Review your list, then ask yourself: Is there anything I want that isn't on this list because I am afraid to hope for it? If so, add that hoped-for item to your list. And while you are at it, write down why you're hesitant to include it. Example: "I hope to buy a house at the ocean. I'm hesitant to want it because I don't know if I can afford it." Just the act of writing down a hoped-for goal is a powerful first step towards achieving it. Your unconscious mind will set to work figuring out a way to bring it to pass because intention is a powerful force.

Study Questions: Think of a big rejection you suffered in the past. Ask yourself: how did it feel to be rejected? How did it affect your self-esteem? Did it affect your willingness to reach out again? When you encounter rejection, what can you do to remember that you are still worthy of love and "good enough" regardless of how others respond?

LESSON 5-Using the Soul to Forgive

"Love is the gesture of sharing. Love extends outward- it gives something of itself, this is the nature of love."

"At the heart of all suffering is the inability to let go."

The love that Hollywood depicts is romantic and passionate. Movies and novels allow us to be swept away in a fairytale where every misunderstood guy turns into a prince, and the heroin is rescued from the perils of real life. Cut to ten years later, and you'll find the same couple drowning in bills, kids, career, and responsibilities-the inescapable duties of life. But for all the changes that time will bring, one thing about their relationship will never change: it will always require them to "give something of themselves." True love isn't self-centered, it is other-centered.

Becoming a parent also requires a selflessness that places the needs of the child first. The nature of love is selfless but many of us struggle to share our time and attention, even with the ones we love the most. While the nature of love is giving, human nature can be self-centered.

Have you noticed that part of maturing is learning to let go of the people you love, and sometimes you must let go whether you're ready to or not? We must let go when people or pets die, because of divorce, when a relationship ends, or when children grow up and leave home. We change jobs, and over the course of a lifetime, we even change friends. The only certain thing in life is change!

Yet we struggle to let go; our hearts don't seem to know when it's time to move on. When Metatron makes the statement: "At the heart of all suffering is the inability to let go," He's referring to grief. Learning to let go is as important as learning to hold on. You've got to let your children do their own thing, you've got to let your partner be their own person, and you have to say goodbye when someone dies. When you hold on too tightly it can be smothering and can drive people away. Or you might become controlling, dominating others to get your way. These are unattractive attributes because they are the opposite of love. Love is an open hand.

"The Christ Consciousness looks out to the world and says, "I can forgive you, because I am complete, totally without flaw, and unforgiveness is a flaw."

Because it's important to forgive, Metatron instructs us to forgive with the consciousness of Christ. What does this mean? There are two parts of a human being: the material "us" (the brain and body), and the immaterial "us" (the Soul). When Metatron says to forgive others using the Christ Consciousness, He means to forgive others using the Soul part of us. But how do we use the Soul to forgive?

It is difficult to forgive others on our own steam because it's impossible to forget what was done. Metatron isn't suggesting that we pretend it never happened. Instead, He is saying to allow that bigger part of us to do the forgiving *for* us. I really like this idea-that we can appeal to the divine consciousness within, asking *it* to forgive. That's so powerful! The Soul always forgives, even when our human mind can't forget. It only makes sense to call on your Higher Self to do the forgiving for you.

Summary Lesson 5:

1. Metatron defines love as unselfish giving.
2. You cannot be hurt by love, but you can be hurt by people who are unloving.
3. The more love you give the more it grows in you.
4. We are here to learn to love each other.
5. The Oversoul is: all loving, accepting, all knowing, relaxed, and in a state of sufficiency.
6. If our real Self is all loving, we only need to connect with it to experience that love.
7. We get disappointed when we are not loved by those we have loved, but true love isn't concerned with how much it gets back, it is unconditional.
8. Unselfish love is agape, or spiritual love, and it's rare.
9. Even though we make mistakes we should keep practicing being loving.
10. We are instructed to love but to "hold on loosely." We are told to let go of both things and people.
11. Demonstrate flexibility and openness rather than control.
12. Loving oneself means accepting your faults and imperfections.
13. Practice gratitude.
14. Be self-efficacious: be your own advocate.

15. The experience of failure is a necessary element of success and more valuable than success for growth.
16. God forgives you because you are blinded by ignorance.
17. Forgive others with the help of the Christ Consciousness.

EXERCISE 5: Call on Your Soul to Forgive

Think of those who have offended or injured you and say: *"I call on the Christ Consciousness within to forgive those who have injured me, including (name). I cannot find the strength to forgive, because my mind remembers, but my Soul wants me to release the hurt. I release (name) by the authority of the Christ Consciousness within me, and I release myself from unforgiveness. Set us free."*

Visualize handing your hurt to God and see what happens to it. The offense may burn up in a fire, it may get buried or fly away, it may vanish, or your Soul may want to talk to you about it. But be certain that your Soul does not want you to carry the burden of unforgiveness any longer. Whenever you've been hurt or offended, call on your Christ Consciousness to come forward, and through divine grace, exercise your Soul's ability to forgive.

Study Questions: It can be hard to forgive, though our Soul is always seeking for ways to resolve grief. Is there a part of you that wants to forgive, and another part of you that feels it cannot? In prayer, ask the Christ

Consciousness to forgive *through* you. In the future, do you think you can use your Soul to forgive when your mind wants to remember?

LESSON 6-Religion & Science

"The story of creation keeps changing with evolving scientific understanding."

"The biggest impediment to human development is believing that what you see is all there is."

We tend to think we know everything there is to know-and this tendency to be too sure of ourselves is not a plus, but a minus, because it keeps us from seeing possibilities. In 1899 the Commissioner of the US patent office declared: "Everything that can be invented has been invented." He made this statement before the lightbulb had even been invented! But you can bet that when he said it, it seemed accurate to him. This is how subjective opinion works: something can seem unarguably true and correct to us; and at that time, it may be. But time marches on, and with it come inventions and discoveries that we never imagined in our wildest dreams. Just as technological knowledge is ever advancing, so does our knowledge of the Divine. If you study history, you'll see that different religions have sprung up and disappeared over time. Religions mutate from the original. Much like biological evolution, spiritual evolution transpires over time in accord with scientific discovery.

"What has been called the Holy Spirit are only the sons and daughters of God. Each of you is this Holy Spirit."

Metatron is challenging modern Christian doctrine by revealing that the Holy Spirit, that third "person" of the trinity are all of God's children. The "holy" spirit is in truth a description of "the spirit of wholeness" or oneness. The Holy Spirit is the Soul.

Summary Lesson 6:

1. Many claim to have divine knowledge, but few do.
2. Humans seek to know their origins.
3. The Egyptians described a multitude of Gods and Goddesses that ruled the universe and came from the Heavens in flying machines.
4. The creation story has evolved to suit different ethnologies.
5. Modern religion has changed to reflect scientific breakthroughs and societal customs and ethics.
6. Forcing people to "convert" is a mistake.
7. Today's religions will seem antiquated thousands of years from now.
8. Christ claimed to be one with Father God.
9. Christ was a projection of God the Father.
10. The Holy Spirit spoken of by Christ are God's sons and daughters.
11. In Heaven, God will appear to you in a form recognizable to you.
12. All religions lead to the same God.
13. God came to earth in the form of Christ to experience human existence.
14. Christ healed to demonstrate His divinity.

EXERCISE 6: Name a Debunked "Fact" About the World

See if you can name a few "facts" that have changed over the years with the help of science (example: It used to be accepted that the world was flat).

Study Questions: Name a few scientific discoveries or technologies that have caused the world to change (such as the telescope). When Metatron says, "each of you are this Holy Spirit," in practical terms, what does that mean to you?

LESSON 7-Your Karmic Team

"Healing happens because the willing subjects have a Spirit Guide or several Guides, even angels working alongside them."

When our bodies heal, we can watch it happening. If we scrape our knee, we watch as a scab develops. If we break a bone, the pain subsides as it heals, and mobilization improves. While we can observe the body's miraculous healing properties, we cannot see our Heavenly helpers, the Spirit Guides and angels who enable our emotional healing. Therefore, we cannot fully comprehend how cared about and protected we are.

"You owe your very life to these helpers, because they are with you throughout your lifetime. From the very first breath you take, they are with you, until the very last breath."

If we owe our lives to these helpers, and they stay with us over the course of a lifetime, we should feel a sense of gratitude for their unseen support. We have not achieved success all on our own, and therefore we should practice humility, keeping in mind that while we cannot see them, they can see us!

"There are also totem animals or spirit animals attached to you, and you may have one, several, or a group of devoted animal helpmates."

Not only do unseen Spirit Guides and angels assist us in life, but Metatron says devoted spirit animals are defending and comforting us with their presence. For animal lovers, this is welcome news, for perhaps pets that have passed on are still near in spirit.

Summary Lesson 7:

1. Angels have not lived on the earth in human form, only Spirit Guides may have lived as humans.
2. Spirit Guides can incarnate but Angels do not inhabit bodies.
3. Angels have more celestial knowledge than Spirit Guides.
4. Spirit Guides work closely with humans to influence, guide and teach them.
5. Your Spirit Guides interact with you daily.
6. The third chakra, the throat chakra, is the psychic powerhouse of the body.
7. Only Spirit Guides can open a human's psychic ability through the chakras.
8. The throat and third eye chakras must open before you can see and hear the spirit world.
9. The Spirit Guides chosen for you at birth will usually accompany you your whole life.
10. You have been spared thousands of incidents thanks to angels who protected you.
11. Everyone has Spirit Guides.
12. God doesn't intervene for you personally; your Spirit Guides and angels do.
13. Totem animals provide you with protection from dark energies.

14. Your Soul continues to evolve on the Other Side.
15. There is free will in Heaven as on earth.
16. The voice of your conscience is your Spirit Guide.

EXERCISE 7: Write a Thank You Note

To contact your Spirit Guides, Guardian Angels and totem animals, write a brief thank you note to them expressing your gratitude for their dedication and protection. Ask them to reveal themselves to you in a safe way so you can be assured of their presence. List what your concerns are and what you'd like their help with.

Study Questions: Has there ever been a time when you felt your life was spared, or something unexplainable occurred that might have been due to an angel? If so, describe it.

LESSON 8-Biases

"If you're always wanting more of something then you are like a hungry ghost."

Although humans do not have instincts the same way animals do, we have genetics and drives that predict behavior, and these are remarkably consistent among humans. While a dog wags its tail when it's happy, humans smile. When a dog is threatened, he will growl and show his teeth. While we don't exactly growl, our body language and facial expressions change enough to indicate to others when we're angry or afraid.

A drive we all share is the propensity to create and to achieve. Our larger brains allow us to plan and execute goals, a higher reasoning ability that separates us from the animals. Once we accomplished a goal, we move on to the next one, which is fine-except that when it's time to relax or to sleep, many people have difficulty slowing the mind. If we don't control the mind, it acts like a hungry ghost. Hungry, because it desires more, and ghost-like, because the desires of the mind can haunt us. The inborn human drive for achievement can be a double-edged sword.

"Religion isn't simultaneous with authentic God consciousness."

Metatron says that religions can be manufactured and can misrepresent God. People may attend religious services but not follow the ideals of their religion. For example, Moses told the Israelites that God wrote the Ten Commandments, but most people have transgressed these laws by coveting (wanting something another has), by taking the Lord's name in vain, or by forgetting to observe the Sabbath (a day of worship). When it comes to religion, actions speak louder than words.

"There are many who cannot see past the material world because they are not prepared to see reality. You will only see what your mind can conceive."

Reality is free of bias; what is real is fact. Psychology tells us we unconsciously harbor biases; it is unavoidably human. For example, humans have preferences, such as: you like vanilla ice cream, and I prefer chocolate. There is nothing inherently wrong with being biased, for it means you have a will, and it's healthy to exercise our wills. The downside to bias is that it can sometimes keep us from seeing the truth. Vanilla ice cream isn't any "better" than chocolate ice cream; it's all ice cream. Unless of course I prefer chocolate, in which case chocolate seems better to me. If chocolate seems better, I automatically value vanilla ice cream a little less. Who is right? Perhaps neither vanilla, nor chocolate is better than the other-perhaps both are valuable, in different ways. Bias can eclipse the true value of things. Because of human bias, we do not always see things as they are but as our minds believe them to be.

Summary Lesson 8:

1. The properties of water include flexibility, adaptability and sensitivity. Be like water.

2. Being still is rare and therefore more valuable than keeping busy.

3. The acquisition of material possessions will never be satisfied.

4. Looking within brings contentment.

5. Some Souls are like hungry ghosts; empty and longing for more.

6. When you turn inward, heartache, loneliness or grief vanish.

7. While there is nothing wrong with enjoying sense pleasures, bliss can be found in deprivation of the senses, as in meditation.

8. Your mind is like a monkey that will cause chaos unless you master it.

9. Religions that claim you can get into Heaven by spreading their church doctrine are mistaken.

10. The Soul evolves over many lifetimes-this is how you get into Heaven.

11. You are "saved" by making good choices.

12. Having a relationship with God has nothing to do with religion.

13. Experiencing God's love directly is genuine spirituality.

14. Most people relate to what is outside of themselves.

15. The devil, demons, poltergeists and ghosts are trapped in low-frequency dimensions. In Heaven, earth is regarded as a low-frequency dimension and you are like ghosts trapped in it.

16. The ego will slow your progress so practice defying it.

17. The spirit world has no regard for time or deadlines.

18. A spirit is composed of light waves, of vibration, and it dwells in a realm of light.

19. Self-realized people do not play games and will require you to speak truthfully.

EXERCISE 8: Identify a Bias

Identify a bias or a preference you have. Example: "I prefer to spend time with women over men." Next, identify why you think you have this bias. Example:

"Women talk about their feelings, and men tend not to." Now, challenge yourself to see the opposite point of view! Example: "Someone might prefer spending time with men because they can be more rational." Finally, reframe your preference as a bias. Example: "Because I enjoy talking about my feelings, I prefer talking to women are sometimes more expressive than men."

Study Questions: Why do you think being productive is valued so highly?

People call themselves a Christian, a Buddhist, a Hindu or a Muslim, but they don't always act in accordance with their religion's mandates. Explain why you think this happens.

When you have a strong preference for something, it is difficult to see the opposite point of view. Identify a few strong preferences or biases that you have. What can you do to be more open-minded about opposing viewpoints?

LESSON 9-The Buddha in The Mirror

"To a certain degree, loving oneself is healthy. But egoic people have a marked lack of one quality: compassion."

Everybody fails-failure is a part of the human experience, but not everyone has allowed failures to soften them. When life pounds us, we can be hardened or tenderized by it. When the ego is in control, we harden our hearts and it prevent us from getting to know others. Only those who have experienced failure are capable of deep compassion.

"Your internal guru will consistently require you to help others, to give, and to be a kinder, more truthful person. Mostly it will show you how to love less selfishly."

Metatron suggests that we listen to our "internal guru." He says our guru will ask us to practice helping, giving, kindness, truthfulness, and loving selflessly.

"The Buddha's life is an allegory; it shows where the seeker should look. He discovered that going within would afford him the peace, comfort and direction he'd been seeking in the outer world."

The Buddha looked for answers to his existential questions in the external world. He left his home and turned to spiritual teachers. He practiced their various spiritual programs of renunciation, traveling to different parts of India in his quest. Ironically, it wasn't until he stopped looking outwardly and started looking inwardly that he achieved Self-realization. It is tempting to rely on other people for answers. While education, books and wise teachers are invaluable, the path to enlightenment leads directly back to us. The Buddha's story helps us see that the Buddha is found in your mirror.

Summary Lesson 9:

1. You want to become enlightened because you don't want to keep reincarnating.
2. Enlightenment is suppression of the ego.
3. Buddha learned lessons, including: the Soul wants to be free, and you may need to leave things and people behind to follow where the Soul is leading.
4. Buddha found four noble truths in the world: death, sickness, old age and suffering.
5. Freedom is found in God.
6. While Buddha renounced money and pleasure, he did not find God until he sat still and listened.
7. Buddha awakened to the truth that the world is an illusion.
8. Enlightenment isn't achieved because of a religion or spiritual teachers; spirituality is an inside job.
9. Suffering caused the Buddha to seek God.
10. Listen more than you speak.

EXERCISE 9: From Your Inner Guru, With Love

Your Inner Guru, or Higher Self, is your source of wisdom. Write a letter from your Inner Guru to you. Have your Guru answer the following: What is your opinion about the way I am living my life? What advice would you give me? What action steps would you suggest I take? What would you say about my health? What would you say about the environment I am in? The people in my life? How would you suggest I could enrich or improve my life?

Study Questions: Name some characteristics of a compassionate person. What are reasons a society should practice compassion? What happens when a society stops showing compassion? Can you name compassionate leaders who have influenced the world for good? Can you think of any teachers, leaders or loved ones whose compassion or generosity touched your life for the better?

LESSON 10-Change Your Thinking

"Every Soul is surprised in the Afterlife Review when they see the immense network of Souls their existence touched."

"Even the smallest act of kindness has a profound effect, too enormous to fathom."

Metatron refers to the Ripple Effect, suggesting that everything you do matters to others. Social Contagion Theory suggests that our behavior is influenced by those around us. Essentially, humans are copycats. According to Social Contagion Theory, if you're in a group that is acting civil, you are more likely to act civil, too. If you're in a group acting out their frustrations, Social Contagion Theory suggests that you will feel freer to act out your frustrations. Humans are easily influenced, so it stands to reason that every behavior of ours, whether we are aware of it or not, has touched someone else and in some way influenced them. Metatron encourages us to act in positive ways because behavior rubs off.

"You are co-creating the outcome of the Human Experiment by the thoughts you think. If the outcome of planet earth is your responsibility, then your thoughts matter."

It's sobering to think that our thoughts can influence the outer world. If my thoughts are predominantly negative, judgmental or even violent, I am projecting that rotten energy outward, superimposing it onto the world. This means that our collective thinking must change if the world is going to change! If there is violence and all manner of negativity running rampant, it is because our individual thoughts have become corrupted. Time for a shift in thinking. Metatron says that each of us is influencing the outcome of our planet by the predominant thoughts we think. But staying positive is a tall order, especially if we are in a difficult or toxic environment. Because the world we live in is filled with negative events and circumstances, the world is in desperate need of more positivity.

Lesson 10 Summary:

1. Christ fore-knew He would be persecuted on earth, but He came anyway.
2. The importance of your life won't be known during your lifetime.
3. Every Soul is surprised in the After-Life Review about the impact their life had due to the "ripple effect."
4. Fear is your only enemy.
5. Don't be afraid of being different.
6. It seems as if the Human Experiment has failed when you see the chaos and violence in the world.
7. The Human Experiment began with great hope for success.
8. The hypothesis of the Human Experiment is that humans will choose to evolve toward Self-realization.
9. The survival instinct is the strongest of all human drives and will probably save the human race.
10. It is common among societies worldwide to believe that God will return from the sky.

11. Many people live as if there are no consequences for their actions.

12. A random algorithm controls the Human Experiment.

13. Because the Experiment's algorithm is random, even God does not know how the human story will end.

14. Collective thought will determine the outcome of the Human Experiment.

15. You cannot control anyone's thinking besides your own.

16. You are a powerful influencer, so focus on transforming your thinking.

EXERCISE 10: Doing Your Part to Be a Positive Person

Think of one thing you could do that would make you a more positive influence. Example: "I could complain less," or, "I could be more grateful." If you made this change, how do you think it would affect your life? How might it affect those around you given the Ripple Effect?

Study Questions: Why does it seem easier to be negative than to be positive? Do you see a correlation between negative thinking and the state of the world today? If every person worked on being more positive, in what ways would the world change?

LESSON 11-Your Invincible Soul

"It (the Soul) is encoded with the plan for your life-the blueprint, the unique lesson which you agreed to, what is known as your Life Mission."

It's reassuring to know that at least part of you knows what's going on, and that part is the Soul. Our minds get confused, but the eternal Soul is like an unerring compass that points in the direction we should go. Metatron says we agreed to the circumstances in this life, however difficult or painful, for our Soul was "encoded" with our Life Mission. The word "encode" means: to convert from one system of communication to another. The mission you brought to earth was successfully converted or encoded, so there's nothing that will stop you from achieving what your Soul came to achieve. Take heart because your Soul is never deterred, confused, and never, ever lost.

"A Soul cannot be lost or destroyed, nor is it unrepairable as you may have been led to believe."

A Soul is composed of energy, and energy cannot be destroyed (Einstein), it only changes form. You've already changed forms: as you grew from an infant into a child, from a child into a teen, and from a teen into an adult. As an adult, you'll transform again from an inexperienced adult into a wizened elder. All of life is a metamorphosis. If a Soul is made of energy, then you cannot be destroyed, and you will always evolve upward.

"Being a spiritual person has nothing to do with where you worship, or even if you worship. A spiritual person follows Spirit-not a church doctrine."

You can be spiritual anywhere, doing anything. The only non-spiritual thing you can do is harm yourself or someone else; that is decidedly wrong. Spirit cannot be contained in a building for a Spirit is free: free of doctrines, free of harsh judgements, free of bias, utterly unchained to human behaviors and thinking. When you have morphed back into your spiritual Self at death, you will be released from confining human ideas of right and wrong, good and bad, and all biases. You will be utterly free.

Lesson 11 Summary:

1. The Soul is an essence of a personality and is energetic in composition. You are an electromagnetic energy field with self-awareness.
2. Souls can communicate after death from one dimension to another.
3. Souls can fly, move through solid objects and travel at the blink of an eye.
4. You co-exist with spirits and appear as a ghost to beings in other dimensions.
5. The Soul does not experience fear and is encoded with your Life Blueprint. It is infinitely wise.
6. Animals have Souls.
7. If a creature is self-aware it has a Soul.
8. All Souls are eternal, even animal Souls.
9. No Soul is lost or "damned" eternally.

10. Reincarnation is the Soul's redemptive method.
11. While sleeping, you transfer information to the Other Side.
12. All Souls go where they belong in the afterlife.
13. You don't go to Heaven to rest, you keep progressing.
14. There are "less-than-positive" near-death experiences.
15. God doesn't send anyone to Hell-their own choices do.
16. Some atheists will go to Heaven and be surprised.
17. Religion and genuine spirituality are not the same.
18. The mind is not you, the Soul is who you are.
19. You authored your life, so all experiences are valuable.
20. Everything that happens serves a purpose.
21. Peace comes from within.
22. What you do in secret determines your character.
23. A strong leader takes into consideration the welfare of others.
24. Your Soul is encoded with a Life Mission.

EXERCISE 11: Responding from Your Soul

Let's pretend that I could wave a magic wand over you and tomorrow morning when you wake up you can stay connected to your wise Soul as you walk through your day. You're able to respond calmly from your Soul instead of reacting. You would be the objective observer, standing apart from the drama of life, totally secure and all-knowing. If you could walk through the day responding as the Soul, how might your day be different? How might the world respond to you?

Study Questions: If you made a practice of responding from a place of Soul vs. mind, how long do you think you could you sustain this shift in perspective? What situations or emotions cause you to lose touch with your Soul? What do you think would help you to stay connected to your Soul?

LESSON 12-Good Medicine

"If new, young minds are willing to depart from what they have been taught at universities and institutions of medicine, if they are willing to become mavericks who dare to ask the questions that scientists laugh at, ridicule and ignore, then there is hope that the brain will be utilized as it should be, as it was meant to be."

Nothing was invented, and no improvements made without questioning the status quo. However, institutions of higher learning, religions, and governments resist change and people quickly become habituated. Even when it isn't in their best interest, people will side with the institution they were taught to respect. When people stop questioning, they have become "institutionalized." When the average citizen stops thinking for themselves, by default, they become dependent upon the institution to make decisions for them.

When someone introduces an invention or a new method, even if it will be helpful, it can be met with resistance by established institutions. Humans like sameness and resist what they don't readily understand. Only the bravest, most advanced Souls will question authority, and to these "malcontents" we owe a debt of gratitude, for they are the inventors, innovators, and forward-thinkers.

"The average person will look up into the night sky in anguish and cry out, "Why don't you care?" while we are looking at you in anguish crying out, "Why don't you care?"

God is blamed for many things. It's understandable, for when the bottom falls out, it seems like God doesn't care. Metatron makes it clear that humanity was gifted with free will, and because of this, angels cannot interfere with natural consequences, or karma. But when tragedy strikes, we look Heavenward. If God has all power, why did He let it happen? Humanity is holding God responsible, while God is holding humanity responsible for the shape the world is in. In the sum of things, Metatron points out that it is our free will, our ability to choose that is responsible for the shape of the world.

Lesson 12 Summary:

1. Your Soul is a transmitter, sending the electronic signal that jump-started you.
2. If humans understood how to create life, catastrophes would occur.
3. Earth is still in the scientific dark ages.
4. Mind-body medicine is not new, the Egyptians practiced it.
5. Medical professionals and healers should keep in mind that humans are holistic. Holistic medicine should be the focus of the future.
6. Universities of the future will teach mind-body medicine, and neurology will unlock the brain's secrets.
7. Medical systems are so specialized so that the integration of mind-body medicine is ignored.
8. The Egyptians used energy to heal, but the Egyptian ruling class used their knowledge to elevate themselves and to suppress the masses, which is why the knowledge was taken from them.

9. The rejection of energetic medicine is a hoax because scientists know that solid matter is composed of energy.
10. The medical community denies advanced energetic technologies because they profit from prescribing pills.
11. If research money was used to develop mind-body science there would not be such a need for hospitals and pharmaceutical companies.
12. Physicians have blocked the knowledge of mind-body medicine.
13. The cosmic community is waiting to see if new generations will investigate mind-body medicine.
14. Heaven does care and knows about human suffering.

EXERCISE 12: A Big Improvement

Tell about a time when you challenged the system or improved upon the way things were being done. Share what the outcome was. Or, tell about a time you took a leadership position. If you've never changed the way something was being done or been in a position of leadership, simply note that.

Study Questions: Discuss a time when you wished God had intervened. At that time, did it seem like it was "God's fault?" Have you ever been angry with God, or lost faith? Do you think it was God you were angry at, or was it really yourself, or someone else?

LESSON 13-Letting Karma Settle the Score

"Letting go of the need to be right is the first step towards more peaceful relationships."

"Never underestimate the human desire for revenge. It is potent and insistent and can rob you of the love and connection you say you want."

Metatron says the need to be right and the desire for revenge can sabotage us. When we allow others to have the last word, we're demonstrating a willingness to live at peace with those who oppose us. While taking revenge might seem justified, it cannot change what hurt you and it prolongs the cycle of pain. We should leave revenge in the capable hands of karma.

"There is only one way to understand someone, and that is to listen to understand."

When people talk to each other they may fail to listen attentively. Often, they are distracted and only half listening. Active listening shows you care.

"You are not a slave to time; it does not rule you. Time is a non-entity; how could it be your master unless you believe it is?"

Your concept of time is culturally influenced, called time orientation. America is hyper-time conscious, because time is said to be money. Americans are raised to watch the clock. At school and work we follow a schedule, and both school and employers give project deadlines. Businesses find timesaving methods so workers can produce more in less time. In contrast, time in Africa is more leisurely and relaxed-they are less clock-bound. Depending upon your time orientation, Metatron's metaphysical explanation about time being false is either a challenging concept (American), or easily grasped (African). For those who feel bound to the clock, Metatron is reminding us that we are supposed to be in control of time and not vise-versa.

"Therefore, live more in the moment, because that's where the joy is. Truly I tell you, laugh instead of cry; life will bring you tears enough."

Mindfulness has its roots in Buddhism, but many religions include some type of prayer or meditation that shifts attention back to the present moment. Mindfulness improves well-being, so the practice has been adopted in the secular world. Schools are utilizing meditation to improve student focus, and counselors teach it to their clients to relieve anxiety. It's increasingly common for mindfulness meditation to be taught as a part of good mental health.

Summary Lesson 13:

1. Angels are an example of unconditional love.
2. For more peaceful relations, walk away from a fight.
3. The urge for revenge is strong.
4. Practice letting go of having to have the last word.
5. Be an active listener.

6. You will seek for Soulmates and you will have many.
7. Ask your angels to purify and cleanse you of the past.
8. As false beliefs pile up, you'll feel the weight of them.
9. Feel emotions, then release them. Don't hang onto negative emotions.
10. In the Life Review you will see that what seemed disastrous at the time later became a blessing.
11. Time is useful, but a false concept. There is only the now.
12. An earthly life equals only a few days in eternity.
13. Take a break from productivity to enjoy life.
14. Heaven is light-hearted and full of laughter.
15. You will participate in Resolution Meetings in the afterlife where you will make peace with those who hurt you. Restitution is the process of making amends for wrongdoing.
16. You will empathetically see through other's eyes and they will see through yours.
17. With 3D holograms, you will rework problems that occurred in life.
18. Live in the present and have a good time.

EXERCISE 13: Letting Go and Letting God

Letting grievances go, making time for exercise and relaxation, and practicing being in the present are ways to increase your happiness. Make goals for your physical or mental health, such as losing weight, working out, or a goal of regular meditation. While you may not be able to change a situation, you can change the way you manage the stress.

Study Questions: How could allowing someone else to have the last word be of benefit to you? Why is allowing karma to settle the score important? Do you feel you are clock-bound? What steps can you take to be more mindful of the present moment?

LESSON 14-Your Life Mission

"Each Soul is encoded with a message that it is to leave with the world, and we call this your Life Mission."

Every Soul has a purpose, a reason they are here. Metatron says your Life Mission is the reason you have incarnated at this time in history. Until you have completed your Mission, you will feel incomplete. Yet if you were to ask people to articulate their Life Mission, most don't even know they have a Mission and aren't able to articulate what it might be.

"Until you have learned the proper use of power, your world will continue to suffer in ignorance of the advanced technologies the Egyptians possessed."

Because of the misuse of power, the Egyptian civilization lost the advanced technologies they had been given. Today, government officials are still misusing their power by exploiting the earth and ignoring the poor for personal wealth. Some things never change!

"The primary law of the original Soul is an acceptance of its "differentness."

For society to improve, individuals must change. An inner change must occur before an outer change can occur. When you are afraid of being different, you are held back from being the original Soul you were meant to be. Fear of criticism can cripple your fullest expression. Acknowledge that being different is okay-be proud of your individuality and try not to fear people who are different from you.

Summary Lesson 14:

1. Ancient Egypt was polytheistic.
2. Be true to yourself.
3. Every Soul has a Life Mission.
4. Originality is not the same as rebellion.
5. The ancient Egyptians had metaphysical technologies that have been lost.
6. The Pharaoh Akhenaten was a hybrid who was visited by aliens.
8. Ramses 111 was a narcissistic Pharaoh who tried to erase Akhenaten's legacy.
9. There are modern day Pharaohs who build their wealth at the expense of the poor.
10. If you are an original Soul, expect to be misunderstood.
11. The laws of the original Soul are:
a. Accept your uniqueness.
b. Leave attachments that restrict you.
c. Don't be afraid to fly solo.
d. Push for progress.

EXERCISE 14: Accomplishing Your Life Mission

Write down what you think your Life Mission might be or what you guess it is (Hint: It is often the lesson you keep repeating). Example: "My mission is to love people, but not to save them." Then, articulate in writing what steps you can take to fulfill your Life Mission. Example: "In order to avoid saving people, I should stop rescuing them and allow them to take full responsibility for their lives and choices."

Study Questions: If you could rate yourself from 0 to 10 on a scale (0 being none, and 10 being complete), where on the scale would you fall in terms of accomplishing your Life Mission? Why did you choose that number?

What is difficult about being different? What is good about being different, what are the benefits of being an original Soul?

LESSON 15-The Body Is Not You

"Because aging is inevitable and an inescapable fact of life, it is essential to your happiness to accept that your body is not "you" in any way, shape or form."

Because we live in bodies, they are precious to us. We care for them, feed, bathe, and exercise them regularly. We dress them, and even show them off to others. We closely identify with our bodies even though we find them to be imperfect. Nevertheless, they are a representation of "us." But do they truly represent "us" or are they a false representation of our truest selves? The enlightened recognize their bodies as a useful vehicle but see the invisible Soul as their identity.

"God does not want anyone to hide their unhappiness or confusion. To represent those undeniable feelings on the outside is not a mistake or sin."

To hide what we feel is deception. If God is truth, then God would not condone deception. When we cannot be ourselves, it is because we are trying to please someone, or trying to avoid criticism or even danger. But God only requires us to be who we are.

"God is always for your liberation. God always wants you to be freer and freer, happier and happier. But how can you be happy if you've been hiding something as fundamental as your sexual or gender orientation?"

God is first and foremost a creative force. To create, expression must be uninhibited. Therefore, as the Supreme Creator, we know God's nature is liberated; free of fear. Because God is liberated, He wishes His creation to live free of fear. Concealing your sexual or gender orientation is the opposite of free self-expression. God is happiest when you can be truthful with yourself and others.

Summary Lesson 15:

1. You are not your body.
2. To be well-adjusted, accept yourself as you are.
3. God does not want anyone to hide questions.
4. Transgenderism and same-sex attraction are foreknown by the Soul and are part of a Life Blueprint.
5. Transgenderism and homosexuality teach by example that being different is okay, and that you are more than a body.
6. Everyone is an aspect of the Creator, so stop identifying people's worth based on their looks or lifestyle.
7. What makes someone good or bad is their thoughts.
8. There are white, grey and dark Souls.
9. Gender is determined by the Soul, not the body.
10. It can feel as if God made a mistake to the gender-questioning person, but God doesn't make mistakes.
11. Transgenderism liberates society from ignorance.
12. Transgenderism makes people think about the real definition of a man or a woman.

EXERCISE 15: Appreciating the You That Isn't You

List some things about your body that you appreciate or like. Example: "People tell me I have a warm smile." Now, list several things about your personality that you enjoy. Example: "I'm confident and outgoing, and that makes people feel at ease around me." Unlike physical features, personality features are more of a choice. If you work hard at improving your personality and attitude, you can! Name one feature of your personality that you'd like to improve ("I'd like to be more patient and less angry").

Study Questions: In your opinion, is it hard to accept your body as-is? Why? Name something that has changed about you over the years, either physically, or in your personality. Describe what impact this change has had on your life. In what ways do you think the Soul different from the personality?

LESSON 16-Learning from Soulmates

"The characteristics of a Soulmate are simple: you can recognize them because they will either be your teacher, or they will be your student."

It is said that in relationships we are either the teacher or the student. If you look closely at the significant relationships in your life, you'll be able to see what role you played. For example, it's only when a couple enters counseling that they become aware of their patterns, the unconscious "intimacy dance" they do. Even friendships have long-standing dynamics and patterns. Usually, one person tends to be the leader and the other the follower. It's important to become aware of the roles you play, and if you don't like the role in the relationship, work to change the dynamics.

"Soulmates will cause you to see your true nature. They will be a mirror that forces you to see who you really are."

Soulmates can bring out the best or the worst in us. We feel free to be ourselves around Soulmates, for they love and accept us as we are. But as the adage says: "Familiarity breeds contempt." We hurt those who love us most because we trust that they will not leave us. Soulmates draw to the surface what needs to be improved within us. Like a mirror, we can look at how we treat them to judge how far we've come. Like Ram Dass said: "If you think you're enlightened, go spend a week with your family."

"It can be difficult to give thanks for the most painful relationships you've had. And yet, the advanced Soul sees beyond the pain to the lesson."

Life lessons are learned over time; maturity is a lifelong endeavor. We learn several ways: by getting enough information or education that we change, or we learn the hard way-when it hurts bad enough and we are forced to change. When life is painful, we must endeavor to find the lesson hidden in the painful circumstance.

Summary of Chapter 16:

1. Feeling strong attraction or immediate comfort with someone could be a karmic tie, also known as a Soulmate.

2. You will have a multitude of Soulmates.

3. The more Soulmates you have the better, because they will allow you to learn lessons quickly.

4. Soulmates can be recognized because they will either be your teacher, or they will be your student.

5. Soulmates force you to see who you really are.

6. Soulmate relationships can be difficult, turbulent, intense and transient.

7. Don't try to force a Soulmate to stay.

8. Walk through life with an open hand.

9. Soulmates can be family, friends or lovers.

10. You may pick troublesome Soulmates as family to cause your Soul to grow.

11. Your gender and personality can vary greatly from one life to the next.

12. When you construct your Life Plan there is complex strategy involved when you write in Soulmates.

13. Most decisions aren't included in your life's "script." Most decisions are free-will.

14. Parting with a Soulmate may feel wrong because you have unfinished business that will be completed in another life.

15. Animals can be Soulmates.

16. Animals can evolve into humans.

17. A human cannot evolve down the chain into an animal. Soul evolution is a forward-moving process.

18. Relationships are the greatest gifts because they are eternal.

19. When you look back at painful relationships ask yourself, "What did I learn?"

20. Soulmates are necessary for your Soul's perfecting.

EXERCISE 16: Learning Life's Lessons

List the significant people in your life, and beside each name, write whether you feel you are predominantly the teacher or the student. Write what you think you are teaching them, and/or what lessons they've been teaching you. Write down why you are grateful for them and grateful for the lesson learned. You may want to share your gratitude with your Soulmate.

Study Questions: Metatron says all Soulmates are important, even the painful ones, because they help us work through our karma quickly. What life lessons do you suspect you are learning? Discuss a life lesson you had to learn the hard way.

LESSON 17-Defeating Fear

"The purpose of living is to realize that none of it is real."

Our problems seem urgent, serious and worrisome. When Metatron says that none of it is real, it sounds impossible. He describes life as if it were a 3-D game, and we are the unwitting pawns. If what our five senses perceive is not reality, what is?

"Changing yourself is the greatest thing you can do. It is more important than trying to change others."

"The pinnacle of evolution is the willingness to change one's self."

The world's social systems are set up to change others. Think about it: Religions are for converting others to a certain spiritual perspective. The educational system is for changing people's thinking. The criminal justice system seeks to punish and rehabilitate the criminal. Yet, Metatron says that intrapersonal change, what happens privately inside of us, is the most important learning we can do.

"How would your life be different if you didn't have to worry about what other people thought or said about you?"

We live in apprehension of other's disapproval. We worry about how we are perceived or what people say about us when we're not around. We may live in a defensive posture because in the past we were the object of criticism, and some of us have even been physically attacked. We learn early to "watch our back." What would it feel like to walk through life without fear of rejection, criticism or abandonment? It's hard to imagine, but Metatron asks us to imagine how our lives would be different if we didn't carry these fears.

Summary Lesson 17:

1. Don't be afraid of death.
2. The finite brain cannot comprehend eternity.
3. Leaving the body at death is like taking off a confining, heavy costume.
4. The purpose of life is to realize that none of it is real.
5. You have come to earth to reclaim your divine nature and to appreciate it in others.
6. Humanity believes it is all-knowing while possessing infantile metaphysical and scientific knowledge.
7. The ego wants to control.
8. Nirvana is when the mind ceases to chatter and stays in the present.
9. Peace, bliss, trust, childlike joy, freedom and spontaneity are the natural state of the Soul.
10. Divinity is at rest, desiring nothing.
11. Every day the goal should be to trust your Soul vs. the ego.
12. All beauty and fear come from your thoughts, thus the world is a result of collective consciousness.
13. If you knew all the loved ones waiting for you on the Other Side, you wouldn't feel alone.

14. The mind is a separating machine-it can only focus on your current life.
15. Changing yourself is the greatest achievement. It is more important than changing others.
16. How cannot know another's heart, motives, destiny or calling.
17. You should not judge, nor do you deserve to be judged.
18. It is best not to harm others for you are connected to all others.
19. The enemy is not one another, but fear.
20. The Akashic Record (The Book of Life) records every thought and action of humanity.
21. Prophets, psychics, mediums and mystics receive spiritual insight from the Akashic Record.
22. There is no quick method of learning to hear your Higher Self other than spending time listening for it.
23. Most people deny the spiritual world for many lifetimes.
24. Without you, all life would stop, and time would come to a halt.
25. Life Themes are lessons you will repeat.
26. The person you've imagined you could be is the real you.
27. Given enough time, even dark energies grow to perfection.
28. All humans feel broken, but not all of you will see it as a gift and make something positive of it.

EXERCISE 17: Role Playing

List all the roles you play in life or have played in the past (example: spouse, parent, daughter or son, caretaker, pet owner, business owner, employee, employer, entrepreneur, parishioner or choir member, group participant, group leader, etc.). Next, look inward and list a few things you'd like to change about the roles you play, being as specific as you can (Example: "In my role as a partner, I'd like to show more patience." Or, "Since I'm a dog owner, I'd like to take better care of my dog by walking him more regularly").

Study Questions: Metatron says that what we consider reality is unreal. If this is true, what is reality? Imagine if you woke up tomorrow and miraculously, you didn't have to worry about rejection, criticism or abandonment. How your life would be different?

LESSON 18-The Best Laid Plans

"Could there be realms and dimensions beyond your human perception in which it all makes perfect sense?"

Metatron explains we live in a multiverse of parallel universes. There are invisible elements that sustain us- microscopic worlds that are just as real as the visible elements. In fact, unseen atomic particles are the building blocks of the entire visible universe. Since there are worlds unseen by the naked eye, could there be other dimensions that science has yet to discover? In "M-theory," there are 11 dimensions. In Superstring theory, there are 10. Theories of modern physics stimulate the imagination, opening new realms.

"Try very diligently not to focus on your worries, for they cannot help you. Focus instead on anything positive. Staying close to God can help you stay positive, because God is a positive force-field."

Negative thinking is limited thinking, while positive thinking is unlimited. Meditation is one way of plugging into that positive current. When you're feeling overwhelmed or defeated, positive energy may be running low. Meditation, chant, prayer, exercise, and being in nature are a few sure-fire ways of recharging your battery and invigorating your Spirit.

"Your Oversoul has already calculated your every move, thought and feeling, even your environment.

Like a plane on autopilot, the course is already set, so enjoy the ride."

Everything that happens to you is pre-known to your Higher Self. Your Oversoul is in constant attendance, presiding over everything you do. It is utterly trustworthy, sustaining you. However, it never interferes or tells you what choices to make, as it honors the power of your individual choices and free will. Take consolation that you are not navigating life alone.

Summary Lesson 18:

1. If you believe this life is the only life, it will seem like a senseless struggle.
2. The next cycle of human evolution is lighter and freer.
3. In the future, accountability will be demanded from governments.
4. In Heaven, every person's motives and deeds will be seen.
5. When you disobey moral laws you will hide from God.
6. The world is confusing, and frightening compared to Heaven.
7. Staying close to God can keep you positive.
8. God loves you as His dear child.
9. Don't be afraid to show yourself to God.
10. Karma is like the symbol of Lady Justice-it weighs and measures each word and deed.
11. You are not anyone's savior.
12. When a relationship ends don't assume it's a failure. You may meet them again in another incarnation.
13. You cannot see the hand controlling your destiny.

14. When you complete this life you may not have to reincarnate again if you learn your lessons.

EXERCISE 18: Exploring Physics

Truly spiritual people are open-minded people. To broaden your horizons, research a modern physics theory such as the Multiverse Theory, Holographic Universe, Parallel Universes, "M-theory" or "Superstring theory."

Study Questions: What was the most interesting aspect of these theories? What did you find most surprising? What implications could these theories have for understanding our universe?
Since your Oversoul is in charge, all that has happened to you is foreknown to it. How does knowing this change your outlook?

LESSON 19-Making Good Decisions

"Making good decisions starts with a clear understanding of who you are, and what you want. You've really got to get clear on those two subjects. You may think the course you're on is the right one simply because you've never stopped to question it."

Humans are creatures of habit. Unless there's a problem, we don't stop to analyze ourselves; we operate on autopilot. A self-aware person has a clear understanding of their values, and this knowledge is essential to making decisions that are right for them. You are a sovereign being. You have the right to live your life as you see fit, unless it harms others. But you cannot live life "your way" until you first deduce who you are and what your values are. Self-awareness is synonymous with happiness. Self-aware people are the happiest people.

"People stay stuck because they don't want to make the "wrong" decision, so they don't make any decision at all. Or they allow someone else to make their decisions for them, which means they are living in a disempowered state. Avoid this trap by making small decisions. Instead of following someone's lead, suggest an alternative, something you would enjoy-then stand by your decision."

Not deciding *is* a decision. There are times when we should make our voice heard, but instead we fall silent because we fear the implications of standing our ground. That silence is a decision not to exercise our sovereign will. When we sacrifice our opinion, we abdicate our will and personal power. Consequently, we live in a disempowered state, in the illusion of "no choice," also called the "victim mentality." The opposite of victimization is taking our power back by making our voice heard. Empowered people look to themselves first when making decisions. Ask yourself: "What do I really want?"

"If I had one wish for you, it would be that you'd say: "So what?" the next time someone makes a mistake, because most mistakes can be corrected."

We all learn from our mistakes, why then do we make such a big deal when we, or others make them? Maybe we've been sold on the unattainable idea of perfection. After all, movie stars look perfect, so shouldn't we be? They are wealthy, famous, always smiling, projecting Hollywood's ironclad image of success. But the truth is, many celebrities are less happy than the average person. They have more stress and less privacy. They have less time to enjoy the simple pleasures of life due to demanding schedules. But they keep smiling, because they have an image to uphold. And that's all it is: an image. Their public persona is an act. We've been taught that mistakes are embarrassing or unacceptable when mistakes are a part of the learning curve of life. Metatron says mistakes are what make us human.

Summary Lesson 19:

1. Most people haven't stopped long enough to ask themselves: who am I, and what do I want?
2. You are a product of what you've been taught.
3. It's difficult to think for yourself because society and your family reinforces pre-programmed messages.
4. Following someone else leads to a dead-end.
5. Routines are comfortable, so most people don't risk much.
6. The "Primary Objective" of reincarnation is to evolve, which includes taking calculated risks.
7. You were sent here for your Soul's growth.
8. Human development occurs in stages.
9. Assess your life's trajectory. Are you where you want to be?
10. You do not owe apologies for changing direction.
11. Know your talents and capabilities and be seeking ways to use them.
12. Part of maturing is the ability to make your own decisions.
13. Voice your opinions.
14. Making mistakes is how you learn. When others make mistakes don't take it too seriously, because you've made them, too.

EXERCISE 19: Core Values

List your core values, such as: Love, Parenting, Spirituality, Success, Community, Wealth, Service, Learning, Peace, Humor, Autonomy, Honesty, Family, Friends, Influence, Creativity, Fun, Travel, Education,

Love and Security. Now prioritize them in order of importance. Values change over time, so the values you have today might be different from those you had in the past.

Think of a mistake that you still blame yourself for. How would it feel to let go of the blame and guilt?

Study Questions: Share your top 3 values. Describe how your values have changed over time and explain why you chose them.

What should you remind yourself of the next time you think about a mistake of the past?

LESSON 20-Religion vs. Spirituality

"Religious dogma that seeks to control will always fear questions and shame the questioner. Fear and shame have nothing to do with spirituality, and spirituality has no association with fear and shame."

Religion isn't the same as spirituality. The dictionary defines spirituality as: "A broad concept with room for many perspectives. In general, it includes a sense of connection to something bigger than us, and it typically involves a search for meaning in life." Spirituality is an individual quest for universal truth, as opposed to a religious methodology. Spiritual individuals dare to question what they have been told and seek to accept themselves and others.

Contrast this with a religious person who may be harboring many unanswered questions but who submits to authority out of fear of rejection, or sadly, out of fear of God. The religious person who experiences guilt and shame is more likely to hide their confusion.

"Being a genuinely spiritual person means you have the freedom to be yourself, and you give other people that same liberty."

Spiritual individuals are accepting and practice open-mindedness. They aren't afraid of being different and avoid judging others. They welcome viewpoints that are different from theirs because they might learn something they didn't know before. They employ logic and reason, and don't reject information just because it can't yet be proven by the scientific method. They are curious and willing to try on new perspectives.

"Whatever you set your focus on will grow, so focus intently and forcefully upon the positives."

Maybe you've heard the expression, "You are what you eat." This principle also applies to what you feed your mind. Meditation, chanting, prayer, reading encouraging books, listening to soothing and uplifting music, watching funny or inspirational movies, laughter, socializing, recreation, exercise and sex are all positive stress-relievers. Enrich yourself to become a more positive person.

Summary Lesson 20:

1. A spiritual person isn't mindless.
2. Spiritual people are: observant, curious, childlike, unafraid to ask questions, and are looking for the truth.
3. What makes you a spiritual person are your priorities, how you spend your time.
4. A spiritual person is content in the present.
5. Christ did not judge.
6. Karma is the return of energy.
7. Karma may happen in this lifetime because of thoughts and actions from a previous life.
8. True spirituality meets the needs of the poor and doesn't refuse the seeker's questions.
9. Fear and shame have nothing to do with spirituality.

10. Being genuinely spiritual means being yourself and giving others that same freedom.
11. Spiritual people are: spontaneous, honest, humble and unconditionally accepting.
12. Spiritual people don't reject science and can tolerate opposing views.
13. Any religion that discourages thinking for yourself doesn't lead to freedom.
14. Fear and freedom are opposing concepts. Love liberates.
15. Spirit always leads you to an expanded viewpoint.
16. Spirituality allows you to use both your mind and heart to obtain answers.
17. Your life is full of elements that your five senses cannot perceive.
18. Faith in what you cannot see is healthy and intelligent.
19. It is naïve to only believe in discoveries of the past.
20. The Higher Self in you knows what is right and wrong.
21. When enduring The Dark Night of the Soul, know it is time for resurrection-new life and new hope will grow.
22. Life Lessons or Themes will be presented repeatedly.
23. Man-made religion is a sacrilege.
24. Christ did not ask for a tithe.
25. Some will be called to be leaders in the forward movement of humanity's evolution.
26. Strive to have a direct experience of God's love.
27. The Holy Spirit is the Soul.
28. The symbol of fire is God's monarch.
29. God has no enemies.
30. Be Diplomatic.
31. In the seven Heavens, Archangels are rulers of Heavenly Kingdoms.

EXERCISE 20: Your Spiritual Plan

Write down your definition of a genuinely spiritual person. Next, write down how you plan to grow spiritually or as a person.

List a few social taboos or stigmas that have changed for the better, including what factors led to societal acceptance. Example: "Interracial marriage was legitimized by the civil rights movement."

Study Questions: Think of a few topics that are not commonly discussed in religious circles. Should they be discussed? Why or why not? Describe a religious person you've known vs. a spiritual person you've known. In what ways do they differ?

Can you describe the characteristics of a pessimist? Can you describe an optimist? How do you feel when you are around pessimistic people? How do you feel when you are around optimistic people? What are the benefits of seeing the glass "half full" rather than "half empty?"

LESSON 21-Renunciation

"Jesus answered very simply how to tell if a person is good or bad; He left no doubt. He said, "For no good tree bears bad fruit, nor does a bad tree bear good fruit" (Luke 6:43). You see, it's very simple to tell a good tree from a bad tree."

Humans are notorious for saying one thing while doing another; it is nearly a human characteristic. In Psychology, this is known as Cognitive Dissonance. As a heuristic, when trying to decipher a good person from a bad one, Jesus instructed us to ignore words and look at the person's actions instead.

"You cannot rescue or change anyone, not even your own family. If you are being dragged down by someone's issues, it's time to move ahead with your life. This may not sound like a compassionate response: you might be surprised that an angel is telling you to flee from a lost Soul. But you are not a savior-it is not your job! The only obligation you have is to reach out to them. If they refuse your help, then you are free!"

Compassion compels us to reach out to those in need. But often, those needing a helping hand will not accept help. Pride keeps them from accepting support or from admitting they have a problem. If they refuse help, Metatron suggests we move on. Why is this? Because everyone is learning at a different rate, and you cannot make anyone learn faster than they want to. As the old saying goes: "You can lead a horse to water, but you can't make it thirsty."

"Renunciation of the material world must happen before a Soul can be saved. It is a common religious phrase to say that God can save a Soul. But while God can offer endless opportunity for redemption, the Soul must save itself. You are saved when you have no attachment to riches and power. You are not "saved" by an act of God; your own hand must untie you!"

Like celibacy, renunciation of money and possessions is observed by ascetics to draw closer to God. Dietary restrictions and fasting are also religious practices that devotees follow. Metatron defines being "saved" as renunciation of riches and power. While many religions believe in a savior, Metatron says the Soul will save itself.

Summary Lesson 21:

1. Angels once looked after humans.
2. Angels possess a limited amount of emotion.
3. Earth is a place to shed negative karma.
4. There will be a battle for the earth. The righteous will be rescued, and dark forces will be stopped.
5. You are part of the struggle between light and darkness.
6. Jesus said to judge a person by her actions.
7. Each person is responsible for his or her own salvation.
8. Dark entities have assumed key governmental positions.
9. The earth is full of light workers who will save the earth and her inhabitants.

10. Worship benefits the devotee. God doesn't need your worship or money.
11. What impresses God is obedience.
12. Listening to your inner guide is rewarded with revelation and spiritual gifts.
13. Many people say they know God, but few are friends of God.
14. Renounce the material world.
15. What saves you from the endless cycle of rebirth is forsaking the ego.

EXERCISE 21: Getting the Support You Deserve

The ego can prevent us from asking for help. Think of something you could use help with right now, or in the future. What is preventing you from getting the support you need? Contact someone who might be able to help and ask them for support. Is there anyone you could reach out to who might need a helping hand?

Study Questions: Riches and power are difficult to release. So difficult that Jesus said: "It is easier for a camel to go through the eye of a needle than for a rich man to enter the Kingdom of Heaven!" (Matthew 19:24). What could you renounce that could lead you to a closer relationship with God?

LESSON 22-Your Rebel Soul

"To fulfill your calling, you must be a rebel. You must not accept the placating and pacifying, for this is corrupt system's way of shutting you up. You must become a change agent, every one of you!"

Change can be difficult. All change, even positive change, is stressful. People side-step "rocking the boat" to go with the flow. Because of this, real injustice can occur. In these moments, it's crucial to speak up so justice will prevail. To remain silent in the presence of evil is to condone it.

"There are two types of people in the world. Those who understand that all are God's children, and people who believe they are more important, more special, more "chosen" than others."

Throughout history, groups of people have elevated themselves due to what psychology calls a "superiority complex." The root of superiority is the ego. In its arrogance the ego separates itself from those who are different. When one group dominates, war can ensue. The solution to this problem of the ego is to see that God loves all equally and doesn't play favorites, only we do.

"Being part of the exceptional crowd sounds glamourous until you ask an advanced Soul about the reality of it. They will tell you they wished to be normal with every breath. Instead, they were asked to be out-standing, standing out."

Everyone wants to be acknowledged as special, gifted or talented. In fact, the two human emotional motivators are the need to be understood, and the need to feel important (Dale Carnegie). However, recognition comes with a price tag. Innovators and leaders are doubted and criticized and must stand up to scrutiny. Sometimes they are maligned and even mistreated. We owe a debt of gratitude to people who have dared to be different for they paved the way for progress.

Summary Lesson 22:

1. You must become a change agent.
2. Your Soul isn't hungry for material things.
3. There are two types of people in the world: those who believe God loves everyone, and those who think they are loved more than others.
4. There will be severe unrest politically and economically. There will be a class war.
5. The poor will turn against the rich who acted without mercy.
6. A sociological awakening will give rise to the second renaissance that will bring global peace.
7. People are the greatest treasures.
8. If you want enlightenment, refuse man-made religious systems, let go of your own agenda, and be a servant.
9. Wherever there is light, darkness will follow.
10. Any person who tries to ruin, disgrace or take revenge is not a lightworker.
11. Dark entities can appear attractive and accomplished, but they are filled with anger and the need to control.

12. When discerning good from bad, ask: Can they admit when they are wrong? Are they humble? Are they willing to live peacefully with others?
13. Be tolerant and do not expect perfection.
14. Lightworkers are the hope for the world.
15. Everyone doing their part to change society for the better will be rewarded.
16. Biological diversity is the natural expression of life.
17. Humanity must evolve towards acceptance.
18. Resistance to inclusion is resistance to unity.
19. Being exceptional sounds glamorous but it can be lonely.
20. You may be a pilgrim Soul sent to make waves.
21. You cannot discover anything new if you can already see it.

EXERCISE 22: Gratitude for Support

Think of a time when you felt different. Perhaps you were misunderstood or mistreated in some way. What was your experience? Did anyone stand with you to support you? Write a thank you note to that person (s) acknowledging your gratitude or find a way to express your gratitude to them.

Study Questions: Describe a time when you voiced your beliefs or opinions and found yourself in the minority. What prompted you to take this bold step? How did it feel to speak your truth? What was the reaction?
Do you think God "plays favorites"? How would you counsel a person who believes one group of people is better than another?

LESSON 23-The Gift of Intuition

"It is a service to humanity to use your intuitive gifts and abilities. Only if it is used for evil is it evil. If intuition is being used to help and heal, it is a gift from God."

It's easy to misjudge things we don't understand. Throughout history misunderstanding has led to persecution of innocent people. Jesus said the way to decipher good from bad is to look at the results people are getting. Are they a positive influence? Inspiring? Creative or insightful? Are they helping others? Labels aren't helpful because they box people in and have been the cause of grievances. Before declaring something (or someone) right or wrong, ask yourself: Is this person producing good fruit?

"People who don't understand the need for meditation haven't discovered the true blessing it can be. Nothing else can give you the insight and profound peace that the Spirit realm can."

To ignore that there is a spiritual aspect of life is to miss a large part of the reason you are here. Sri Ramakrishna said: "God realization is the purpose of life." There are different methods of connecting to the spirit world. You can pray (talk to God), meditate (listen to God), or chant (helpful to reduce karma). Whatever method you choose, building a spiritual practice is important for reducing stress, improving mental well-being, and reducing negative emotions such as anxiety, depression, worry and anger. Research shows that people who have a spiritual practice are happier and live longer.

"Many declare themselves healers or religious leaders before they've submitted themselves to God for thorough inspection. Don't be quick to claim your leadership status because, to whom much is given, much is required" (Luke 12:48).

Leadership should be taken seriously, because leaders wield influence and power. Good leaders consider how their decisions will impact others and try to harm as few people as possible. This is a sobering principle: "To whom much is given, much is required." This means the more we are given, the greater our responsibility.

Summary Lesson 23:

1. There is nothing evil about psychics, they provide a service for humanity.
2. Don't argue with a persecutory person, avoid them.
3. The intuitive gift is a tool.
4. The issue of good and evil requires a moral sophistication yet to be developed by humanity.
5. Humans tend to dwell on evil and even blame their problems on the devil.
6. If intuition is being used to help and heal it is a gift from God.
7. Everyone should desire to be more intuitive and develop their psychic abilities.
8. Christ had psychic powers.

9. Because psychics are human, they are bound to make mistakes just as you have made mistakes.

10. As humanity evolves, the average person will develop psychic abilities.

11. Psychic ability is the gift of deciphering the world of thought.

12. Those who are both psychics and mediums have taken the oath of a Bodhisattva.

13. When the world stops persecuting those who are different it will be ready for a new phase of enlightenment.

14. Intuition can be the product of rebirth.

15. If you're not seeking the truth you're not doing anything that has meaning.

16. The serious seeker is rare.

17. Light workers should refrain from comparing and rise above petty differences.

18. Becoming a leader shouldn't be entered into lightly.

19. If you are a psychic, you are blessed, but it can seem like a curse because of skeptics.

20. A way of protecting yourself is to bind the angry words to the person who spoke them.

EXERCISE 23: Use Your Intuition

Intuition is the subtle cue to listen to your Higher Self. It can be a gut feeling, an instinct you have, or a strong impression. Declare: "I AM an intuitive being. When I feel the intuitive nudge, I'll listen and see what results I get."

Study Questions: Do animals have intuition? Do people have intuition? Does everyone have the same amount of intuition, or is it a gift? Is intuition an ability that anyone can develop? Why is listening to your intuition important? Tell about a time you listened to your intuition and it proved to be correct.

LESSON 24-You Are What You Think

"There will be no way to avoid the inevitable, because you are on a crash course with destiny. When soulmates are involved, it's destiny-an agreement you forged on the Other Side."

Some things in life were meant to happen, and some people you were meant to meet. These unavoidable circumstances and relationships were pre-planned on the Other Side, even if you cannot consciously recall these agreements. They are Soulmate contracts.

"For anything to be created, your intention must be fixed, you must hold the thought long enough for the various components and pieces to materialize."

Persistence is key to creating any finished product. Think about the chair you sit on: there was a person who invented the chair. A manufacturing company then built the chair, and a store sold the chair. Getting this chair to you was a process that required precision. If the chair's creator had given up before bringing the chair to market, you'd be sitting on the floor! Most worthy ideas are abandoned before they have a chance to succeed. Stand your ground long enough for something good to take form.

"This is why positive thinking is so important-you can create negative entities through sustained negativity."

Have you ever walked into a room and quickly sensed something was wrong, the air so thick you could "cut it with a knife?" You can sense negative energy. How is this possible? Because sustained negativity is a powerful force, just as sustained positivity is. Words are creative forces, bending energetic fields either way. Think positive thoughts to be a positive force.

Summary Lesson 24:

1. Destiny will draw Soulmates to you.
2. The "Law of Attraction" (Byrne, 2006) means the more you focus on something the faster it is magnetized it to you.
3. Thoughts are a self-fulfilling prophecy, so endeavor to think positively.
4. In Heaven, you will study and practice constructing by thought.
5. Thought forms can be created unconsciously.
6. Thought forms are created out of mass opinion.
7. Because of strong negative mass opinion, thought forms influenced the Germans to adopt Hitler's agenda.
8. Thought forms are agenda-driven entities without a will of their own without a Soul.
9. Negative thought forms aren't to be feared for they must obey forceful commands.
10. A positive command is hundreds of times more powerful than a negative command.
11. You cannot avoid destiny; you can only delay it.

EXERCISE 24: Positivity Score

Think about the words you've thought or spoken today. Have they been mainly positive and uplifting, or did they bend towards the negative? If you gave yourself an overall positivity score for your day, what number would it be? If you were to give yourself a positivity score for the past, what number what it be? What can you change to make your life more positive?

Study Questions: Why is it sometimes difficult to be positive? When people are positive, how do you react? When someone is being unnecessarily negative, how can you shift the energy?

LESSON 25-The Multiverse, Parallel Universes & Holographic You

"You are a multi-dimensional being, just as God is, and you exist perfectly intact on the Other Side, while simultaneously living an earthly life, completely oblivious to the fact that "you" are operating on other planes."

A hologram is a real looking 3D image produced by a laser. Is it theoretically possible that you could be projected to more than one place at a time? Dreaming is evidence that bilocation is possible, as during sleep your consciousness is in the dream world while your body continues to operate without your conscious knowledge. Similarly, your earthy projection functions completely unaware of other versions of you operating elsewhere in the universe.

"I'm aware all this sounds fantastic to your ears, perhaps blasphemous, perhaps ridiculous. But keep in mind that what you accept as fact today was once thought impossible and ludicrous yesterday."

Science has proven that there is a vast microscopic world that we cannot perceive with the five senses. Before the invention of the electron microscope, we could only hypothesize that there were energetic forces. Religions have a long history of persecuting, and even sentencing to death scientists and prophets for their theories and discoveries. Skepticism is healthy, for we must use our reasoning abilities, but we must be open-minded skeptics.

"There is an Over-Self, or Over-Soul that is the most advanced form of you on the Other Side."

If there is a smarter version of you that orchestrates your many lives, what good news! It's a relief to know that you are experiencing but part of your more intelligent self. When you feel inadequate perhaps it's because you are not functioning at total capacity. It's reassuring to know that the Oversoul is masterminding your life's journey and this more advanced version of "you" knows where you need to go. If your Oversoul is so advanced in intelligence that it can organize your projections, perhaps you don't need to be "in control" as much as you think you do.

Summary Lesson 25:

1. Life is a virtual programmed reality.
2. You are a biogenetic experiment projected across time and space.
3. You are a hologram, a projection of your Oversoul.
4. You are a multi-dimensional being, as God is.
5. You exist on the Other Side and projections of you are operating in multiple dimensions.
6. There are parallel universes within the multiverse.
7. An artificially intelligent machine called the Re-Creator produces various projections of you.
8. Your divine parents created your original Soul-seed.
9. Father and Mother created the Cosmic Karmic Drama.
10. Human characteristics are attributed onto God, humanizing God.
11. What is scientific fact today was once thought impossible.

12. Get "impossible" out of your vocabulary for you are limiting yourself.
13. It is appropriate to worship both Father and Mother God.
14. There is perfect harmony among different species in Heaven.
15. When you return to Heaven you will be aware of yourself as your Oversoul.
16. In the afterlife, a scanning machine will project a 3D review of your earthly life.
17. The many projections of you allows your Oversoul to develop at an accelerated rate.
18. When you have completed all incarnations you will return to the Orion constellation.
19. Your Heavenly home can be seen by the naked eye, the seven brightest stars that form an hourglass in the Orion constellation.
20. A hologram is a representation of a figure produced by a laser beam. You are a hologram.
21. You are taking part in a computer-like program.
22. In Heaven, Father, Mother and children share power.
23. Christ taught that the Holy Spirit resides in each person. The Holy Spirit is the Soul of each person.
24. God wants humanity to succeed.

EXERCISE 25: Letting Go and Letting God

In what areas of your life do you tend to worry? Can you trust that your Oversoul is in charge? What benefits would you receive by worrying less and trusting more?

Study Questions: It's strange to think that a more intelligent version of ourselves is orchestrating our destiny. Does knowing this make you feel relieved or concerned? Why? What would be the advantage of having many projections of you operating simultaneously? What questions would you like to ask your Oversoul?

LESSON 26-The Oversoul

"In this present life you are here to work out one dominant character flaw, which is why the same lessons keep coming back to you. These character lessons are called Life Themes, wherein similar problems and scenarios keep resurfacing, just with different faces."

Have you noticed that you have repeated lessons throughout your life? These lessons are called "Life Themes," and they repeat until you have mastered the lesson.

"You may have had occasions of deja vu when one life crossed another; the strong feeling that you've been there before, or had the same conversation, but you don't know why. This phenomenon is the result of other projections having arrived there ahead of you."

Deja Vu is a universal phenomenon so there must be an explanation for it. Metatron says it is due to crossing paths with your other projections operating in parallel universes. There is a cosmological theory called "multiverse", and this physics theory states there is more than one universe, and within these universes we are living parallel lives.

"It's important to listen to the stirrings of your Higher Self, because it is calling your other selves to higher consciousness. Simply put, if you want to be happier, be your next self."

If there are other projections of yourself, those selves are likely to be different than the projection you're experiencing now. Other selves are operating with slightly higher consciousness. If you are feeling the pull to change some aspect of yourself, you should listen, because it's a direction you're headed anyway, and will only increase your happiness.

Summary Lesson 26:

1. The world and time is an illusion.
2. You will be reunited with all parts of your Soul in Heaven.
3. Re-birth is when your Oversoul projects you into new realms.
4. The Oversoul is the totality of you.
5. Life Themes are character lessons that repeat until you learn them.
6. Enlightenment is moving from one dimension to the next while still earthbound.
7. Déjà vu is when projections of you arrive at the same place, but the sequence of events are slightly different.
8. The combined experiences of all your projections are stored in your Oversoul.
9. The Human Experiment tests to see how spiritually intelligent each projection can become.
10. Other projections of you have already become a more advanced version of you.
11. Relationships form your character. How you handle yourself in relationships defines you.
12. It takes more strength to acknowledge a weakness than to ignore it.

13. Strive to be at peace with everyone.

EXERCISE 26: Your Life Theme

Define what you think your Life Theme or life lesson is. Ask yourself: Have I learned it, or is it a lesson I am still working on?

Study Questions: Think back to the most painful lessons you've encountered in life. In retrospect, can you see that while you may not have understood it at the time, there was in fact a lesson to be learned? Share what Life Theme you think you might have, giving an example from your own life.

LESSON 27-Cosmic Concerns

"Why scoff at the overwhelming odds that humanity is not alone?"

Most people would agree that the thought of aliens is a scary. But why? Because we do not know if they will be friendly or not! If they possess technology advanced of ours, we might not be able to defend ourselves against their superior weaponry. Metatron makes it clear that we are not the only species inhabiting the cosmos, but reassures us that Father and Mother God, as well as the angels, are protecting humanity from bad aliens.

"Evil is the blatant disregard for the rights of others."

When one group of people forces their agenda upon another group, they have transgressed human rights. Forcing your beliefs on others is moral robbery, for you are taking away another person's right to choose.

"A Cosmic Religion will unite all beings. In the past, religions caused harm, or separated people one from another. This is not God's intention for His Children."

There are so many religious doctrines that it is nearly impossible to imagine a worldwide religion wherein all people are valued and honored equally as God's children. What a wonderful world that would be!

Summary Lesson 27:

1. There is intelligent life on other planets.
2. You deny the existence of UFOs because you are afraid of alien superiority.
3. There are both good and bad aliens and angels.
4. The Universe is under attack by bad aliens, but Father and Mother God maintain control, protecting the earth from invasion.
5. Bad aliens are abducting humans for experimentation and reproduction.
6. Do not fear the bad aliens, God is ultimately in control.
7. There are good aliens who abide by universal law and promote harmony.
8. In Heaven there is a Cosmic Religion.
9. Evil is the blatant disregard for the rights of others.
10. Bad aliens want to impose their agenda on planet earth.
11. The "Grey Alien Agenda" is to create a hybrid race, part human and part alien so humanity will adopt their agenda and leadership.
12. Ask the angels for protection, for they serve humanity.
13. All Souls have the same value whether they are human, animal or alien.
14. You can make amends in Heaven for wrongs done so there is no hopelessness in Heaven.

EXERCISE 27: A Cosmic Religion

If there is going to be a Cosmic Religion in the future, one that unites and honors all people, what are some of the principles you think it should teach?

Study Questions: What are your beliefs about aliens? Do you think there are good aliens? Do you think aliens might have an agenda for humanity? If so, what do you think their agenda is?

Metatron defines evil as the blatant disregard for other's rights. Why is forcing your beliefs on others wrong?

LESSON 28-Why Meditation

"Meditation is the process of self-inspection. It is a method for correcting character flaws, or at least a means to see what those flaws are."

Changing ourselves is difficult because we cannot clearly see what needs to be changed. We are too close to see our own flaws. Meditation allows us to pull back from our problems and see them in a new light.

"You are not here to produce something. You are not here to impress somebody. You are here to figure out who you are, and to use your talents, gifts and abilities in service to humanity."

Society assigns us our identities. We take on roles such as: daughter, wife, mother and employee or employer, but this is not our primary identity. Before we took on any roles, we were first and foremost a child of God.

"The mind can be opened through the gentle application of meditation, or it will be opened through painful lessons. God does not wish anyone to suffer, but everyone must learn the same lessons of humility."

People change when one of two things happen: When it hurts bad enough, or when they choose to change because they get enough information or education. Most people don't change until it hurts bad enough. We choose how we will learn our lessons: the easy way, or the hard way.

Summary Lesson 28:

1. You deserve love because your true nature is lovely.
2. When you shut others out you also shut out God's love, for God is in each person.
3. Meditation is like the headlights of a car, shedding light on the journey ahead.
4. Meditation is a process of self-inspection to correct character flaws and control the mind.
5. A congruent person is empowered and confident.
6. Meditation is a course in both humility and capability.
7. Power, riches and possessions do not equal morality.
8. Material possessions cannot give you peace because you must have more things to be happy.
9. Peace is the absence of striving for more.
10. The ancient methods of the yogis are sure-fire ways of attaining more happiness and satisfaction.
11. Humanity's history could be titled: "master's and slaves" because mankind has enslaved one another.
12. You are to overcome physical drives, not to be controlled by them.
13. In the age of Aquarius, females will be elevated for their peacemaking abilities, and all people will be treated equally.
14. The afterlife is the great equalizer where karma is satisfied.
15. There are Hellish realms where the evil Soul goes to redeem itself. The underworld is worse than a nightmare.
16. God does not eternally punish anyone due to His forgiving nature.
17. Meditating on your blessings increases gratitude.

18. The mind is a separating machine, but you are part of the whole.
19. Addictions can separate you from others.
20. Love is togetherness.
21. The disappearance of separateness is nirvana.
22. In pure consciousness there is no separateness.
23. It is important to question, because trusting others to make your decisions is to assume they know better than you do what is best for you.
24. A larger male brain does not mean males have superior intelligence. Brain size does not determine intelligence.
25. Physical strength has allowed men to dominate.
26. Disciples were men conditioned by the society in which they lived.
27. Earth is the most paternalistic planet in the galaxy.
28. Omitting the knowledge of Divine Mother has resulted in violence and oppression.
29. Ask your angels and Spirit Guides to open your mind to new ideas.
30. Regrets happen because of not listening to reason.
31. Self-realization is rejection of the egoic self.
32. Purge yourself of stress often.
33. Being in nature, laughter and meditation are stress relievers.
34. The spiritual person can laugh at themselves and life.
35. God is displayed in nature's diversity.
36. God is in everything and everything is in God.
37. Even the evilest people believe they are doing the best they can.
38. You may be skeptical of angel messages, but because you haven't received a message doesn't mean you might not, or that someone else can't.

39. Humanity struggles with doubts about God and a lack of peace.
40. Humanity lacks moral development.
41. Rather than turning inward, humanity has turned outward in its search for happiness.
42. You are the answer you seek.

EXERCISE 28: To Meditate or Not to Meditate

Meditation is defined as a method of self-inspection used to remove character flaws. If you've never meditated before, to complete this exercise, give it a try. Whether you've tried it before or meditate regularly, complete a meditation session, then answer these questions: What obstacles to meditation did you find, such as: mind chatter, distractibility, or finding quiet time? Did you achieve a sense of calm and inner peace during, or after meditation? In what ways was the meditation helpful?

Study Questions: Most people have tried meditation, some without even realizing it, because there are many ways to meditate. Journal writing can be meditative because it is self-reflective. Chanting mantras has been used for centuries in the East as a way of achieving peace and relieving stress. Being in nature also gives you time to reflect upon life and is a guaranteed stress reliever. Talking to a counselor, a trusted friend or a family a member can also be stress relieving, because talking out your feelings is therapeutic. Exercise is also therapeutic for mind and body. What are your preferred methods of stress relief?

LESSON 29-The Stuff That Dreams Are Made Of

"What appears to you as a dream is in fact occurring in another dimension, this is why dreams can seem so real-they are!"

Dreams are produced by slower brain waves, and information comes from the subconscious. It has long been suggested that dreaming is astral projection activated by the pineal gland.

"In dreams, you must encounter evil as well as good, just as you must experience rain to appreciate the sunshine."

There seems to be a reason for evil, because not only do negative forces manifest on earth but evil is encountered during nightmares. Metatron compares evil to bad weather, making the point that without the rain we wouldn't appreciate the sunshine.

"The presence of evil is better tolerated in the dream world than in the awakened state. When you've had a nightmare, it's exposing you to negative energy disguised in different forms."

Metatron says we are "exposed" to negative energy, suggesting that the presence of evil is allowed for our growth. In the dream state, we are not traumatized by evil like we would be if we encountered those forces in the material world. The dream world acts as a buffer and is a more humane way to encounter evil.

Summary Lesson 29:

1. In Theta (REM sleep) you enter a dimension where wrongs can be made right.
2. What appears as a dream is really happening in another dimension.
3. The purpose of dreaming is wish-fulfillment.
4. You can only access the first Heaven in Theta sleep.
5. Recollections of dreams have been reorganized by the waking mind.
6. In dreams you encounter evil so you will learn the nature of evil.
7. Evil is better tolerated in the dream state, which is why evil is largely confined to the dream world.
8. You'll never understand the meaning of dreams due to interference of the left brain.
9. Your dreams are a peek into the first Heaven.
10. Deceased loved ones leave earthly troubles behind.

EXERCISE 29: Rest Easy

In nightmares you may have witnessed ghosts, monsters, aliens, evil people, scary animals, or death. Nightmares all have one thing in common: they are scary! Upon waking, we are relieved to find it was only a dream and we are safe. How do you feel about sleep and dreaming-do you look forward to sleep and find your dreams interesting, or do you feel uneasy about sleep and worry about nightmares? How does this new information make you feel about bad dreams?

Study Questions: Have you had dreams that felt realistic? Do you think some dreams have meaning? Why do you think God tolerates evil in the world? Why do you think we encounter evil in our dreams?

LESSON 30-The Akashic Record & The Future

"The collective unconscious, also known as the Universal Library or Akashic Record, stores every action, thought and feeling that all entities across space and time have had since the inception of its respective race."

Psychiatrist Carl Jung was the first to popularize the concept of the Collective Unconscious. Jung described it as an invisible universal library. A famous medical intuitive, psychic Edgar Cayce said he read from the Akashic Record while in a state of unconscious trance. Metatron validates the authenticity of a Universal Library known also as the Akashic Record.

"Your karmic team that may include your Guardian Angels, ancestors and the loved-ones on the other side from past lives may lend a listening ear and assist your (Spirit) Guide in which way to turn you."

It's easy to feel alone, for we are far from our Heavenly home. Metatron assures us that our karmic team supports and guides us and assists one another in heading us in the right direction. The Bible calls these "ministering spirits" (Hebrews 1:14).

"First, to plug into your Spirit Guide who has access to all the answers, you must listen for them, and be able to hear them. Second, you must see yourself as a benevolent force, and a force to be reckoned with!"

We are divine beings who can be a benevolent force in the world. We should have every confidence that our Guides and angels will guide and protect us.

"The Butterfly King and the Rainbow Mother will emerge to lead humanity, and there will be no more fear, no more tears, no more war, no more destruction of planet earth or taking of innocent lives."

Prophets of the past such as Nostradamus had visions that could be broadly interpreted. It is unknown if Metatron is speaking literally about the names of these benevolent rulers, or figuratively, but by their leadership, humanity will rid itself of the dark forces that have caused so much suffering, evil and war.

Summary Lesson 30:

1. The Akashic Record is an intergalactic library that stores every action, thought and feeling that all entities across time and space have had.
2. Our civilization is being monitored and recorded.
3. Humanity's greatest misconception is to think our behaviors only affect ourselves.
4. Metatron is the keeper of the Akashic Record and the Human Experiment.
5. Angels and aliens are monitoring humanity, allowing us to learn from our mistakes and to develop, and this is the will of God.
6. Divine Mother, The Counsel of True Judges and planetary leaders are assisting humanity to develop intellectually and spiritually.

7. It is hoped that humanity will evolve into peacemakers.
8. Heavenly beings watch you like people watch television programs.
9. The Akashic Record exists because of technology you do not yet have.
10. Progressive ideas that advance civilization are implanted during Delta sleep.
11. Spirit Guides access the Akashic Records and implant ideas as you sleep.
12. Your karmic team includes: Guardian Angels, ancestors and loved ones from past lives who help your Spirit Guide.
13. You develop powers of reasoning by solving problems.
14. Humans were created with a free will to see how far they can develop.
15. Humanity will evolve into a great species due to divine DNA and because your brain's capabilities are yet to be explored.
16. If you have a problem, remember there's an answer for it in the Akashic Record, and your Spirit Guide can access it.
17. You cannot solve your problems when you're unplugged from your power source.
18. To solve problems, listen for the voice of your Spirit Guide.
19. The brain's central duty is your protection and survival.
20. Information from the Other Side will stretch your mind's ability to believe it.
21. Self-growth is the primary reason you are here.
22. Remind yourself that new and different is okay.

23. When the brain is overloaded it rejects anything new.
24. Recharge by withdrawing from stress.
25. Your Soul is a cosmic spaceship and a treasure chest.
26. The earth is in a phase of purification as deception is purged.
27. Non-violence must become the standard before a new earth phase can occur.
28. During the deconstruction, evil will rise to the surface and evil plans and institutions will be revealed.
29. People of many religious faiths, nations, tribes and societies will again esteem ancient wisdom.
30. Those who have been spiritually asleep will wake up.
31. Organized religion will end, and a genuine worldwide spirituality will exalt the four elements of nature and worship the Soul. It will protect the animals and care for the earth.
32. The symbol of the butterfly and the rainbow will be revered. There will be a Butterfly King and a Rainbow Queen.
33. By the year 2050 light will overtake darkness. Thereafter, the Butterfly King and Rainbow Mother will lead humanity and there will be an end to violence and bloodshed.
34. Criminals will live underground in caverns until their sentence is served.
35. There is a plan to save the earth from destruction, and Heaven's plan will not fail. God is in control.

EXERCISE 30: Heavenly Guidance

Have you ever sensed you were being guided, protected or rescued by unseen forces?

If your Spirit Guide or an ancestor you respected were to offer their advice, what advice might they give you right now?

Study Questions: Do you think that the Akashic Record is where intuitive and psychic information comes from? Knowing that you have your own karmic team should be comforting, for it means you're receiving support from the Other Side. What do you think you need to do to tune into their wisdom?

Finally, is it comforting to know that there is a happy conclusion for humanity? Who do guess that these two benevolent rulers could be?

Bibliography

1. (2001). The Holy Bible, English Standard Version® (ESV®) Copyright © 2001 by Crossway, a publishing ministry of Good News Publishers.

2. (1887). John Emerich Edward Dalberg Acton. Letter to Bishop Mandell Creighton.

3. Henry Ford. Quote by Henry Ford. Goodreads. Retrieved from: https://www.goodreads.com/quotes/978-whether-you-think-you-can-or-you-think-you-can-t--you-re

4. (1914). Sigmund Freud. *On Narcissism.* Retrieved from: http://www.sigmundfreud.net/on-narcissism.jsp

5. (1893). Oscar Wilde. *Lady Windermere's Fan.* Quote Investigator. Retrieved from: http://quoteinvestigator.com/2015/07/26/serious

6. (2003). Rhonda Byrne. *The Secret.* Atria Books/Beyond Words Publishing.

7. (2001). Neville Goddard. *The Power of Awareness.* Dover Publications, Inc., Mineola, New York. The Holy Bible, English Standard Version® (ESV®) Copyright © 2001 by Crossway, a publishing ministry of Good News Publishers.

8. (2016). Joyce Meyer. Retrieved from: http://www.joycemeyer.org

9. Eldridge Cleaver. Goodreads. Retrieved from: https://www.goodreads.com/author/quotes/42661.Eldridge_Cleaver

10. (2011). *Queen of Heaven.* Retrieved from: https://thequeenofheaven.wordpress.com/

11. (2007). *Oh Father-Mother Birther of the Cosmos? The Aramaic New Testament.* Retrieved from: http://aramaicnt.org/?s=Oh+Father+Birther

www.ingramcontent.com/pod-product-compliance
Lightning Source LLC
Chambersburg PA
CBHW032031150426
43194CB00006B/235